A PAYROLL TO MEET

ARRANGED TO SUIT

A PAYROLL TO MEET

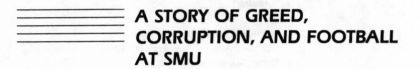

A STORY OF GREED, CORRUPTION, AND FOOTBALL AT SMU

DAVID WHITFORD

Macmillan Publishing Company
NEW YORK

Macmillan Publishing Company
866 Third Avenue, New York, NY 10022
Collier Macmillan Canada, Inc.

Library of Congress Cataloging-in-Publication Data
Whitford, David.
    A payroll to meet: a story of greed, corruption, and
football at SMU/David Whitford.
    p.   cm.
    Includes index.
    ISBN 0-02-627191-5
    1. Southern Methodist University—Football—
Economic aspects.
2. Sports—Texas—Corrupt practices—Case studies.
I. Title.
GV958.S69W48   1989
796.332′63′097642812—dc20   89-8010   CIP

Macmillan books are available at special discounts for
bulk purchases for sales promotions, premiums, fund-
raising, or educational use. For details, contact:
    Special Sales Director
    Macmillan Publishing Company
    866 Third Avenue
    New York, NY 10022

10 9 8 7 6 5 4 3 2 1

PRINTED IN THE UNITED STATES OF AMERICA

*For Mom and Dad
and for Sara*

CONTENTS

ACKNOWLEDGMENTS AND SOURCES

TO THE EXTENT that I was able to turn up fresh material on the SMU football program, I am indebted to the huge volume of reporting on the subject that has appeared in *The Dallas Morning News* and the *Dallas Times Herald,* and on WFAA-TV in Dallas. I owe special thanks to Skip Bayless, Doug Bedell, Danny Robbins, Jack Sheppard, and John Sparks, whose combined efforts over the years tell much of the story of what happened at SMU. Each generously shared his knowledge and insights with a newcomer. I wish to thank also the staff of the SMU sports information department, which never turned down a request for information or assistance; the librarians at the Texas-Dallas archives of the Dallas Public Library; and especially Lee Milazzo and Virgina Bols of the SMU archives, for their helpfulness, professionalism and good humor.

My principal source for post–August 1985 developments was *The Bishops' Committee Report on SMU,* a forty-eight-page document which summarizes the results of an investigation by a special committee of bishops of the South Central Jurisdiction of the United Methodist Church. Wherever possible, I augmented the facts presented in the report with my own interviews.

At places in the narrative I have made use of material from other books. For sections dealing with the institutional history of SMU, I relied heavily on *Southern Methodist University: Founding and Early Years* by Mary Martha Hosford Thomas (SMU Press, 1974). Books on the history of Dallas which I found useful are *Dallas, USA* by A. C. Greene (Texas Monthly Press, 1984); *Dallas Public and Private: Aspects of an American City* by Warren Leslie (Grossman Publishers,

1964); and *Dallas: An Illustrated History* by Darwin Payne (Windsor Publications, 1982). *NCAA: The Voice of College Sports* by Jack Falla (NCAA, 1981) was the source of much of my material on the history of football and its ties to colleges and universities. For the history of SMU football, I referred often to *Mustang Mania* by Temple Pouncey (Strode Publishers, 1981).

I benefitted also from many articles published in *D* magazine and *Texas Monthly*, among them: "The Decline and Fall of the Southwest Conference" by Paul Burka (*Texas Monthly*, September 1974); "Sherwood Blount's First Million" by Nicholas Lemann (*Texas Monthly*, October 1979); "The Abrasive Candidacy of Bill Clements" by John Merwin (*D*, March 1978); "Passing the Bucks" by Jan Reid (*Texas Monthly*, September 1983); "No Man's Land" by Richard West (*Texas Monthly*, December 1980); and "Why Do They Hate Us So Much?" by Lawrence Wright (*Texas Monthly*, November 1983), which taught me more about Dallas than any other single source. Lawrence Wright's article led me to his wonderful book, *In the New World: Growing Up with America 1960–1984* (Knopf, 1988).

Much of this book is the result of interviews with more than eighty current and former SMU players, coaches, professors, administrators, and alumni, many of whom prefer that their names not be mentioned. They know who they are and how grateful I am for their help.

Jim Atkinson, David Bauer, Paul Fichtenbaum, and Ned Leavitt helped get me started on the subject of SMU football. Bill Rosen, my editor, pulled me through to the end. For whatever merit this book may possess, I am beholden to Peter Griffin, who, as always, gave freely of his keen editorial insight and answered all my calls for help; and most of all to Sara Donovan Whitford, my in-house editor, who gave up her job in New York for a year of sacrifices and uncertainty in Dallas and made everything possible.

Some of this material appeared in a very different form in *Sport* magazine.

PREFACE

DALLAS WAS COLD and gray and wet. The rain that came on Monday and fell lightly all day Tuesday had given way in the night to a thickening fog. By dawn on Wednesday, February 25, 1987, the campus of Southern Methodist University was wrapped in a blanket of mist.

Had the sky been clear, one could have climbed the wide steps to the portico of Dallas Hall—the college's oldest building—and, turning, seen the clustered glass towers of downtown Dallas four miles to the south, "neither citadels nor churches, but frankly and beautifully office buildings," as Sinclair Lewis had it. But on this day SMU was cut off from its surroundings, an improbable Southwestern oasis of brick and slate, thick with native live oaks, green in winter.

The SMU campus is divided down the middle by Bishop Boulevard, which runs north from Mockingbird Lane straight at Dallas Hall. Over the last three quarters of a century, as buildings were erected on either side of the half-mile boulevard and the yellow prairie was replaced by grassy, hedge-trimmed quadrangles, the founders' vision of what a college campus ought to look like took shape. It was their wish that the dominant architectural style at SMU be Georgian, in imitation of Harvard Yard, and so it is. Even the new $5 million parking garage, which houses what may be the most extensive collection of Porsches, BMWs, and Mercedes-Benzes of any college in America, is faced with red brick—an aesthetic choice well suited to a college, and a city, whose image is something more than its substance. The centerpiece of the campus, appropriately, is the copper dome over Dallas Hall, and the highest point is the steeple of Perkins chapel. Ownby Stadium, at the foot of Bishop Boulevard, is no more than a single, brick grandstand, partly obscured by trees. The effect is somber, dignified, well heeled—hardly the image of a football factory.

Yet SMU produced a national champion in 1935 and played in the Rose Bowl. Doak Walker, who won the Heisman Trophy in 1948, was an SMU Mustang. So were Kyle Rote, Raymond Berry, Don Meredith, Jerry Levias, Craig James, Eric Dickerson, and a hundred others who went on to play professional football. Their exploits helped make SMU football too big for Ownby Stadium. In 1948 the Mustangs had moved to the Cotton Bowl with its seventy thousand seats, and from there in the 1970s to Texas Stadium, home of the Dallas Cowboys. From this quiet campus at the edge of wealthy, all-white Highland Park had arisen a decade ago an affliction known as Mustang Mania, which had taken over the town. And there had been a time—from 1981 through 1984—when the Mustangs' overall record of 51-5-1 was the best of any college football team in the country.

Football was the reason why today there were gathered on campus more than two hundred reporters, including representatives from virtually every major newspaper in the United States. The National Collegiate Athletic Association had promised to announce the result of its latest investigation into allegations of illegal payments to SMU players. For the seventh time since 1958, SMU faced a possible probationary term—a thirty-year legacy of scandal and corruption unmatched in intercollegiate athletics.

The 1986–87 academic year had been planned originally as a yearlong celebration of the seventy-fifth anniversary of SMU's founding. From its beginnings as a little-known denominational institution with a regional misssion, SMU over the past two decades had made significant progress toward achieving its goal of national stature. The cover story in the December 1986 issue of *D*, Dallas's city magazine, was a glowing, fourteen-page special report on SMU's prospects. The number of endowed faculty chairs, it was noted, had almost doubled since 1981, and freshmen SAT scores were sharply up. In the lead paragraph, governor-elect Bill Clements, SMU class of '39 and chairman of the board of governors, had predicted, "We are now talking in terms of SMU in the future as being at the same level as a Duke or a Stanford. We are just now taking the final step."

By the time the magazine appeared on newsstands, the birthday party had been spoiled. On November 12 a Dallas television station had aired a stunning interview with former SMU linebacker David Stanley, who admitted receiving $25,000 from an SMU assistant coach in 1983 and monthly payments of $750 through December 1985.

The date at which the payments stopped was the critical detail in Stanley's story. If he was telling the truth, that meant that payoffs had continued after the announcement of SMU's last probationary term in August 1985. Since then, the NCAA had devised a tough new penalty aimed at crippling repeat offenders. The stakes had never been higher. No longer was it a question of how many football scholarships the Mustangs might lose, or whether they would be banned from television appearances and bowl games. Now the issue was survival. A guilty verdict would make SMU the first college to receive the "death penalty."

PART I

1 BIRTH OF A SALESMAN

WESTERVILLE, OHIO, is close enough to Columbus that today one would call it a suburb. Forty years ago, when Ron Meyer was a boy, Westerville was more like *Our Town*, with its handsome brick business district, tree-lined side streets, and modest, hardworking Methodist and Presbyterian citizens. Westerville was at one time the headquarters of the Anti-Saloon League of America; the original brick building still stands between the library and the old high school on State Street. After the turn of the century, at the height of the temperance movement, campaign material printed in Westerville and distributed throughout the United States was so voluminous that Westerville became known as the Dry Capital of the World. Fifty-five years after the repeal of Prohibition, residents of Westerville still can't buy a drink without leaving town.

George Meyer was the star center on the Westerville High football team in 1932. After high school, he married Mary Harsha, the 1933 homecoming queen, and they settled in town. George was tall and good looking and he dressed to kill. Over the years he worked at lots of different jobs—credit manager for a finance company, truck driver, used-car salesman—but he had trouble holding on to any one of them for long. He played guitar in a wedding combo called the Five Flats. One of the members of the band smiled recently when he remembered George, but then he shook his head and offered that the man was not dependable. Then he tipped his elbow by way of explanation. Sometimes, former neighbors say, George made scenes. More often he just wasn't around. His kids would be playing in a ball game, a family friend remembers, all the other dads would be there, and George would be somewhere else. If Westerville was dry, George generally was not.

Much of the burden of raising a family fell to Mary, who did what had to be done. She went to her boys' ball games and cheered. With only two years of college, she worked part-time as an elementary school teacher because the family needed the money. She raised four children in a frame house on College Avenue, almost by herself, and only when they were all grown and on their own did she finally say good-bye to George. Mary thought kids should grow up with a father, no matter what.

Yet, if Westerville had not been such a small town, few would have guessed at the turmoil in the Meyer family. The kids were all achievers. Vic, the oldest, was the star, a student and an athlete whose accomplishments earned him admission to the Naval Academy. Suzy and Patti were the babies—pretty homecoming queens like their mother, smart enough to go to college on scholarships and earn advanced degrees.

Ronnie was the golden boy, a little wild, perhaps, but a charmer. When he got in trouble, people patted him on the head and smiled. Although he was small for his age, the other kids looked up to him. When the gang sneaked into the Otterbein College gym on weekends, it was Ronnie who scaled the wall, squeezed through the window, and opened the door for everybody else. He claims to have made the first solo ascent of the Otterbein Avenue water tower.

In school he was hugely popular, a better athlete than a student but not a bad student. He played all sports in their seasons, earned ten varsity letters, was all-conference in football, basketball, and baseball, *and* was voted class president every year. Girls adored him. In the Westerville High yearbook for 1958, Meyer's junior year, Bob Arnett willed "his football helmet and padding to Ronnie Meyer for protection from the weaker sex." Boys who understandably might have been jealous or resentful competed for his friendship.

The land-grant colleges of the Midwest have long been Meccas for homegrown athletes, none more so than Ohio State. Ronnie Meyer felt the pull. The 1950s were glory years for Ohio State football—the Buckeyes produced two Heisman Trophy winners (Vic Janowicz in '50, Hopalong Cassady in '55) and won two national championships ('54, '57)—and Meyer grew up worshiping Woody

Hayes, the Buckeyes' legendary coach. (Years later, as head coach of the Indianapolis Colts, Meyer briefly wore a suit and tie on the sidelines because, he says, that's the way he remembers Coach Hayes.) He became an Eagle Scout, an accomplishment he pooh-poohs with the explanation that uniformed Boy Scouts were admitted free to Ohio Stadium as ushers. Even after Meyer and his friends grew too old for scouting, they were not above getting out the old uniform on certain fall Saturdays and driving down Route 3 to Columbus.

As a senior Meyer led the basketball team into the district finals. On the afternoon of the decisive play-off game, students joined hands and snake-danced around the school building, then wound their way through town. "That was a big thrill for Westerville at the time," remembers Ray Dusenbury, who was a year behind Meyer at Westerville High and is a teacher there now. "A lot of people thought that because of football and basketball, Ronnie would go to Ohio State. The people in town would talk, 'Next year we'll go down to the horseshoe and watch him play.' Well, okay, but nothing ever came of it. I'm sure at the time it was a great disappointment."

One evening in the winter of 1958–59, Coach Hayes drove to Westerville for a basketball game, specifically to scout Meyer. He saw a skinny, crew-cut kid, about five ten, whose legs poked out of his shorts like sticks. Meyer wasn't fast, he wasn't strong, he was just a good athlete. Not quite Buckeye material.

Otterbein, a small college in Westerville affiliated with the United Evangelical Brethren, would have been thrilled to have Meyer, only his ambition was larger than that. If Ohio State didn't want him—that was obvious—there were other fine schools in the Big Ten. An opportunity arose that summer from an unexpected source, a young Purdue man, George Steinbrenner. Steinbrenner, whose father owned Great Lakes Shipping, had a growing reputation in Columbus as a deal maker. Evidently overstepping what authority he possessed as a onetime graduate assistant on the Purdue football staff, Steinbrenner led Meyer to believe he could arrange a scholarship.

In the fall of 1959 Ronnie Meyer left Westerville for West Lafayette, Indiana, and Purdue University. He was seventeen years old and had no money. He had a wife, Carolyn (a Westerville High homecoming queen, like all the Meyer women), whom he had married soon after graduation. Carolyn was pregnant. The baby was due in February.

WHEN MEYER ARRIVED AT Purdue, he went immediately to the football office to inquire after his scholarship. Nobody there knew who he was. Nobody knew anything about a scholarship. Steinbrenner wasn't around. ("Of course," Meyer remembers, "after the fact—I'm there, I make it—my junior year, he walks up, 'Aw, great job, Ron, knew you could do it!' ")

Meyer considered going home. He had spent a summer working as a plumber's assistant in Westerville. Is that what he wanted to do with his life? Maybe he thought about his dad, George Meyer, the football hero who married the homecoming queen and slowly drowned himself in drink.

Not knowing what else to do, Meyer became a pest. Day after day he showed up at Coach Jack Mollenkopf's office, pleading for a scholarship, begging for a chance. Mollenkopf also received a long-distance phone call from a hardworking mother in Westerville who made demands on behalf of her son.

On February 23, six days after Meyer's eighteenth birthday, his wife gave birth to a boy, Ron, Jr.

Football practice resumed in the spring. Meyer's name was buried in the depth chart, under defensive backs. If he could make it as high as third team, Mollenkopf promised, he would have his scholarship.

"I did it," Meyer says now. "I look back and I don't know how I did it, I really don't. I just did it."

MEYER WAS SMART AND TOUGH. He made the most of what modest talent he possessed. Eventually he became a star, a team leader. His last two years, he led the squad in minutes played and called the signals on defense.

"He was not the quickest or fastest guy in the secondary," says Dale Samuels, who was Meyer's defensive-back coach at Purdue. "He wasn't in the plans for our team, and yet every time there was a scrimmage and a big play happened—a good hit or an interception—you'd look up and there he was. He would have made it wherever he went, just because of his tenaciousness, cockiness, and smartness."

Meyer majored in physical education. As a senior he won the Big Ten Medal of Honor, which recognizes athletic and academic achievement. By then the coaches on the Purdue staff had already begun to look upon Meyer as one of their own. "I don't think there was a question in anybody's mind that here was a coach," Samuels says. "If that's the profession he wanted to pursue, he would make it."

MEYER BEGAN HIS COACHING career as a graduate assistant under Mollenkopf at Purdue (GAs are compensated with scholarships rather than a salary while they pursue a graduate degree). After one year Meyer became head coach at Penn High School in Mishawaka, Indiana—the traditional second step—where his team was 5-4-1. Then it was back to Purdue for the next six years as a full-time assistant.

A typical assistant coach in a major-college program has two jobs; he is both a coach and a recruiter. Often it is not easy to see the connection. In his role as a coach he appears to stand around in skintight shorts with a whistle around his neck and clap hands, pat butts, click stopwatches, blow whistles, holler, glower, sulk, cheer, and spit. The top assistants are the offensive and defensive coordinators; they are strategists, theoreticians, masters of minutiae, plotters, and planners. Like any other member of the faculty, a coach must do research in his field, advance his reputation, and know how to hold the attention of undergraduates. Unlike a professor, a coach also has to go out on the road and round up students for the university.

A recruiter is not a coach but a salesman. His knowledge of football rarely comes into play. Not when he is out banking frequent-flyer miles, driving roads that are not on the map, enthusiastically requesting of Billy Blue Chip's mom a second serving of deer-meat chili (even if he has already had dinner that night), and always smiling.

At Purdue, Meyer emerged as a salesman deluxe. Good-looking, charismatic, knew your name, knew your wife's name, did every-thing right. If he was the best-liked assistant at Purdue, it was because he made an effort. As soon as the game was over he was shaking hands with parents, talking to players on the other team, walking up to opposing coaches and saying, "Good game!" Some people thought it was phony, but others weren't so sure. At least Meyer was no Elmer Gantry; he seemed genuinely to believe in his product.

Meyer landed players; in 1969 he personally recruited Otis Armstrong, Dave Butz, and Darrell Stingley. All three were later chosen in the first round of the NFL draft. He made friends who could help him. One was Gil Brandt, player personnel director for the Dallas Cowboys. Brandt traveled all around the country scouting players. He met young college coaches every day. He remembered Meyer. It seemed to Brandt that Meyer always had time for a smile, a handshake, a double check to make sure Brandt had the roster, the game film, the personal insight he needed. "Certain people jump out at you," Brandt said later. In 1971 he offered Meyer a job as a Cowboys scout.

After twelve years in Indiana, Meyer was ready to move on. Only the year before he and Carolyn had gone through a divorce—she got the kids (Ron, Jr., and Ralph), the furniture, and $120 a month; he got the '69 Caprice and the credit-card bills from Penney's and Sears. Meyer was thirty now, still a lowly assistant coach. It was time to make things happen.

THE YEAR WAS 1971, the Dallas Cowboys were America's team and Meyer was part of it. His first year in Dallas the Cowboys won the Super Bowl. Everybody in the organization, even scouts, received a Dallas Cowboys diamond Super Bowl ring. Meyer put his on and kept it on (and wears it to this day). If you met Ron Meyer, you met his Super Bowl ring, even if he had to scratch his nose by way of introduction.

Years later, when Meyer was hired by SMU, Bob St. John, a columnist for *The Dallas Morning News*, wrote about playing pick-up basketball with Meyer at Cowboys training camp. "One thing I hated him for was that he was always dressed properly," St. John wrote about his friend, "wearing new tailored-looking shorts, shirts, shoes, and socks. Though we'd play most every afternoon for an hour or so, his socks never fell down around his ankles. I ask you . . . How can you completely trust a man who runs and jumps all over the place and never has to pull up his socks? He also shot too much. Just because he was a fine athlete and would hit maybe two of every three jump shots didn't mean he had to keep shooting."

As much as Meyer was thrilled to be a part of the Cowboys organization, he missed coaching. After a couple of years outside the loop, he grew restless. No doubt part of the reason he had taken the scouting job was because somewhere in the back of his mind he thought it might lead to a job on Tom Landry's staff. Now he wasn't so sure. He was married again, to his current wife, Cindy, and was ready to start a new family. Scouting kept him on the road too much. So when he heard about an opening for head football coach at Nevada–Las Vegas, he asked Landry and Brandt if they could put in a word for him.

LAS VEGAS, NEVADA, whatever else it may be, is not the sort of place where football legends are born. The town is too new, not like Canton, Ohio. The climate is too hot, not like Green Bay, Wisconsin. There are too many other things to do, not like Tuscaloosa, Alabama. But Las Vegas is where Ron Meyer landed in the spring of 1973.

He was only thirty-two, still unknown, and he got the job because a lot of other coaches who could afford to be choosy did not want it. The UNLV Rebels were still in NCAA Division II at the time, a level below the best. They were coming off a record of 1–10. University officials were beginning to ask themselves if it was right, after all, that UNLV even have a football team. Meyer signed a contract that carried him through one season and not a day beyond. Either turn the team around or that was it—for Meyer, for his staff, and for the program.

With so much else happening in town, the first thing Meyer had to do was make a splash. He had inherited from his father a certain way with clothes. The point was to make people notice, not worry whether they approved of your taste. When Meyer appeared at a function in what his staff fondly referred to as his Cisco Kid outfit—black pants, black buckskin vest (with fringe), tossed-salad shirt—he stood out, even in Las Vegas. On game days he dressed himself and his staff in red polyester slacks and argyle sweaters. Everything about the man—the two-tone shoes, the way his neatly trimmed hair hung down over his ears, the razor-sharp trapezoid sideburns—said *mod*.

Of course it was a show, that was the whole point, and Meyer was the star. Problems arose and Meyer attacked them. Attendance was one problem. Fans were forever whining that the stadium was too far outside of town. So Meyer *walked* there one day from the Strip, seven miles, TV cameras in tow. Image was another problem. The Rebels were losers, everybody thought so. But Meyer looked like a winner. Everywhere he went, he carried a one-hundred-dollar bill in his wallet, wrapped around all the little bills, so that when he paid for something, anything, a soda, a pack of gum, he always peeled back a one-hundred-dollar bill first.

Meyer took advantage of what he had. UNLV had lots of pretty girls. So he organized a cadre of coeds whose job it was to welcome recruits on campus visits and make sure they enjoyed their stay. "People liked his style," says Tina Kunzer, a former hostess, now women's athletic director at UNLV. "He was good-looking, he was young, he said what he wanted, and he got it done. That kind of made him bigger than life."

Backstage, Meyer was sweating, working fifteen-hour days, running his staff hard. You worked for Ron, you made the most of each day. First meeting, 6:00 A.M. If you made it home for the eleven o'clock news, you were lucky. In between, you sat and you worked. If you were tired, maybe Ron didn't mind if you laid down for a minute, *underneath your desk*. "We'd be under those commercial desks," remembers John Chura, a former assistant coach, "catching a few snoozes, and one of the other coaches would come in and say, 'So and so's here,' and then they'd explain, 'He's fixing his desk.' That's how we'd wake each other up."

Meyer's first year as head coach, the Rebels ran their record to 8–3. The second year, 1974, was even better—11–0 during the regular season, 12–1 after losing in the semifinals of the Division II national play-offs. It was the sort of spectacular reversal that hard work alone could not have accomplished. Meyer needed players who were winners, and he got them. The best known was Mike Thomas, a super blue-chip running back who left the University of Oklahoma and transferred to UNLV. Thomas was later NFL rookie of the year for the Washington Redskins.

Wayne Nunnely, who became head coach at UNLV in 1986, was

a player in 1973 when Meyer took over. "That first spring here," Nunnely remembered, "We had, oh, about sixty or seventy players out for football. That fall we probably had about one hundred thirty guys out. They brought all kinds of guys in from all over."

Later, when Meyer ran afoul of the NCAA, Nunnely, for one, was not surprised. "No," he says, "because I felt, uh, things moved awfully fast here, too. There were a lot of players in here really fast. That's as far as I'll go on that one."

2 THE GLORY YEARS

FOOTBALL WAS INVENTED in the ancient colleges of New England, spread to the Midwest, and later flourished on the West Coast. The South, especially the Southwest, was the last region of the country to produce teams that achieved national recognition. Southern Methodist under Coach Ray Morrison in the 1920s was the college that put Texas football on the map. Morrison created a national sensation by dramatically exploiting the most revolutionary and lasting innovation in the history of the game, the forward pass.

The rule that allowed for advancing the ball through the air was introduced in 1906 as part of a larger effort to end the bone-crushing monotony of the game and make it more interesting for the fans. It was thought that the old rules placed a disproportionate emphasis on brute strength. By creating a neutral zone at the line of scrimmage separating the teams by a space equal to the length of the ball, increasing the distance required for a first down from five yards to ten yards, and allowing the ball to be passed, the rule makers hoped to "produce a game affording broader strategic possibilities." E. K. Hall, chairman of the football rules committee, writing in the 1928 *Football Guide*, stated that it had partly been their aim to "remove the premium on mere weight and to develop greater opportunity for speed, agility and brains."

Most teams were slow to take advantage, especially in the East, where the old run-and-kick style prevailed among the established powers for many years to come. But west of the Appalachians—at lesser-known colleges such as St. Louis University, Notre Dame, and

Oklahoma—pioneers began to explore the consequences of the new rule. An early display of passing prowess—one that created an instant national reputation for an obscure Indiana college—was Notre Dame's 35–13 aerial bombardment of Army at West Point in 1913. The Irish scored all five of their touchdowns on pass plays while gaining an astonishing 243 yards in the air. "Football men marveled at this startling display of open football," *The New York Times* reported.

Ray Morrison must have been enamored of the pass at an early age. Although accounts differ, some football historians credit Morrison with inventing the Statue of Liberty play—where the quarterback poses as if to pass as the runner circles back and takes the ball out of his hand—while a student at McTyiere School for Boys in McKenzie, Tennessee. Morrison played his college ball at Vanderbilt between 1908 and 1912, competing, as was common in those days, until he was twenty-seven years old. He weighed less than 160 pounds but could run and throw with the best, and in his senior year he made Grantland Rice's all-America team.

SMU started playing football in 1915—the same year it began offering instruction in the liberal arts, theology, and music in a single college building in Dallas's Highland Park—and Morrison was hired as the first coach. After only two years, having compiled a record of 2-13-2, he was fired, reportedly told by Robert Stewart Hyer, the president of SMU, that "pressures from downtown make it necessary for me to ask for your resignation." However, Morrison returned to SMU in 1920 as coach of the freshman team. When the varsity job opened up again in 1922, Morrison got a second chance.

"When I found myself with a team that averaged only 166 pounds per man," Morrison later recalled, "I knew that I couldn't win any games by brute force, and I had a good passer in [Logan] Stollenwerck. We began to experiment with that and found that we could be quite accurate and decided in four downs we could complete two passes, and in that time we could make ten yards. . . .We passed on first down, second down, third down, and we found it paid off."

Morrison's electrifying attack employed laterals, passes, and trick plays originating from every corner of the field. Taking advantage of the fact that there were no official standards governing the shape of the football, Morrison commissioned a leather-goods company in Nocona, Texas, to design a new football with a sharp point, more suitable for throwing than the cumbersome bladders preferred by other teams. (The Nocona football was later used by Sammy Baugh, who set numerous passing records at Texas Christian University in the 1930s.) His receivers wore blue wool jerseys with "stick-um stripes" on the chest. Jimmie Stewart, a self-described "speed merchant," who along with Blink Bedford was a favorite target of Stollenwerck, opted against the stick-um stripes ("I caught it with my hands"); Stewart chose not to wear a helmet, either, preferring to streak bare-eared down the sidelines in pursuit of flying footballs. Sportswriters of the era dubbed the display SMU's "Aerial Circus."

Before long, SMU was piling up wins. The undefeated 1923 team, led by the so-called Immortal Ten, scored 207 points to the opposition's 9 and captured SMU's first SWC title. The Mustangs won their second title in 1926, the year they traveled to Columbia, Missouri, for their first intersectional game outside the Southwest. And in 1928 over seven hundred players, coaches, and fans journeyed five days by train from Dallas to West Point for a showdown with Army.

Allison Danzig, covering the game for *The New York Times*, filed this page-one sports report on October 6, 1928:

> "In one of the biggest extravaganzas of forward passing and loose handling of the ball ever put on by football teams of major caliber, Army eked out a bare 14–13 victory over Southern Methodist University of Dallas, Texas, today in one of the first big intersectional engagements of the season.
>
> "A gathering of 18,000 spectators sat through three hours of such bewildering and spectacular aerial pyrotechnics as to leave them exhausted from cheering and so surfeited with the display that they must have had their fill of forward passing for the season.
>
> "From the opening minute of play the fireworks started popping, as [SMU's Ira] Hopper threw a 26-yard pass to [Ross] Love that put the ball on Army's 35-yard line, and from then on it was an afternoon of mad, reckless passing, fumbling and intercepting....It was nothing for them to throw the ball thirty and forty yards down the field ... and

during the afternoon so many passes were completed that it was impossible to keep track of them."

SMU's near upset of powerful Army hastened acceptance of the forward pass by offensive strategists around the country, and made the Mustangs famous. In the years that followed they took their show on the road, playing before huge crowds at Nebraska, Notre Dame, Navy, Syracuse, and UCLA. "Overnight," wrote Horace McCoy of *The Dallas Morning News*, reporting on the Army game, "the Southern Methodists burst into some measure of fame; a trite storybook quotation, but a genuine fact."

IN 1935 SMU WON the Knute Rockne trophy, which in the days before wire-service polls was an acceptable basis for laying claim to the national championship. The game of the year—indeed, one of the most memorable college games ever played—was against TCU in Fort Worth. It matched two unbeaten teams in a battle for the SWC championship and a trip to the Rose Bowl. NBC radio broadcast the proceedings live from coast to coast, the first such broadcast to originate from the Southwest. After SMU jumped out to a 14–0 lead, Sammy Baugh brought TCU back to tie the game in the third quarter. SMU finally won on a fourth-quarter, fourth-down, thirty-nine-yard desperation heave from Bob Finley to Bobby Wilson, who jiggled the ball, then clutched it firmly and fell into the end zone. Sportswriter Grantland Rice, who was there, called it "one of the greatest football games ever played in the sixty-year history of the nation's finest college sport."

For SMU it was the end of an era. Ray Morrison had gone home to Vanderbilt in 1934, replaced by Matty Bell, and for the rest of the 1930s and through the war years, SMU dropped out of the national picture.

THE END OF WORLD WAR II signaled the birth of a national sports culture. Returning GIs bolstered war-thinned rosters. Bowl games grew in number and offered bigger purses. Air travel opened up exciting new intersectional match-ups. One of the first places the spotlight fell was on a five ten, 170-pound backfield sensation from SMU named Ewell Doak Walker, Jr.

Doak was a local boy. He grew up within walking distance of

the SMU campus and used to hang around the practice fields on Mockingbird Lane while the Mustangs went through their drills. His favorite player was fullback Harry Shuford, one of the captains of the '35 national championship team. When Walker enrolled at SMU in 1945, he made sure to get Shuford's old number 37.

Walker almost didn't make it to SMU. His friend and teammate at Highland Park High School was quarterback Bobby Layne, who had graduated a year earlier and was playing for the University of Texas. Layne leaned hard on Walker to join him in Austin, but Walker chose to stay close to home, partly because Rusty Russell, his old head coach at Highland Park, had recently been hired as SMU's top offensive assistant. Walker and Layne both became collegiate all-Americans. Together they went on to brilliant careers in the National Football League and were later inducted into both halls of fame, college and pro.

Doak Walker was exactly the sort of player of 1906 rules committee had in mind when it tried to fashion a more open style of play. He wasn't big, he wasn't muscle-bound (except in the neck and shoulders), and he wasn't fast. His game depended on cunning and quickness. He kept the opposition off balance. He excelled at all the wide-open skills: passing, pass-catching, and broken-field running. Walker was best known as a back but he also punted, kicked extra points, returned punts and kickoffs, and intercepted passes.

The happy convergence of so many skills in one blue-eyed, square-jawed hometown boy soon attracted a fanatical following to the Mustangs. After the 1947 season SMU abandoned on-campus Ownby Stadium (capacity: twenty-three thousand) and moved downtown to the Cotton Bowl. The big stadium at Fair Park had opened in 1930 and was originally intended as a showcase for Texas high-school football. It boasted modern reinforced-concrete construction, sixty acres of parking, and for the comfort of the forty-six thousand fans, redwood bleachers. In 1937 the first Cotton Bowl Classic had been played there, an event that was slow to catch on (perhaps because Dallas is colder in January than the other major-bowl cities, Miami, New Orleans, and Pasadena) but in recent years had begun attracting sell-out crowds. Now that the Mustangs were taking over as regular tenants, construction began on an upper deck, which would add almost thirty thousand seats by the time it was completed in 1949, Doak Walker's senior year. Average attendance at SMU home games that season would surpass sixty thousand. Total attendance for eight home games would be the highest in the nation.

Walker's career was interrupted by a stint in the army in 1946, but in 1947 he returned with a vengeance, leading the Mustangs to their sixth SWC championship and a number-three national ranking. He was an all-American on his way to becoming an American hero, and in September 1948 *Life* magazine put him on the cover, which made it official. Walker posed in his red SMU jersey against a Texas sky almost as blue as his eyes. (According to one informal tally, Walker appeared on forty-seven magazine covers over a period of two years.) "Walker is so good," *Life* trumpeted to the nation, "that even Texans find it difficult to exaggerate his remarkable talents as a signal caller, passer, runner, blocker and kicker in SMU's versatile single-wing formation."

The 1948 Mustangs more than lived up to their press clippings. Walker, only a junior but judged the best college player in the country, was awarded the Heisman Trophy by New York's Downtown Athletic Club. SMU breezed through the season, winning its seventh conference title and finishing ranked among the top ten nationally. *Life*, which ordinarily was as prone to exaggerate as any Texan, had been right after all; SMU was "just about the slickest football team in the country."

DOAK WALKER WAS THE right player at the right time for SMU. His improbable exploits, his modesty (after missing much of the '49 season with injuries, he wrote a letter to *Collier's* magazine, asking that he not be included on their all-America team), and his obvious wholesomeness rekindled for an eager, postwar generation of national sports fans an enthusiasm for SMU football forgotten since the days of Ray Morrison and his Aerial Circus. In 1950 a nine-minute newsreel entitled "Football's Mighty Mustangs"—featuring Kyle Rote, Walker's younger backfield mate, also an all-American—played in movie theaters around the country.

After that SMU fell off sharply. Over the next quarter century—from 1951 until 1976—SMU won less than 44 percent of its games. Of course there were stars who played for the Mustangs in those years: Raymond Berry (1953–54), Forrest Gregg (1953–55), Don Meredith (1957–59), and Jerry Levias (1966–68), who was the first black scholarship athlete in the Southwest Conference. With Levias, SMU won another SWC title in 1966. But for the most part, the fifties, sixties, and early seventies belonged to the conference's two big state universities, Texas and Arkansas. Between 1959 and 1973, Darrell Royal's Longhorns or Frank Broyles's Razorbacks won thirteen of fifteen SWC titles. The Texas-Arkansas game invariably fell at the end of the season and often was carried on national television. Frequently it had a bearing on the national championship.

Meanwhile, the private colleges in the SWC—Rice, Baylor, TCU, and SMU—struggled against stiff odds to stay competitive. What had once been easy to overlook—that SMU, for instance, was a provincial, church-owned college with fewer than five thousand undergraduates—began to seem like an insurmountable obstacle. How could it possibly compete with the huge enrollments and vast resources of the public schools—Texas, Arkansas, Texas A&M, Texas Tech, and Houston?

In Dallas a generation of fans grew up with the idea that the Mustangs, more often than not, were losers. These were fans who had never heard of Ray Morrison. Their memory of Doak Walker was dim. For them the word *slick* may have evoked images of oilmen or Elvis or flashy automobiles, but it had nothing to do with SMU.

WHEN THE SMU JOB opened up after the 1975 season, every big-name coach who was approached turned it down. Lou Holtz, who had accepted the last time SMU had an opening and then backed out, wasn't interested. Johnny Majors and Hank Stram said no. Darryl Rogers said yes, then thought it over and changed his mind. The next name on the list was Ron Meyer, the former Cowboys scout, who was promoted for the job by his old boss, Gil Brandt, and Cowboys president Tex Schramm.

"Ron would have crawled to Dallas on his hands and knees to get that job," says a friend.

3 SNOW JOB

STEVE ENDICOTT WAS AT his desk in the football office of the University of Miami one late-winter day in 1976 when the telephone rang. It was Ron Meyer, calling long-distance.

Endicott had met Meyer only once, at the coaches convention in Kansas City. That was several months ago and they had not talked since. Now Meyer was telling Endicott that he had a new job, head coach at Southern Methodist. Was Endicott interested in joining him?

Endicott was twenty-six years old, just starting out. A talented and versatile athlete from Grants Pass, Oregon, he had earned ten varsity letters in high school and played in three statewide all-star games his senior year (in two, football and basketball, he was named most valuable player). At Oregon State he played quarterback in the fall and third base in the spring until a shattered wrist ended his dream of becoming a professional athlete. In 1972 he joined the football staff as a graduate assistant.

Endicott never had to put in time as a high-school coach. He came to Miami in 1973, was hired after one year to coach the freshman team, and was promoted one year later to varsity assistant in charge of quarterbacks and receivers. Now he was listening to an exciting offer from Meyer.

Endicott was tempted. No one, least of all the current Miami staff, had an inkling of what Miami would become several years down the road under Howard Schnellenberger, who would transform the Hurricanes into a national power. In those days Miami was just another second-tier program, overshadowed in its own backyard by Florida and Florida State. There was not a lot of money to build with, nor was there much interest from the fans. Endicott was not very familiar with SMU—he had seen them on TV a couple of times—but if what Meyer was telling him was true, this sounded like his ticket to the big time.

"I'll tell you," said the raspy, crackling, high-pitched voice at the other end of the line. "Dallas is the greatest city in America. It's got good players, the Southwest Conference, good crowds, everything."

Endicott was sold.

SEVERAL WEEKS LATER, Endicott was sitting by the door in a dingy meeting room beneath the west grandstand of Ownby Stadium on the SMU campus. Nearby sat Pat Jones, twenty-eight, an up-and-comer off of Frank Broyles's staff at Arkansas who would later become the head coach at Oklahoma State. They were, respectively, the new receiver coach and the new defensive line coach at SMU, and they were about to get their first close-up look at the 1976 Mustangs.

Silently they watched as, one by one, the players filed past them and took their seats. They watched with the alert, critical eyes of cattle ranchers inspecting the herd, looking for size, signs of unusual strength, or a certain way of moving that suggested talent. They were giving these players the so-called eye test, which is a part of every coach's vanity; he is supposed to know, on first sight, whether he sees a football player or some other lesser species. So Endicott and Jones watched, until the door closed, and then they looked at each other as if to say, What *is* this?

Where were all the linemen? Nervously they scanned the room, searching for the six three, 270-pound studs, the guys who lived in the weight room and had made themselves into bulls. A few had some size, granted, but they looked soft. Probably the best-looking specimen they saw was a big Irish lineman named Jim Duggan, who eventually would change his name to Hacksaw and find fame and fortune on the pro-wrestling circuit. Where were the graceful, loose-framed athletes whose speed was apparent even as they walked? Jones and Endicott decided there might be one guy in the room who looked like a natural linebacker. Later they learned he was an undersized defensive tackle.

When Endicott thought about what Ron Meyer had told him on the phone he had to wonder if *any* of it was true. Good players? C'mon. The team was coming off of a 4–7 season, and now they would have to find thirteen new starters to replace the departing seniors. Good crowds? Uh-uh. The Cotton Bowl could accommodate more than seventy-five thousand fans; the norm in recent years was about one third of that.

Not that he was bitter. Endicott was young and ambitious and he probably would have taken the job no matter what. Still, Meyer had done a snow job on him.

MIKE BARR WAS A twenty-five-year old graduate assistant at Purdue moonlighting as a player-coach for a semipro team called the Lafayette Generals when he heard from Ron Meyer. "I'm looking for a young guy," Meyer told Barr. "Would you be interested?"

Barr was single. He didn't know the first thing about SMU—not even where it was—but when Meyer told him Dallas, he was sold. "Everyone knew Dallas had glamour," Barr explains, "and of course Meyer kept saying, 'Hey, Barr, it's got the best-looking women I've ever seen.'" So Barr packed his few belongings, hopped in his Plymouth Gold Duster, and headed south.

With Barr's arrival in midsummer 1976, Meyer's staff was complete. They weren't *all* single, not *all* of them had blond hair, but it is easy to understand why people would remember them that way. They tended to be young, outgoing, and charismatic, qualities that rated high in a fast-growing Sunbelt city like Dallas, Texas. Meyer's offensive and defensive coordinators—Larry Kennan and Steve Sidwell—were both thirty-one years old. Jim Anderson, Dante Scarnecchia (a carry-over from the previous SMU staff), Steve Endicott, Pat Jones, and Barr were in their twenties. All but two (Jones and Scarnecchia) were northerners and westerners who had never played or coached in the Southwest Conference. They knew little about Texas football and less about SMU.

Even those who came from less prestigious programs agreed that the SMU facilities were surprisingly poor. Everything—offices, locker rooms, meeting rooms, what passed for a weight room—was housed within a fifty-year-old, brick-walled grandstand at the south-east corner of the SMU campus, Ownby Stadium. Those who were unable to find a house or apartment right away made Ownby Stadium their home. Most of the staff lived for a time in a dank, win-dowless, second-floor locker room outfitted with bunk beds and known affectionately as the sub. They would start work early in the morning and keep going until late at night, and then they would go to the sub and shut the door and lie there in the stuffy blackness until it was time to go to work again. Coaches who awoke in the middle of the night and left the sub to visit a refrigerator stocked with beer and soft drinks would sometimes find Meyer—in skivvies, with a towel over his head—still at his desk.

Yet they had a common goal, a sense of mission, and it was an exciting time. Meyer was able eventually to hustle up some apart-ments by appealing to generous alumni. They all drove courtesy cars donated by local dealers and bought gas with university credit cards. They ate free meals with the players. After work maybe one of them would go buy a couple of six-packs and they would sit around the sub and entertain each other. (Once they were chewed out, dutifully, by Dick Davis, the athletic director, for leaving too many beer cans lying around.) Or else they would go by The Point After, a sports bar on Greenville Avenue where SMU coaches are always welcome.

There was a feeling, shared by Meyer and all the members of his staff, that they were in on something big. What made it thrilling was that everyone in Dallas, whatever his game, felt the same way. The city's economy in 1976 was shooting off sparks in every direc-tion. Immense fortunes were being made in banking and real estate, fueled by the Texas oil boom (the price of oil had shot up 75 percent in 1974, to $6.95 a barrel, on its way to a high of more than $35.00 a barrel in 1981). Dallasites who shared in the general prosperity fervently believed that the wealth and power of a nation were shift-ing inexorably to the Southwest, and that Dallas—Big D!—was stra-tegically placed to take maximum advantage. The signs were everywhere: spanking new office towers downtown, whole new communities leapfrogging to the north, a new airport (the biggest in the country), the Dallas Cowboys (America's Team), Dallas women (sexy, savvy, and blonde), and "Dallas," the TV show, which created an intoxicatingly evil Dallas myth for television viewers around the world.

WHEN AN EIGHTEEN-YEAR-OLD boy is deciding which among several scholarship offers to accept, he takes into account scores of small considerations. People matter. Attitudes matter. Distance from home matters. He cares about the city where he will be living, what the campus looks like, whether he can make the grade in the classroom, what the girls look like, where the team plays, how big the crowds are, who the opponents will be, what style of offense the team runs, what the uniforms look like, how many upperclassmen are ahead of him at his position, how many games will be televised, how many players on the team make it to the pros, what the weight room looks like. He may care about what programs of study the university has to offer.

These are questions that come up during recruiting. SMU coaches had a hard time answering some of them. Facilities? Nothing to brag about there. Big crowds? Well, no. Pretty girls? Sure, except that SMU had very few black women students; many black players who later came to SMU, including future NFL star Eric Dickerson, chose to spend their weekends forty miles up the interstate in Denton, home of North Texas State University, where the student population was more diverse and the party scene more varied. What about academics? SMU is good but probably not the best in the Southwest Conference; Rice has a better reputation, the University of Texas has more to offer. The team? The team was terrible. Recruits who chose SMU were giving up a better chance of going to bowl games, appearing on television, and playing in front of big crowds at any number of other schools. For some, admittedly, SMU's lack of recent success was a selling point—it meant they could expect to play as freshmen—but not many high-school stars consider it a plus to be part of a team that loses all the time.

SMU was a good example of what can happen to a college team once it starts losing. Without the leveling factor of a draft—the mechanism used by professional leagues for distributing fresh talent to the teams who need it most—the tendency in college athletics is to keep moving in the direction one happens to be going. In SMU's case, a losing record made it hard to recruit talented high-school players, which made it doubly hard to improve, which kept fan interest low, which limited income, and so on.

But a team that has won once will often find it easier to win again. Like a perpetual-motion machine engineered to operate on positive feedback, the tendency is to accelerate. The key is getting started.

"We sat down as a staff," a former assistant remembers, and said, 'Okay, you guys, why would you come to SMU? What does SMU have that nobody else has?' And what it came down to, one thing about SMU—probably the biggest thing—we're in Dallas! We're in Dallas, Texas! We were selling, 'Guys, the one thing SMU has that nobody else has is Dallas, Texas!' "

The SMU coaches had a statistic which showed that a large majority of college graduates eventually settle within so many miles of the city where they went to school. They told you that first, then they rattled off every Dallas superlative they could think of: Dallas is the seventh-largest city in the United States, and among the fastest growing; Dallas has more major corporate headquarters than all but two American cities; Dallas has more blacks in management positions than any other city in Texas; Dallas has the nightlife; Dallas (take our word for it) is the best city in the best state in the best country in the world. "If Lubbock is so great," Meyer used to say, flashing his diamond Super Bowl ring, "why aren't they the Lubbock Cowboys?"

OUT ON THE TOWN—in swank restaurants and bars on McKinney Avenue, at late-night clubs along Greenville Avenue, and on the golf course at Bent Tree Country Club (guest privileges courtesy of real-life J. R. Ewings)—Meyer and his kiddie corps of tow-headed assistants felt like players in the big show. During recruiting forays into backwater conference towns like Waco (Baylor), Lubbock (Texas Tech), and College Station (Texas A&M), they had a tendency to carry themselves like ambassadors from Rome. If that rubbed some folks the wrong way (other coaches, mainly), Meyer couldn't have cared less. The last thing he or anyone else on his staff aspired to be was a good ol' boy.

On the other hand, no amount of fervor or swagger on the part of the SMU football staff, no pride in Dallas, could alter the simple fact that the SMU football team was not very good. Senior quarterback Ricky Wesson and junior running back Arthur Whittington were proven performers, both of whom went on to play professionally, but they were exceptions.

Meyer had been hired in late January, only a few weeks before national signing day. There had been little time to recruit. An earlier start would have helped, although with SMU's poor reputation and Meyer an unknown, it was probably inevitable that his first class contain more uniform fillers than players. In fact, of the original twenty-five high-school seniors and one junior-college transfer signed by Meyer within a month after he was hired in 1976, only seven were still around four years later as seniors. The rest were swept away by a rising tide of talent as SMU steadily improved.

The star of that first class was a speedy five eleven, 175-pound running back from Little Rock Central named Emmanuel Tolbert. Normally a player with Tolbert's credentials would have been snapped up by Arkansas as a matter of territorial entitlement. That Tolbert was not, some of the SMU coaches suspected, was because he happened to be black. Arkansas, slowly integrating in the 1970s under Coach Frank Broyles, was simply letting too many good black players get away. Meyer, whose eye for talent was color-blind (and who appreciated speed above all), made Tolbert his first signee. He converted him to wide receiver and started him as a freshman. Tolbert, who would become an all-American in 1978, was the first in a long line of outstanding black athletes aggressively recruited by Meyer and his staff.

Still, the Mustangs weren't going anywhere until they could get a lot more good players. Meyer knew that better than anyone else. In the meantime he did what he could.

He designed a new uniform. It had red, white, and blue stripes on the pant legs. It said SMU across the chest. It had a galloping Mustang on the helmet. "We had a lot of kids during recruiting," a former assistant remembers, "who would say, 'God, you guys got good-looking uniforms.' This isn't a bigoted comment ... but they appealed to the black kids. They weren't so conservative, like the old [University of] Texas orange shirts and white pants. I mean, our uniforms had some *pizzazz* to 'em!"

Everything was triple-striped—the pants, the socks, the shoes, the helmet. Everything matched. Recruits who visited the SMU campus were invariably led into the locker room by Meyer for a private viewing. "What's your number?" he'd say. "Ninety-nine? Here, try this on. Hey, you look great! It's perfect for you."

The uniform had to be worn just so, socks pulled all the way up to the knees, auxiliary pads in place. One of Meyer's pet peeves was the sloppy habit so many players had of writing their numbers *on the outside of their elbow pads*. They were only trying to keep track of their equipment, Meyer understood that, but couldn't they write on the *inside* of their pads? Meyer had to insist.

Team-picture day was the worst. Meyer and the photographer would take forever to set up the perfect shot, and when it was over, Meyer would suddenly realize that one of the coaches wasn't wearing a wristwatch. "Alright, *everybody* take their watches off," he'd bellow, and they'd line up and do it again.

"Everybody take their rings off!"

MEYER MADE HIS DEBUT as head coach of the SMU Mustangs on a Saturday night, September 11, 1976, downtown at the Cotton Bowl. SMU was opening against the Horned Frogs of Texas Christian University and Meyer was nervous, not only because it was his first game but because he felt he had to make at least a good showing. If the opponent had been Texas or Arkansas, the pressure would have been more manageable; no one expected SMU to compete with the big state universities, not right away. But there were three other private schools in the Southwest Conference besides SMU—Baylor, Rice, and TCU—and Meyer knew that against them there was no such thing as a grace period. "We're going to beat TCU in that opening game if we have to drop the stadium on them," Meyer had predicted.

Some of the staff members were secretly worried that the truth about the SMU football team was worse than they had imagined; SMU was sure to lose and it would not be pretty at all. It didn't help their confidence when Meyer, during the critical last week of practice, spent hours choreographing the Mustangs' grand entrance into the Cotton Bowl. Meyer had a vision: He saw his team running full speed out of the tunnel, single file, and then splitting off in equal groups at evenly spaced intervals for pregame calisthenics, like a marching band. The split was to happen simultaneously across the entire field.

The assistant coaches thought he was out of his mind. It would take hours to get the damn thing worked out. No matter how hard they worked, there was always the danger that on game day somebody would screw up—just one guy, that's all it would take—and then everybody would be off and running down the wrong yard lines. But Meyer was insistent and so they had practiced, hard, every day. Even now, minutes before they would take the field, no one was sure if it was going to work.

The last thing Meyer did before the game, as he would for all games to come, was call his coaches together for a private conference. They would squeeze into a bathroom or a shower, anywhere a dozen big men could be alone, and Meyer would tick through the five or six points he wanted to drive home. Then they would put their fists together, just like the players, and Meyer would say something like, "Let's go out there, let's win this game," and they'd all yell, "Break!"

Tonight, their first game together as a staff, nerves were especially taut. Meyer was wrapping up what he had to say when suddenly his eyes locked in on his defensive coordinator, about neck level.

"Sidwell!" he shouted. "You got the wrong shirt on!"

Meyer had taken extraordinary care in outfitting his assistants. They all wore individually tailored, diamond-patterned, bell-bottomed slacks with white sweaters, white shoes, and a red shirt. Each coach owned two sets of red shirts—one for practice, another for games—and while the shirts were almost identical, Meyer absolutely could tell them apart. Sidwell must have had his mind on something else (football?) when he got dressed this afternoon.

"I can't believe it! It's the first game! You got the wrong shirt on!"

THE MUSTANGS GALLOPED into the Cotton Bowl in tight formation, spread out crisply in straight lines across the field without a single wrong turn, and broke into a tight, sharply executed calisthenics routine that would have reminded the fans of breakdancing if breakdancing had been invented yet. "Hey, we weren't worth a shit," a former assistant admits. "But our kids, boy, they *thought* they were tough shit, all lined up across the field in a perfect line, just *perfect*."

SMU beat TCU that night, 34–14. Meyer understood how important it was to make a good first impression and he was relieved to have succeeded. But one week later in Tuscaloosa, SMU was crushed by Alabama, 56–3. Six players suffered season-ending injuries. Meyer knew now, if ever he had any doubt, that a long road lay ahead.

4 THE I-45 CONNECTION

MEYER'S AMBITION FOR SMU was nothing less than national prominence on a level with Southern Cal and Notre Dame, two private institutions of roughly comparable size and academic standing that more than hold their own in the world of big-time college football. This was a radical notion in the 1970s but Meyer wasn't crazy. SMU had what he called "embers of greatness"—the dimly remembered glory years of the 1920s, the national championship in 1935, Doak Walker's Heisman Trophy in 1947. If it had happened before at SMU, it could happen again. The closer he looked, the more clearly he saw what looked like a sleeping giant.

He made recruiting the top priority. Most college teams routinely scale back their Friday workouts, partly to preserve players' strength for Saturday's game but also in order to give assistant coaches time to travel to Friday-night high-school games in their respective recruiting territories. Meyer went one step further, sending his assistants away early on Thursday so that they would have all day Friday before the game to make contacts, look at films, whatever had to be done. Mike Barr, whose territory was West Texas, can remember leaving practice at 4:30 on a Thursday afternoon, boarding an airplane at 5:30, arriving in Odessa (350 miles west) at 6:30, recruiting all day Friday, attending a game that night, and returning to Dallas on a 6:30 flight Saturday morning in time for the SMU game.

On Fridays, when most of the assistants were out of town, Meyer ran practice with help only from his two coordinators, Larry Kennan and Steve Sidwell, who were conveniently assigned to recruit Dallas and nearby communities. By design, they were probably the least effective recruiters on the staff—X-and-O men, not salesmen. If they needed help with recruiting in Dallas, Meyer was there.

Kennan and Meyer working together were responsible for signing SMU's first Texas high-school superstar, Mike Ford. It was one thing for the Mustangs to sign Emanuel Tolbert—who, after all, was ignored by Arkansas—and quite another to sign, one year later in 1977, an all-state quarterback who was heavily recruited by the University of Texas.

Ford was a local boy from Mesquite, a suburb on the eastern edge of Dallas that, though sliced through with interstate highways and overrun by subdivisions, still manages to retain some of the flavor of the Old West. Ford stood six four (taller in his cowboy boots), weighed 215 pounds, chewed tobacco, and was a classic, drop-back passer. In his first year at SMU, Meyer had replaced the Mustangs' run-oriented wishbone offense with a pro-style I-formation, which permitted a more varied and open attack. He knew that the best chance SMU had of beating teams that were bigger and more talented was with the pass. (It was also more exciting for the fans; Meyer had to worry about that, too.) Ford was perfect for the I. He was also well known around the state. If SMU could sign him, the pass receivers and running backs would follow.

Ford had wanted to be a Texas Longhorn all along. He had a friend from high school who was already in Austin, which helped, but really for Ford, as for most Texas schoolboys of his generation, it was no contest. If the Longhorns would have him, that was where he wanted to go.

SMU started after Ford early, the summer before his senior year. This was not usually done in the Southwest Conference. Meyer, though, was an outsider. He didn't play by anybody else's rules. One summer he personally visited more than seventy recruits, an act of aggression that may or may not have paid dividends in the fall but definitely spoiled a lot of other coaches' summer vacations.

Larry Kennan worked hard to lay the groundwork. He and his wife took the trouble to get to know Ford's parents. During the 1976 Mesquite football season, Kennan was in the stands every Friday. Meyer was with him the night Mesquite played Highland Park, a big game that they lost despite a brilliant performance by Ford.

Afterward, Ford came home to find a raucous party under way. The SMU coaches were there—they had sat with Ford's parents at the game—and, as Ford remembers, everyone was drinking and hollering and listening to country music. Ford shook hands with Meyer but he didn't stick around for long. The loss to Highland Park had been hard on Ford and he was in no mood to chat.

Later when they talked at length, Meyer told Ford what any high-school quarterback would have wanted to hear: that SMU would throw the football; that he would have an opportunity to come in and be the starting quarterback right away, as a freshman; and that he would be famous—everybody in the country would know who he was by the time he was nineteen. Ford believed him.

SMU was helped unexpectedly when Fred Akers replaced Darrell Royal at Texas midway through recruiting season. Royal was a legend, winner of eleven SWC titles and three national championships during his twenty-year reign as head coach. Akers, who would last eleven tumultuous seasons before he was fired in 1986, was not Royal. People who met him for the first time often found his manner abrasive. Players called him Frantic Freddy.

Akers wanted very badly to sign Mike Ford. Soon after he was hired, he sat down to a home-cooked breakfast in the Ford's kitchen. He had brought along Ken Dabbs, his recruiting coordinator, and Alan Lowry, a former Texas quarterback. "I listened to him talk for about three hours," Mike Ford remembers, "about what the burnt orange *had done*, and he didn't never say anything about what we was gonna do. And I said, 'I can tell right now, I need to start lookin' elsewhere to go to school.' "

Mrs. Ford was pushing hard for SMU. She hoped her boy would stay close to home. She thought it might aid the cause if SMU knew something about Texas's recruiting strategy. With that in mind, she called the SMU football office, made a connection, and hid the telephone under the couch. Akers never knew it, but Mike Ford was not the only one who heard his spiel that day.

Mike Ford made an oral commitment to attend SMU on New Year's Eve 1976, six weeks before national signing day in February. He called Meyer from a party and gave him the good news. "I've made up my mind, Ron," he said. "I'm coming to school there. Go get us some help."

* * *

MEYER HAD COME TO Dallas believing that the only way to win big at SMU was by recruiting coast to coast. It would be a struggle at first, he knew, but if a small school like Notre Dame could pick and choose from among the best high-school players in California, New Jersey, and Florida, why not SMU? Then he had realized he didn't have to do that; there were more than enough top-drawer players in Texas to take him as far as he wanted to go. Eventually he narrowed his sights even more. Most of the players who would carry SMU to national prominence in the early 1980s were recruited from a narrow corridor along either side of Interstate 45, the 292-mile stretch of highway connecting Dallas in the north with Houston in the south and ending at Galveston on the Gulf of Mexico.

In fact, as Meyer used to say, he probably could have won a national championship with his pick of the top high-school recruits from *Dallas County alone*. But the Mustangs had a reputation in Dallas. They were losers. Mike Ford was the notable exception; most top players who had a choice did not want anything to do with SMU. So in the beginning, Meyer looked south, focusing his attention on the powerful inner-city high schools in Houston, where SMU was hardly known at all.

LUTHER BOOKER, HEAD COACH at Houston Yates, has been coaching at black high schools in Houston long enough to remember when his best players had two options if they wanted to play college football: Enroll at a black school in the Southwestern Athletic Conference (SWAC), such as Prairie View A&M, Texas Southern, or Grambling; or, if they were venturesome (and truly among the elite class of athletes), seek a scholarship from one of the big state universities in the Midwest or the West, such as Michigan, Colorado, or UCLA. The latter were a small minority. Until the late 1960s most black athletes from Texas or anywhere else in the South who played college football played at black colleges. Typically, facilities were second-rate, exposure was limited, and opportunities to advance to the pros were few.

As long as the SWC was segregated, nonconference schools that did recruit black athletes were free to pick and choose. "You know," Booker says, "UCLA or USC or Michigan, they didn't have a lot of difficulty recruiting in this area. They came here and just took what they wanted. They had no competition. 'Wow, you mean I can go to Michigan?' Gone. 'California, are you kidding?' Gone. After Levias . . ."

Jerry Levias turned Texas football upside down, opening up a new era of intense competition among SWC schools for the services of black athletes. Levias came from Beaumont, a steamy Gulf Coast city eighty-five miles west of Houston. Beaumont owes its status as a modern industrial center to nearby Spindletop, the world's first great oil gusher, which spewed thousands of barrels into the Texas sky on a winter evening in 1901. Together with the cities of Port Arthur and Orange, it defines an area known as the Golden Triangle. The term refers to the region's considerable industrial clout, but when college recruiters speak of the Golden Triangle, they're talking about football players, not petrochemicals. Beaumont, a city of just over 120,000, once had sixteen native sons earning a living in the National Football League. The city promotes itself as the Pro Football Capital of the World.

As a boy Levias played football on the same sandlot in the Pear Orchard section of Beaumont as Bubba Smith (who starred at Michigan State and later with the Baltimore Colts) and Mel Farr (UCLA, Detroit Lions). What he lacked in size (five ten, 170 pounds), he more than made up for with speed, (he ran the hundred in 9.5), quickness, and agility. As a running back at Beaumont Hebert High, he scored twenty-six touchdowns his junior year, seventeen as a senior. In the summer of 1965 he turned down offers from almost one hundred other colleges to sign with SMU, becoming the first black scholarship athlete in the history of the Southwest Conference.

Why was SMU the school that broke the color barrier? Partly, it was a question of market forces. On the supply side, there was an imbalance: a shortage of white athletes with the skills to play major-college football and a large surplus of blacks. Demand was uneven. Texas and Arkansas, the traditional powers, lagged several years behind in the recruitment of blacks, in part because they were able to sign more than enough top white players. Texas, in fact, was the last college in the country to win the national championship with an all-white roster, in 1969. But for SMU integration was a practical necessity.

Luther Booker remembers attending a coaches clinic in the early 1960s where he heard Hayden Fry, the SMU coach who signed

Levias, predict that the private schools in the Southwest Conference would be the first to integrate. "Because just dealing with predominantly white athletes, they didn't get the choice," Booker says. "The choice was going to Texas, Oklahoma, A&M, the big state schools. The small private schools just couldn't compete without using the black athlete."

BY 1977, ALMOST A DECADE after Jerry Levias graduated from SMU, assistant coach Steve Endicott (who is white) looked sufficiently conspicuous on his first recruiting trip to Houston Kashmere High School (which is almost all black) that a student asked him if he was a narc. That was fine, as far as Meyer was concerned. Let them think what they want, as long as they remember who you are. Meyer says the main reason he hired Endicott in the first place was because of his hair. He wanted people thinking, "Endicott, the blond guy, right? From SMU?"

Other SWC schools were recruiting at Kashmere in the late 1970s (Texas A&M, University of Houston), but none made it a priority like SMU. "He [Meyer] didn't give me the idea that I could only give him one or two [players]," says Johnny Felder, the former head coach at Kashmere. "When he talked to the coaches he let them know, 'This is a new day. We're depending on this school.'"

Between 1977 and 1979 SMU signed eight players from Kashmere: Anthony Smith, an all-state receiver, and his brother Gary, all-city at the same position; Lee Spivey, an all-state offensive lineman; Harvey Armstrong, an all-state defensive tackle; Eric Ferguson, an all-American linebacker; Michael Charles, an all-state running back; Stanley Godine, a defensive back who was one of three high-school seniors in 1979 (together with two other SMU recruits, Eric Dickerson and Craig James) to receive unanimous can't-miss ratings in the annual *Texas Football* magazine poll of SWC coaches; and Don Pettaway, a basketball player who made such a strong impression on Endicott when he saw him one day in the gym (the eye test) that SMU offered him a scholarship. With the exception of Pettaway—whose promising career ended sadly when he drowned the summer after his freshman year—all were major contributors to SMU's early success.

Endicott, whose recruiting territory was inner-city Houston, was probably the strongest recruiter on the staff after Meyer. "He made a great impression on me," says Armstrong, now with the Indianapolis Colts. "This young, blond-headed guy who was very energetic, very talkative. He just had a lot of spunk in him, like he should still be playing football. It wasn't like he was always trying to put pressure on me—'Come on, sign with SMU'—it wasn't that. He just made you feel so comfortable around him. Other guys did not make you feel that way."

The Texas A&M recruiter in Houston was Dan LaGrasta. Most of the players thought he was nice enough; he just failed to connect with them the way Endicott did. LaGrasta had a habit of coming up on players from behind and grabbing them affectionately by the neck. "He thought the guys enjoyed it," says Armstrong. "I hated it."

"The recruiters were mostly white," says Gary Smith, "and I just felt like they . . . well, they just tried to overwhelm you with everything. Like, 'This is the greatest thing that we're fixing to give you that you've ever had.' It got to be bothersome. Or they would put down other schools. It seemed like they always had to be saying something and they didn't know what to say. [Endicott] was real down to earth, real easygoing. Everybody really liked him. He seemed to really care about the players. He was sincere."

THE OTHER KEY MEMBER of the SMU recruiting team in Houston was Robin Buddecke, a local stockbroker. Buddecke was in his midthirties, compactly built, an energetic, ambitious man who had achieved success in life well beyond what had been expected of him. Buddecke's involvement in SMU recruiting had nothing to do with school ties (he attended Lamar University). His loyalty was to Meyer, with whom he had much in common. They met for the first time in 1976 at the home of Burnie Miller, Buddecke's neighbor and a member of Meyer's original staff. "We sat up practically all night," Buddecke remembers, "and got heavy into the Scotch, and we talked football. To me that was great, I loved it, and listening to Ron I immediately liked him."

Buddecke was raised during the 1950s in Beaumont, believing in racial segregation. Long after he moved to Houston, he still could not have found his way to Kashmere High without a map. "I don't think that I had ever met a black kid," says Buddecke, "other than seeing them in a store or having them mow my yard. I had never sat down and talked to a black kid for more than thirty seconds in my whole life."

Buddecke's life changed dramatically when he began accompanying Endicott on recruiting visits to Kashmere and Yates. Together they roamed the halls, exploring what for Buddecke was an "alien world."

"It was tough for me at first," he says, "but once I got over that it was a very natural thing. I wasn't intimidated, I didn't have any ill feelings, I wasn't embarrassed or anything, I was just fascinated."

One of Buddecke's first assignments was to nail down commitments from several Houston-area recruits on signing day in 1977. "That really got my juices cranked up," Buddecke says. "That was the part that I really liked. Not just signing a kid—getting it done. Making the sale. Getting the order closed and signed. There's a great deal of adrenaline pumping when you do that."

In time Robin Buddecke became the unofficial SMU station chief in Houston. He met Meyer and Endicott at the airport. He went along on school visits. He joined them for dinner in the homes of recruits, then followed up after they returned to Dallas. He took care of details: making sure they had cars when they were in town; arranging for an apartment with a telephone where they could set up a field headquarters; locating an alumnus with a private airplane when they needed to be somewhere in a hurry.

On Friday nights during football season Buddecke and Endicott would go to games. "It wasn't so much that we had to see them play," Buddecke says. "It was a matter of making sure they knew we were there. We would get there in time for the pregame and always get down on the fence, someplace close, where the player you were recruiting could see you. That was essential. It was real important to them; if you didn't care about coming to their game, then to hell with you. So we always came. Then we would leave there and try and catch another game, try to get there right before halftime. As the player came off the field, you would position yourself so that he sees you. If you didn't expose yourself to him, then you would go up in the stands, make sure you find his girlfriend or his mother or a teacher, somebody you knew would tell the player, 'Oh, I saw Mr. Buddecke.' Very important. And then we would go to the third game and make sure we were there at the end, to shake hands or whatever."

Buddecke got a kick out of all that. He liked working with Endicott and Meyer and was flattered to be in their confidence. The gossip he picked up—what this kid was really like, where that kid was leaning—was all good stuff for sharing with friends and clients. Later, he would begin to see a financial advantage in helping out with recruiting, but for now, Buddecke was just having fun. So he was willing to take the next step; to do the things that would not have met with NCAA approval, had the NCAA had any idea what was going on.

Buddecke says the first time he saw money pass between a coach and a high-school football player was during the summer of 1977. "Ron came down," he says, "and so it was Ron, myself, Endy [Endicott], and maybe another coach. We were recruiting at Kashmere. We talked to a bunch of kids that day. I can't pin it down but it was maybe twenty or fifty bucks or something like that we gave one of the players. I don't even remember who it was now but it did strike me as, *hmmmm, well.* I was sort of getting the idea at that time that this was more than a selling job."

A coach gave a twenty-dollar bill to a seventeen-year-old kid. Whoever the kid was, he probably doesn't remember the details today any better than Buddecke does. It was nothing more than a first step, a small one, and if it has any significance now, it is only because of what we know was waiting at the end of the road. In time, the twenty-dollar bills would become one-hundred-dollar bills. The casual contacts and occasional gifts would be formalized into a virtual payroll. Eventually, paid athletes would bring SMU SWC championships, bowl games, a run at a national title, and, in the end, ruin.

5 EXPENSES

LIKE ANY SMALL, unknown company trying to enter a new market, SMU's first problem in Houston was how to convince their major customers that it meant business. "Basically," says Anthony Smith, one of the first Kashmere players to sign with SMU, "nobody really had hardly heard of SMU." When Eric Dickerson—who is from Sealy, forty miles west of Houston—was first approached by Endicott in the summer of 1978, he had no idea that SMU was even in Texas.

Robin Buddecke, the stockbroker, had had experience with cold prospects. This game was played a little bit differently but he knew what to do. "In the early stages," he says, "they wouldn't even let us in the door. I mean, you couldn't even call them on the phone. They didn't want anything to do with SMU. SMU was like The Citadel, it was some unknown quantity. So we had to be up front. We basically bribed players to come visit. We handed out small amounts of cash, twenty-dollar bills, not thousands or anything like that. You wouldn't say, 'Here, I'm giving you twenty dollars with the understanding that you're gonna come visit and you're gonna sign with us.' The way I approached it in my own mind was, 'This kid is my son, he has a date tonight.' What do I do? I reach in my pocket and give him a twenty-dollar bill. It was not done with the [idea] that we're gonna buy players, that was not the angle at all. We wanted to show them that we had some class, that we had the wherewithal to take care of them."

Buddecke's willingness to part with medium-size bills gained him a measure of notoriety. One incident stands out. It took place in December, Buddecke remembers, either 1978 or 1979; in any case, after SMU had become firmly entrenched at Kashmere. He left the office early one day and swung by Kashmere for the afternoon, dressed, as usual, in a coat and tie and wearing a fur-collared Burberry raincoat. He entered the school through a side door that opens on to a covered quadrangle, where students congregate between classes. "I was bouncing in," remembers Buddecke beginning to laugh, "and there was a whole cluster of them—they were standing around almost in choir formation—and as soon as they saw me coming around the corner (Buddecke is laughing so hard now he can barely talk), they burst out with a rendition of 'Here Comes Santa Claus'!"

EVERY YEAR IN DECEMBER, after football season, high-school players begin making their official paid visits. The NCAA allows prospects to visit no more than five campuses, so competition among recruiters to make what amounts to the first cut is intense. "When we got into the official visits, that's when we kind of went overboard," says Buddecke. "That's when we really started to get serious about this thing.

"Number one, you might get a commitment out of a kid to come up there but that doesn't mean he's gonna get on the plane and show up. This is true with everybody. You have to baby them. I mean, you gotta pick them up, take them to the airport, get them their tickets, and put them on the plane—bye-bye—and have somebody at the other end to pick them up. Let's face it, your official visit has got to be your close. It's got to be when you put your best foot forward, when you do what you have to do. All that other stuff is the movies but this is the senior prom. So my job was to make damn sure I got those kids on the plane and make damn sure they were *happy.* You pass them a few bucks, you know, 'Oh, this is just in case you have any problems.' It's like packing your kid off to summer camp, visit to grandma, same thing. I'm sure their parents gave, too. I just sweetened the kitty a little bit. I never had a kid turn it down. I always did it right and I took pride in doing it right."

Buddecke says the money he handed out to players at the airport was usually between $50 and $100 per person. Sometimes there were extra benefits. "In a very few special cases," says Buddecke, "a few players would get a small wardrobe for the weekend. Oh, pair of slacks, maybe a sport coat, maybe a leather jacket, couple of shirts, shoes. We're not talking about Brooks Brothers or anything but we're not talking about Wal-Mart, either."

Once in Dallas, chances are the player would be introduced to another booster—one with strong paternal instincts of his own—who would be happy to help him pick out a souvenir gold chain for his girlfriend or something nice for his mother. Then maybe there would be a free dinner at Tony Roma's, owned by Dallas Cowboys owner and SMU booster Clint Murchison, and later a tour of the music clubs on Greenville Avenue, hosted by a current member of the team. The NCAA limit on entertainment expenses—even today, only $20 per player—was routinely exceeded. "If you go out on Greenville to party," says Buddecke, "you go out in style."

SMU WAS BY NO MEANS the only villain in Houston in the late 1970s, or even the biggest. The violations Buddecke describes were routine. If SMU was sometimes more flagrant than its competitors, that was because SMU entered the race at the back of the pack and had to make up ground. But nothing SMU did was new. A lot of recruiters handed out small amounts of cash. A lot of them followed players around, picking up tabs. That was the way it was done.

In fact when it came to the more serious violations—cars, big money, expensive clothes, things that were offered as part of a package deal in exchange for a player's signed commitment—SMU, in the beginning, was actually cleaner than most. This was not necessarily because SMU respected the rules and the others didn't; SMU just didn't have the cash.

Eric Ferguson, who came close to signing with Texas A&M, used to chide the SMU recruiters for being "pikers" compared to everybody else. Harvey Armstrong, who says he was offered a new car by a school in the Big Eight Conference, claims SMU was, at best, "competitive in the Southwest Conference. SMU wasn't the bad guy on the block."

Player after player describes turning down better offers from other schools in order to sign with SMU. "The going thing in Houston," says Anthony Smith, one of the first players recruited by SMU in 1977, "was, 'Hey, man, take the money, get you a car.' You wanted to be proud of being a great athlete and you wanted to let it show. It was manifested in cars, nice clothes. So I had that thrown my way. I was supposed to sign with this particular school. I was offered a brand-new Ford of my choice and five thousand dollars on the table. It was out there. Nothing but hundreds. Five thousand dollars. Right there. Bam. And then the promise on the handshake that I could come down to the Ford place and pick out the Ford of my choice. I had some people ... they weren't even the coaches, they'd say, 'Anthony, I'm down here to do whatever it takes to get you to come to my school.' That just scared me. I was like, 'Damn!' I'd go home, I'd think about it, 'Hey, I could use a car and nice clothes.' Because you wanted to be seen. That was just the going thing.

"But the ironic thing about it," says Smith, "SMU was probably one of the most straight-up schools. Endicott said, 'We don't have a whole lot of money. I can't offer you all this stuff that everybody else is.' "

No one who saw Ron Meyer operate ever would have believed that SMU was cash poor. He always made a point of looking prosperous. He still carried a one-hundred-dollar bill everywhere he went; once, on a visit to Baytown Sterling High, east of Houston, he pinned one on a bulletin board where other coaches had left their business cards.

Meyer *was* Dallas: cool, urban, sophisticated, and somewhat overblown. When he walked the halls at Kashmere in his alligator pumps, he made the competition look like so many buffoons in cowboy boots. "Meyer was flashy, flamboyant, well dressed," says Richard Frank, a Kashmere assistant. "He was wearing clothes kids in this neighborhood could relate to—a pretty leather jacket with a turtleneck and a diamond ring or two; they could relate to that. Or a nice, bright, pretty sport coat with an expensive tie and shirt. He didn't come in looking like a hen. He came in looking like a rooster. As the kids would say, he was clean."

Luther Booker has a vivid recollection of the first day Meyer visited Yates. "He had that black hair rolling back at the time," Booker says. "Three-piece suit. It was cold out, he had on a heavy overcoat. He made a very strong impression but he said very, very little. The air that he had when he came in, I wouldn't have thought he was a coach. Tell you the truth, he looked more like the godfather."

MEYER'S IMAGE HELPED make up for SMU's lack of funds. It lent some authority to the vague promise, often repeated, "We're gonna take care of you." But in order to follow through on that promise,

SMU needed substantially more money than it had. The money could not come only from the heavy hitters; it had to come from small and medium-size contributors, too. And it had to be available whenever it was needed to cover the many expenses not ordinarily accounted for in the athletic-department budget. For that to happen, someone had to build an organization. This, according to Buddecke and other SMU boosters, some of whom asked not to be identified, was Meyer's unique skill.

"Ron Meyer built the organization," says one of the nine SMU boosters who were banned from any association with SMU athletics after an NCAA investigation in 1985. "He's the one that built the organization to do the funding for the football players and then went out and recruited the football players and funded them. He set it up initially. Dave Smith (Meyer's predecessor) was not able to do that."

Among the names frequently mentioned in connection with the origin of the fund are two ex-SMU athletes who would later play a big role in SMU's demise under Bobby Collins, Meyer's successor: George Owen and Sherwood Blount. Both would be among the nine banned boosters. But according to sources familiar with how the slush fund worked, neither was instrumental in its creation. "They were basically bagmen, that's all they were," according to a booster who asked not to be identified. "I mean, they were just delivering the bucks. They could raise some money. I'm sure they probably did. But they were not the instigators. They were not the ones who put the thing together. Ron Meyer is the one that basically got these people together and said, 'Here's what we can do and here's how we can do it.' "

Down in Houston, Robin Buddecke raised some money on his own from local sources. Not all of the two dozen or so serious SMU boosters in Houston were contributors to the fund. Some provided summer jobs for players, others donated their cars or airplanes during recruiting, still others attended the periodic luncheons at the Racquet Club and occasional dinners at River Oaks Country Club mainly to hear the recruiting gossip. But there were always two or three who were willing to go one step further.

"You didn't have to go into any great detail," Buddecke explains. "Just common sense tells you that there are expenses that are not accountable for, period. Remember, we're talking about business-men. I mean, I didn't approach anyone who was on salary working for Exxon. The people that were able to contribute were people in construction and other businesses who were in a position to know that if you're gonna get that sewer line laid, you have to talk to the county engineer; take him out to lunch, show him ten thousand dollars on the table, and you get your sewer line approved. We're not talking about anything that was foreign to them. Usually those kinds of guys were the ones who would step up."

By 1978, Meyer's third year at SMU, there was enough money in the fund to have a significant impact on recruiting. The action was still centered in Houston. Most of the cash that was distributed there passed through Buddecke's hands. When he needed money in a hurry and could not immediately contact a source, he took out a loan. According to Buddecke, even Meyer occasionally borrowed money to handle emergency expenses. "We basically had to run a debtor-type situation," Buddecke says. "We would borrow money from a bank, take loans, Ron and I. Ron made several, I made a bunch. They weren't big loans. They were five-thousand-dollar, ten-thousand-dollar loans."

Most of the money to pay back the loans came from Dallas. Buddecke traveled there frequently to meet with clients, and so it was convenient for him to take care of recruiting business at the same time. Sometimes, Buddecke says, he received money directly from Meyer. More often, he would go to Bobby Stewart.

ROBERT HENRY STEWART III is an example of what *D* magazine calls "straight Dallas establishment." He was raised in tony Highland Park, graduated from SMU in 1948, and immediately went to work for Empire State Bank in Dallas. In 1951 he joined First National Bank as a cashier in the business-development department. Banking is in Stewart's blood: His grandfather was chairman of First National and his father was on the board; an uncle was chairman of Manufacturer's Hanover in New York.

Stewart rose quickly up the ladder at First National: vice president in two years, senior vice president six years later. After nine years, at age thirty-five, he became the youngest bank president in the United States. By then Stewart was being called "the light of the future in Dallas," and was acquiring a national reputation as well. He turned down cabinet posts under Presidents Nixon and Ford and was said to be a candidate for treasury secretary under President Carter.

Stewart was a longtime member of the SMU board of governors—the most powerful governing body in the university—and became its chairman in 1976. By then he was also chairman and chief executive officer of First International Bancshares, the bank holding company that grew out of First National. His office was on the fifty-sixth floor of the new fifty-six-story First International Building, then the tallest building in Dallas.

Stewart was a fan of SMU football. So were a lot of his rich friends. That made Stewart an ideal fund raiser. On numerous occasions between 1977 and 1981 Robin Buddecke visited Stewart's office. Usually, Buddecke says, Stewart would reach into his desk drawer, take out a thick envelope, and hand it to Buddecke. If Stewart wasn't there, his secretary would be expecting Buddecke and she would hand him the envelope. Inside the envelope were one-hundred-dollar bills.

NOT ALL OF THE MONEY went directly from the the wallets of wealthy boosters to bagmen like Buddecke and into the hands of the players. There were legitimate recruiting expenses that had to be met—gas for the car, phone bills, maybe a meal with a potential contributor. And players' needs varied. From 1978 on, the most common arrangement in Houston was not a large up-front payment, or a car, but an agreement to make modest continuing payments directly to the player's family. Several hundred a month from September to June ($2,500–$4,500 per year) was usually all it took. Then if the family wanted to buy the player a car, they could afford it—and the NCAA would be none the wiser.

Once a month Buddecke drove from house to house through some of the poorer neighborhoods in Houston, like an insurance collector; only Buddecke wasn't collecting, he was paying. "I would make my little rounds," he says, "and they were so appreciative. You had a sense that, 'God, I'm really doing something nice, I'm being a really good guy.' I really felt good about it. And I think the players really appreciated it. It was like you were taking care of business for them, making sure their families were taken care of. It was just a good way to do it."

"And," says Buddecke, "if the NCAA would come to you and say, 'Did you give this *player* money?' [and you said,] 'No,' a lightning bolt wasn't gonna come flashing down on you."

Other monies were handed out in Dallas on an as-needed basis. If a player had to have a new set of tires for his car, or his battery went dead, or he was surprised with a phone bill he couldn't pay, then there was always someone willing to help out. This is what SMU coaches meant when they promised a player, "We'll take care of you."

Taking care of your own is a tradition as old as college football. Many SMU boosters are bitter because they believe that the University of Texas, for example, which has a reputation for being relatively honest, is at best honest only until their players arrive on campus; then they take care of them like anybody else. SMU— because it is unable to attract players without making payments in advance—gets caught, and Texas doesn't.

The practice is often justified on humanitarian grounds. After all, many scholarship athletes are poor. When Ron Meyer was still at Nevada–Las Vegas, he had a rule requiring that players wear dress shoes on team trips. Once, the story goes, when a player arrived at the airport in sneakers, Meyer berated him in front of his teammates. Later Meyer learned that the sneakers were the only shoes the player owned. He immediately apologized and gave the player $50 to buy a new pair.

But there are reasons other than charity why a coach might do something for a player. A booster explains: "I don't care who [the coach] is, if a player has a problem—his car is broken down, his mother's sick, she needs medicine—and he needs cash, I guarantee you either the coach would get it for him or he'll send him to somebody who will take care of him. There is no way on God's green earth that a football coach is gonna let a valuable commodity be screwed up in the head because he's having an outside problem. When all these holier-than-thous say, 'Oh, we're clean, we don't do that,' bullshit. If they don't take care of their players, there is something wrong with them."

At SMU, players were taken care of in many different ways. If the player was a star, chances were he had a special relationship with a particular booster: Eric Dickerson with Buddecke; Craig James with Sherwood Blount; Mike Ford and Harvey Armstrong with George Owen; Michael Carter and Ricky Bolden with Ronnie Horowitz (a University of Texas graduate who, like Buddecke, recruited on behalf of SMU out of loyalty to Ron Meyer).

"I know that George [Owen] didn't have anything but good intentions for the people he was helping," says Mike Ford. "If you cut the man's arm, he'd bleed red, white, and blue, you know what I'm saying? I imagine every school in the country's got their George Owen; 'By God, I'm gonna do what I gotta do to help Tom, Dick, and Harry.' I don't think the world would go around if there wasn't people like that."

Players without a sugar daddy of their own could still get cash when they needed it. Many went to Steve Endicott. "He was like my father figure," says Anthony Smith. "You know, 'Hey coach, I'm going home this weekend, is there any kind of way I could get some gas money?' When you needed money, someone would provide it."

"If I had to be dependent on my parents to tide me through my own four years," says Gary Smith, "boy, it would have been tough."

Not all of the players who went to Endicott for help came from poor families. One ex-player says he went to Endicott on at least two occasions—once after several weeks of losing bets on profootball games and once after an expensive night on the town with friends—simply because he preferred not to ask his father for money. Endicott took care of him.

Another ex-player, a transfer student, says that whenever he came up short, he asked Coach Meyer for help: "If I needed a hundred bucks or something, I went to Meyer. I just went, 'Hey listen, something's come up, I need this and I just don't know how to take care of it, being in the position I'm in right now.' And he said, more or less, 'Well, why don't you come back to the office tomorrow,' and that's all he said. And I went by and his secretary said, 'Oh, there's something here for you,' and handed me the envelope. That's how I did it."

As the team improved, there were always more opportunities to make money. Many players sold their complimentary game tickets, a common practice, especially when tickets are in demand. "You could get fifty dollars a ticket pretty easily," says a former SMU receiver. "When it came to a big game, you'd have guys calling you early saying, 'Look, man, I gotta get some tickets, pay you whatever.' "

Depending on the game, some players say they received as much as $150 per ticket, or a total of $600 for the four free tickets the NCAA allows each player. Selling tickets, even at face value, is a violation of NCAA rules.

And then there were the occasional pennies from heaven. An ex-player from Houston describes how once after a game he received $500 in the mail from a Houston doctor whom he had never met; the cash was wrapped in a newspaper clipping that featured the player's picture. "You had a great game," the doctor wrote, "I know you can use this." Another ex-player describes how once, while dressing after a big game, he discovered that the toes of his shoes were stuffed with cash.

SINCE 1986 RON MEYER has been the head coach of the Indianapolis Colts. Whenever he is asked, he denies having any knowledge of improprieties committed during his tenure at SMU. Recently, in his office at the Colts' training complex northwest of Indianapolis, he was asked again.

Meyer looked prosperous, as always. He had come out from behind his desk and was sitting cross-legged on the couch, dressed like the chief executive of an international perfume conglomerate: European-cut blue pin-striped suit, pink shirt, red tie with blue paisleys, a pink silk hanky. A gold chain dangled from his wrist.

Is he responsible for what happened at SMU? Did he pay players? Was he aware, at least, of what was going on?

"No," Meyer said quietly, covering his mouth with his hand, tensing his eyebrows, staring straight at his questioner with black-blue eyes. "No, nothing like that."

ROBIN BUDDECKE WONDERS how Meyer could say that. "Did Meyer actually sit in front of you and tell you he didn't make any payments?" Buddecke asks. "He said that with a straight face? God!"

Later, Buddecke would reconsider: "When Ron told you, 'No, I did not *pay* any players,' now that I think back on it, I don't really remember seeing Ron do that. Maybe in all honesty that is true. Did he *know* about it? Of course. He can't deny that. I mean, there's no way. That was the key to our organization. That's why he was successful—if you want to call it that—and the other guy, Collins, wasn't. We knew that Ron was the ultimate decision maker and we all accepted that, whether it was me or George [Owen] or anybody. Ron had control and that's what made the thing work."

6 GOOD ON THE HOOF

MEYER'S FIRST TWO SEASONS as head coach at SMU were indistinguishable, to most observers, from the bleak years that preceded them. But in 1978 he began to make some headway. SMU opened at home against TCU and won (for the seventh year in a row), 45–14. Then Meyer and his young squad embarked on a hellish, three-game road trip. First stop, Gainesville, Florida, where SMU shocked the University of Florida, 35–25. One week later in Happy Valley, SMU was narrowly defeated, 26–21, by Penn State, the top-ranked team in the nation. The following Saturday, Meyer went home to Columbus for a game against Ohio State—still coached by his childhood hero, Woody Hayes. With many of his old Westerville buddies looking on, Meyer's Mustangs out-gained the Buckeyes by two hundred yards, missed a game-ending forty-eight-yard field goal, and settled for a 35–35 tie.

It was disappointing to go home with a 2-1-1 record when they had come so close to being 3–1, or even 4–0. Yet the idea that SMU—just two years after the humiliating loss to Alabama at Tuscaloosa—could hold its own against some of the top teams in the country was more than enough (at this point) to satisfy the boosters.

Mike Ford, a sophomore in 1978, and playing his second year as quarterback, was just beginning to realize his predicted stardom. Against Ohio State he completed thirty-six passes—one shy of the all-time SMU record—for 341 yards. By season's end he had emerged as the nation's leader in total offense with 2,957 yards. His favorite receiver was junior wideout Emmanuel Tolbert, who caught sixty-two passes for 1,041 yards and eleven touchdowns. Tolbert finished second in the nation in receiving and was a first-team all-America selection of the Associated Press.

Despite brilliant individual performances by Ford and Tolbert, the Mustangs finished 1978 with a record of 4-6-1. Yet it was a triumph. The three SWC victories (TCU, Baylor, and Rice) were what mattered most. Meyer's first goal—supremacy among the league's private schools—had been met. Finally, the players, mostly freshmen and sophomores, could see a bright future.

MIKE HARVEY, AN SMU business-school professor who served as faculty athletic representative for ten years, remembers sitting with SMU president James Zumberge in the press box at the Cotton Bowl while SMU played Rice in 1977. The game was going well for the Mustangs—they were slaughtering the Owls, 41–24—but Zumberge, a former chancellor of the University of Nebraska, was angry. Spread out beneath him were almost 65,000 empty seats; the crowd of 6,918 was smaller by far than what many players were used to in high school. Harvey recalls Zumberge turning to him and saying with conviction, "This will never happen again."

Zumberge's thinking, according to Harvey, was this: "You can't have any part of the university that's significantly below the level of the other parts of the university or it will pull the good parts down. You can't have a bad law school—you improve the quality of the law school or get out of it. The visibility and public-relations value of sports meant that you couldn't get out of it. He understood the environment he was in. Notre Dame, everybody's heard of it. 'Good school.' It's really a pretty crummy school. But there's a national reputation at that school that helps them attract faculty.

"I think it's necessary, when you're not a prominent university, to get the publicity like Notre Dame gets, so that over time you can evolve into—if all goes well—a prominent university. We're not a prominent university. We're a second-tier liberal-arts school. Nothing wrong with that. You can get an excellent education here. But if you're trying to aspire to a higher level of visibility and education, the only way you can do that is by public relations."

Attendance at SMU football games had been low for twenty years. The average in 1977 was only 26,635, a 38-percent drop from 1959 (the year before the Cowboys arrived) and less than half of the more than sixty thousand fans per game who streamed into the Cotton Bowl in 1949 to cheer Doak Walker and Kyle Rote. As a result, the SMU athletic department suffered substantial operating deficits—between $200,000 and $1 million a year throughout the decade of the 1970s.

In the fall of 1978 President Zumberge hired Russ Potts as the new SMU athletic director. His mandate: to revitalize fan interest. Potts came from the University of Maryland, where, in 1971, he had been the first full-time promoter ever employed by a university athletic department. Thanks in part to Potts's promotional zeal, the Maryland radio network had grown from one station in 1970 to fifty-five in 1977. Record ad sales had fattened the game program from fifty-five pages to 202, and attendance at football and basketball games had increased by leaps and bounds. By the time Potts left Maryland for SMU (and brought along his assistant, Brad Thomas, to be his promotions director) more than thirty colleges around the country had hired their own version of Russ Potts. He had created a new profession.

One of the first things Potts and Thomas did was invent a slogan: Mustang Mania. By the fall of 1978, Mustang Mania was on buttons, plastic cups, T-shirts, billboards, posters, pocket schedules, and car bumpers all over Dallas. All this occurred well before Mustang Mania actually existed. For that, Potts had to fill the Cotton Bowl with Mustang Maniacs; not easy given the fact that even if every living SMU alumnus from every corner of the globe were to attend the same game, there would still be empty seats.

Potts was resourceful. He knew that an empty seat never bought a hot dog, never bought a program, and worst of all, was likely to come back next week. The first game against TCU in 1978—a "nothing" game, by any reasonable standard—became the Jerry Lewis Bowl. A portion of the proceeds went to the Muscular Dystrophy Association. One hundred seventy-five thousand balloons were released. Jerry Lewis showed up. So did 41,112 fans.

Potts and his thousand-watt sidekick, Thomas, ran the major-college equivalent of a minor-league baseball franchise. They gave away hats and T-shirts, sponsored ten-thousand-dollar cash scrambles at halftime, brought in the San Diego Chicken, and convinced fraternity members to dress in tuxedos and escort female patrons to their seats. "Just stuff," says Thomas, "just *stuff.*" Mostly, they passed out a lot of free tickets; once—against Baylor in 1979 at Texas stadium—they passed out so many they had to turn back ticket holders at the gate.

Statistically, the results were impressive. After SMU's long road trip at the beginning of the 1978 season, the Mustangs came home to the eleventh largest crowd in regular-season history: 64,871. Average attendance at SMU home games in 1978 jumped to 51,960, up 95 percent in one year. According to officials at SMU, it was the third largest single-season increase in the history of college football. How much of that represented an actual increase in paying customers is anybody's guess.

IN 1979 SMU's recruiting and promoting and spending finally struck a fire. Even casual fans of college football will recognize the two biggest names in SMU's recruiting class of that year: Craig James (running back of the New England Patriots) from Stratford High School in Houston; and Eric Dickerson (Indianapolis Colts) from Sealy, a town of 3,785 on the interstate fifty miles west of Houston. Either one by himself would have been a spectacular prize for any college program. That SMU was able to sign *both*—somehow convincing the two most talented high-school running backs in the state that their best interests lay in splitting time in the same backfield—stunned the rest of the conference.

There were other prizes in the same class: Charles Wagoner, a running back from Dallas Carter High, who outplayed Dickerson and James in fall practice but broke his neck early in the season and had to give up football ("He would have played eight years in the NFL," says Steve Endicott); Stanley Godine, the top-rated defensive back in the state from Houston Kashmere; Michael Carter (San Francisco 49ers), a nose tackle from Dallas Jefferson High; and linebackers Gary Moten (49ers) from Freeport and Kevin Chaney from Dallas Jefferson. Overall, the SMU class of '79 was rated number one in a 1986 *Texas Football* magazine analysis of the best SWC recruiting classes since 1976. According to *Texas Football*, "This is the group that changed the face of Southwest Conference football for the 1980s."

With Craig James—who could have gone to college anywhere he wanted—SMU was plain lucky. Craig's girlfriend (now his wife), Marilyn Arps, was one year ahead of him at Stratford High. They had been going out together since Craig was a freshman. When it came time for Marilyn to choose a college, she and Craig talked things over. As Craig remembers, Marilyn was interested in North Carolina, Duke, LSU, Texas, and SMU. Craig knew he didn't want to leave the state; and at that point in his career, he didn't think he would ever be good enough to play for the Longhorns. That left SMU. Marilyn liked SMU because she had a sister who was there. Craig didn't know much about it—only that when he was a little boy playing football with his friends, the customary insult after a dropped pass or a missed tackle was something like *Smoooo!* Craig thought he had a good chance to make it at SMU, even if he wasn't offered a scholarship.

Meyer and Endicott met with James at his home early in the summer of 1978. By then, James's play as a junior (757 yards rushing, sixteen touchdowns) had made him a top prospect. This was to be only a get-acquainted session, but as soon as Meyer formally invited James to attend SMU, James said, "Hey, I'm coming."

Meyer's shock, he later told James, was such that when he left the house he asked Endicott, "Are you sure this guy is as good as we think he is?"

He was better. In his senior year James rushed for 2,424 yards, scored thirty-four touchdowns (five on pass plays), and led his team to the class-AAAA state championship. Interest in James reached new levels. Other colleges used Eric Dickerson's growing interest in SMU as an argument for James to go elsewhere. James was also an outstanding baseball player (his brother Chris is an outfielder with the Philadelphia Phillies), and by the spring of his senior year, he was hearing offers of $150,000 to turn pro.

But in the end James stuck by his commitment to SMU. "I was going to SMU long before they even knew who I was," James says, "and that is a fact, the very hardest truth there is. It wasn't going to take any wining and dining to get me there."

ON THE SAME DAY in the summer of 1978 that Meyer and Endicott first met Craig James, they also drove to Richmond, a town of fifteen thousand, southwest of Houston on the Brazos River. Richmond was settled in 1822 by members of the Stephen F. Austin colony— the Old Three Hundred—and today is the seat of Fort Bend County. Endicott and Meyer drove several blocks past the turn-of-the-

century silver-domed courthouse to a pure white, beautifully re-
stored Victorian home, which belongs to Robin Buddecke. They had
an appointment there that afternoon with Eric Dickerson.

If there was a player in Texas who was more highly recruited
than Craig James it was Dickerson, who may have been the most
highly recruited player in the country. Dickerson was fast (9.4 in
the hundred), lean and muscular (six three, 207 pounds). After he
switched from split end to running back in the fourth game of his
sophomore season, he went on to rush for 5,889 yards in his high-
school career. Already he was being compared to two former Texas
high-school running backs who won Heisman Trophies as the best
college football player in the country: Texas's Earl Campbell (1977)
and Oklahoma's Billy Sims (1978).

Buddecke had made initial contact with Dickerson through Paul
Albert, an SMU player from Bellville, near Sealy, who had known
Dickerson in high school. Earlier that summer, Albert had brought
Dickerson over to Buddecke's house to shoot pool in the parlor and
talk informally about SMU. Today, Eric was coming back with his
stepfather, Robert, to meet the coaches.

Outsiders found Dickerson's family situation hard to figure out.
Apparently, Eric never knew his real father. He was raised by his
great-uncle, Carrie Dickerson, who died while Eric was a junior in
high school, and his great-aunt, Viola. Robert, the stepfather, lived
with Helen, Eric's real mother, in the house next to Eric's aunt's in
Sealy. Together with Eric's grandmother, Mae Shaver, who lived in
Houston, they made a close and loving extended family. Eric's childhood memories are happy ones.

The meeting at Buddecke's house went well. They ate barbecue
and got to know one another, and after it was over, everyone agreed
that Eric and his stepfather had seemed pleased.

Once football season began, either Buddecke or Endicott or
Meyer made sure he was at each of Eric's games. All the usual
politicking and jockeying for position that goes on whenever
coaches and boosters attend a high-school game was that much
greater in the case of Dickerson. Eric's stepfather was a popular
man in the stands with recruiters from all over the country; so
popular, in fact, that the SMU recruiters sometimes found it hard
to get close to him. As a result, Buddecke and Endicott usually
wound up with the women—Helen, Viola, and Mae. They were

building relationships that would later play an important role in Eric's decision.

Once or twice a year on fall Saturdays, SMU piled all the most important Houston-area recruits in a motor home and drove them up to Dallas to see a game. "It was really great," says Buddecke, "because it gave us a lot of time to spend with the kids. They had a little fun, drank their soda pop. No beer, nothing like that. We really tried to play it as straight as we could." In Dallas they would all watch the game together and afterward go down to the locker room to meet the coaches and the players. Then it was back to the motor home for the five-hour return trip to Houston.

Such an excursion was planned in the fall of 1978 for Dickerson, Stanley Godine, Michael Charles, and several other top recruits. They left Houston early on a Saturday morning heading north on I-45 and made it as far as Conroe—less than an hour out of town —when the motor home broke down. Buddecke knew he had a serious problem. Here they were at a service station next to the interstate in a broken-down motor home that happened to be filled with some of the most prized—and recognizable—high-school football players in Texas and they weren't supposed to be there. "This was obviously not an event sanctioned by the NCAA," Buddecke says, laughing. What to do?

There was an airport in Conroe. Buddecke had a little cash. So he called some taxicabs, carted everybody to the airport, and chartered two private planes. Some of the players had never flown before.

"I called Meyer," says Buddecke. "He said, 'What the hell are you doing?' I said, 'We're on our way, we're flying. Just have somebody at Love Field to meet us.' And so we put them on Cessnas and off we went. It turned out to be a great weekend. I think it impressed them, you know?"

One by one, all the other schools that had been in the running for Dickerson were falling out of the race. Texas Tech—which through shrewd, hard recruiting came close to pulling off an upset—lost out when Dickerson decided that Lubbock was just too small and too far away. The University of Texas—increasingly desperate under Fred Akers to sign top players the way it had under Darrell Royal—eliminated itself. A Texas recruiter reportedly told Eric that if he signed with Oklahoma, he would never be able to find work in Texas, which only made Eric mad. On his official visit to Oklahoma, Eric had met a girl, and for a while it looked as if love might make him a Sooner. But the girlfriend was evidently not happy living in Norman, and in the end it was she who convinced Eric he would be better off someplace else.

As signing day approached, so confident was Buddecke of Dickerson's intentions that, with less than one week to go, he backed off. Up to this point, Buddecke says, SMU had done nothing for Dickerson beyond "the usual, just trying to make sure he knew we were for real and we were gonna take care of him. There was never any major money negotiated or anything like that."

When Buddecke dropped Dickerson off at his house in Sealy for the last time, he told him, "Eric, it's really been a pleasure to recruit you. I'm not gonna call you again and I'm not gonna talk to you. I have told you everything I can possibly think of." Then he drove back to Richmond, thinking Dickerson was in the bag.

On Saturday morning, February 10, four days before SWC signing day, newspapers published a picture of Eric Dickerson's brand-new 1979 Pontiac Trans Am—gold with a black firebird on the hood—together with a report that he had committed to Texas A&M. "I was dumbfounded," says Buddecke. "My first reaction was, 'How could I have been so wrong?' He made me look like a fool. I could have met any offers, all he had to do was let me know. I would have found a way."

According to Buddecke, he had just hung up the phone that morning after consulting with Meyer ("he wasn't very happy") when Eric's mother, Helen, called. She sounded as surprised as anybody at Eric's decision to attend A&M and asked for a meeting with Meyer. Buddecke told Helen, "We are ready to talk. We are ready to do anything you want." They agreed to meet the following day, Sunday, in Richmond.

Buddecke immediately called Meyer. "We're back in the picture," he told him. "You and Endy get down here. And be ready, we're gonna have to do something. If we don't do it, it's over."

The next person Buddecke talked to, he says, was Mae Shaver in Houston. Helen had told him that the Trans Am was registered in Robert's name. Buddecke's advice to Mae was that she borrow money from her bank, transfer the car to her name, and assume responsibility for the payments herself. Buddecke says his motive in suggesting this plan was to protect Eric's eligibility. Mae, he says, could plausibly afford to buy Eric a new car; Robert could not. If the car was registered to Mae, there would be no way for the NCAA to prove that Eric had accepted an illegal inducement.

Bob Minnix was the enforcement representative assigned to Texas and Louisiana then as part of the NCAA's Operation Intercept, a program designed to monitor the recruiting of top prospects. He happened to be sitting in Coach Ralph Harris's office at Sealy High School when Eric drove up in his new car. Minnix was so impressed he asked Eric for a ride around the block before he asked him any questions.

Minnix's subsequent investigation determined that the car was indeed registered to Mae Shaver, who told him she had bought the car for Eric. "I had a real problem with that," Minnix says. Today Minnix says he has no doubt that the car came from Texas A&M. "Eric told me as much," Minnix says. "He said, 'If I told you where the car came from, is that gonna be a problem with me going to another school?' I said, 'What do you mean?' He said, 'I have no intention of going to Texas A&M.'"

On Sunday evening, February 11, Meyer, Endicott, and Buddecke met with Eric, his mother, Helen, his aunt, Viola, and his grandmother, Mae, at Buddecke's house in Richmond. Eric's stepfather, Robert, was not invited and did not attend. According to Buddecke, all present wanted Eric to go to SMU, including Eric. Several options were discussed, including giving Eric a substantial annuity, which Buddecke says was Meyer's proposal. In the end, though, according to Buddecke, Eric's family agreed to a much simpler arrangement, similar to the ones negotiated for other Houston-area players and their families. The deal, says another party involved in the negotiations, was for "not much more than two hundred dollars a month," a figure Buddecke confirms. The same source adds that once Dickerson proved his value on the playing field, his "leverage" improved and so did his deal.

Thereafter, Buddecke added Mae Shaver's Houston home to his regular monthly rounds. Eric Dickerson drove his brand-new Trans Am to Dallas and kept it most of the four years he was there. Somewhere an Aggie was grinding his teeth.

GOOD THINGS WERE HAPPENING all over. Following the hopeful conclusion of the '78 season and the spectacular recruiting class of

'79, donations to the Mustang Club increased threefold. SMU's endowment was fattened with $10 million in contributions, and applications for admission grew 20 percent—all of it attributed by President James Zumberge to Mustang Mania. Finally, SMU announced that, beginning with the 1979 season, it was shifting its home schedule to Texas Stadium, home of the Dallas Cowboys.

Texas Stadium is in Irving, ten miles from the SMU campus, in the center of a large patch of concrete near where three expressways converge. SMU had experimented with a limited schedule at Texas Stadium once before, in the early 1970s, but it had not worked out. In fact, the three games SMU played there in 1973 failed to attract a *total* of fifty thousand fans.

That was before Mustang Mania and before Ron Meyer, who, with his Cowboy connections, his Super Bowl ring, and his slush fund, had begun to attract the kind of players who attracted big crowds. Certainly no one was more pleased at the Mustangs' impending move than Clint Murchison, Jr., who not only owned the Cowboys but also Texas Stadium. Murchison was closely associated with George Owen, whose role in SMU recruiting in Dallas was similar to that filled by Buddecke in Houston. Murchison's involvement in the turnaround of the SMU football program was well known, and now he stood to profit financially. Conservative estimates of Murchison's share of the gate for SMU games, plus parking and concessions, add up to more than half a million dollars per year, which went a long way toward retiring the substantial stadium debt.

The promise that they would be playing in the same arena as the Dallas Cowboys had an intoxicating effect on Texas schoolboys, and Meyer made the most of it. He made the stadium tour a highlight of every campus visit. Recruits were led through the Cowboys dressing room (not the same one used by SMU, though no one ever said so). They were permitted to linger in front of Tony Dorsett's locker. Afterward, out on the stadium floor, Meyer posed for a photograph with each and every player beneath a backdrop of the player's name, in lights, on the Texas Stadium scoreboard. The cumulative message was unmistakable: *We're gonna be champions. I know how to get this* (Meyer indicating his Cowboys Super Bowl ring). *I know how to be a champion. I can take you there.*

"The damn team," a booster remarked about the '79 Mustangs, "it was almost as if in four years you took a high-school team and replaced it with a pro team. I mean, they just looked good on the hoof."

STILL, THE FIRE FLICKERED. Mike Ford and safety Blane Smith were injured in the second game of the 1979 season against TCU, and both were lost for the year. James rushed for over seven hundred yards (sixth in the SWC), but Dickerson, who was hobbled by an unlucky succession of bruises, twists, and pulls, never really got going. All told, injuries forced substitutions at twenty-five starting positions over the course of the season. SMU's final record in 1979, 5–6, was a bitter disappointment for players, coaches, and fans.

When SMU—after winning its first four games—suffered back-to-back losses to SWC opponents Baylor and Houston in 1980, Ron Meyer and Steve Endicott (now offensive coordinator) decided something had to be done. That's when they benched Mike Ford and replaced him with a freshman from nearby Highland Park High, Lance McIlhenny, for the Texas game.

Ford was surprised and angry and hurt. His decision to attend SMU had helped put it on the football map. But that was three years ago. With running backs like Dickerson and James and a big offensive line made up of run-blocking specialists, it didn't make sense any more to keep putting the ball in the air. What Meyer needed now was an option quarterback, one who was nimble and levelheaded and could consistently deliver the ball into the hands of the running backs. That was not Mike Ford and that was all there was to it.

For many SMU fans the Texas game on October 25, 1980, is among the happiest memories of their lives. Texas was undefeated and ranked number two in the nation. SMU, unranked, with a record of 1–2 against SWC opponents, was starting a freshman quarterback who was making his college debut. Keith Jackson and Bud Wilkinson, who were calling the game for ESPN, struggled at the outset to provide fans with a reason to stay tuned.

They needn't have worried. McIlhenny confidently guided the SMU offense in one ground-eating sequence of plays after another, rolling right, rolling left, keeping the ball himself or pitching wide to Dickerson or James. The game breaker was a forty-six-yard sideline touchdown scamper by James on a pitch from McIlhenny. Meanwhile, the experienced SMU defense held its ground. Final score: SMU 20, Texas 6.

During the second half of 1980 and for the next four seasons, the Mustangs accumulated a record of 45-7-1, won three SWC championships, finished in the national top twenty for five straight years (the last four in the top ten), and played in four bowl games, including the Cotton Bowl in 1982, when they defeated Pittsburgh, 7–3, and were ranked number two, finishing as the only undefeated major-college team in the country. Lance McIlhenny went on to become the winningest quarterback in SWC history. Dickerson and James became the Pony Express. All three graduated, and were replaced by stars of nearly equal stature, and still the Mustangs won. It was the most glorious episode in the history of SMU football.

SEVERAL DAYS AFTER the Texas game, Chris Rentzel, a Dallas attorney who was a second-string SMU receiver in the late 1960s, left work early so he could stop by Ownby Stadium and watch the end of practice. It was a beautiful day, crisp and blue, and Rentzel was still overflowing with excitement. As he stood on the sideline, Meyer sidled over his way.

"Congratulations again, Ron!" Rentzel considered himself Meyer's friend. "What a big win!"

But Meyer wasn't thinking about the Texas game. He had something else on his mind. "Hey, uh, you talked to anyone yet?" Meyer asked. "Anyone talked to you yet?"

"No, what about?"

"Oh, this NCAA deal we've got."

Later, Rentzel would describe the experience of hearing Meyer mention the NCAA, so soon after the big win over Texas, as akin to "taking an elevator up as fast as you could go and then cutting the cord and letting it drop."

"Ron, what are you talking about?" Rentzel asked as the elevator plummeted. "What NCAA deal? What's going on?"

PART II

7 HARMFUL EFFECTS

THE FIRST WHITE SETTLER in Dallas was a Tennessee lawyer turned speculator named John Neely Bryan, who came down by foot from a trading post at Preston Bend on the Red River in 1841. Bryan laid claim to 640 acres of black-earth prairie centered on a limestone bluff overlooking the Trinity River (near the spot later called the "grassy knoll" by the Warren Commission). He was banking on that bluff one day becoming the head of navigation, the site of a bustling river port connecting North Texas with the Gulf of Mexico.

It never happened. The Trinity then, as now, was a shallow, twisting, congested stream, unnavigable over much of its 550-mile course. Throughout Bryan's lifetime and on into the twentieth century, the Trinity has suffered repeated dredgings, explosions, debris fires, and other attempts, all doomed, to free its flow and open the floodgates of wealth Bryan envisioned for himself and the city he founded. Consequently, while Dallas grew from Bryan's homestead into a regional metropolis—the seventh largest city in the United States—it had no help from the Trinity. Today, people who live in Dallas are proud of the fact that their city has no apparent reason for being—no river to speak of, no ocean port, no natural defenses, no abundant resources. Even the popular assumption that Dallas is rich in oil is false. Dallas bankers (before the bust) financed drilling projects in Texas and around the world, but no one ever found oil in Dallas County until 1986, and then only sixty-eight barrels.

From the beginning, every step forward in the development of

Dallas has been accomplished only with pushing, prodding, boosting, plotting, wooing, scheming, and promoting on the part of Dallas businessmen. Dallas became the capital of Dallas County in 1850 not because it was the logical site, but because John Neely Bryan promised free ferry service to county residents and donated land for a courthouse. When it became known that the proposed route of the Houston and Texas Central Railroad did not include a stop in Dallas, local businessmen gave the H&TC 115 acres of free land, a right-of-way through the center of town, and $5,000 cash; in 1872 they got their railroad. One year later—thanks to legislative trickery and a pot sweetener amounting to $100,000 in bonds—Dallas got a second, intersecting railroad, the east-west Texas and Pacific. Overnight, Dallas was transformed from a small town on the North Texas prairie into a commercial crossroads. In 1875, before the T&P pushed west, Dallas enjoyed a brief flowering as the world's busiest market in buffalo hides. The railroads made Dallas an important grain market and helped it become, by 1900, the largest inland cotton market in the world.

Dallas has fought for every advantage. In 1913, against all odds, it won designation as the site of one of twelve regional banks in the Federal Reserve system. At the time it was the smallest city chosen. Thanks in large part to the initial influx of capital provided by the Fed, Dallas has since developed into a regional center for banking, finance, and insurance. In the 1930s Dallas outbid Houston and San Antonio for the right to host the 1936 Texas centennial celebration, despite the fact that Dallas has no ties to early Texas history and did not even exist in 1836. The six-month exposition attracted ten million visitors from around the world, sparked a boom in the local construction industry, and helped keep the Dallas economy afloat during the worst years of the Depression.

THE FIRST PROTESTANT minister to invade Catholic Texas was a Methodist circuit rider named William Stevenson, who crossed over the Red River from Arkansas in the late fall of 1815 and preached at a place called Pecan Point. Soon thereafter, the first Protestant church in Texas, also Methodist, was organized in the community of Jonesborough in present-day Red River County.

By 1910 there were more than a quarter-million members of the Methodist Episcopal Church South (formed in 1844 after a split with northern Methodists over slavery) living in Texas. Southwestern University—established by the Methodists in Georgetown, Texas, in 1873—was no longer adequate to serve the denomination's needs. After considering and rejecting a proposal to simply move Southwestern to a larger city, the decision was made to build a new university somewhere in Texas. Dallas was an obvious choice. As early as 1905 Wallace Buttrick, executive secretary of the General Education Board of New York, had told Robert Hyer, president of Southwestern, "It is the best unoccupied territory in the South. Someday someone will build a university in Dallas and you Methodists are the people who should do it."

Dallas businessmen were quick to recognize the potential for gain. Apart from any contribution a university might make to the cultural and intellectual life of the city, there were financial and publicity benefits to consider. During an early campaign aimed at raising funds to attract Southwestern University to Dallas, a banner draped across Main Street proclaimed, WE NEED $400,000 TO GET SOUTHWESTERN. WILL BRING FROM 3,000 TO 5,000 STUDENTS HERE AN-NUALLY AND MILLIONS OF MONEY. But nothing was ever handed to Dallas, and the University was no exception. Fort Worth, thirty miles west, was equally aware of the benefits. The two went toe to toe in a battle over who could do the most for the Methodists.

Dallas made its pitch on February 2, 1911. The touring Methodist delegation was presented with three alternatives. The most attractive included a $300,000 cash grant (raised by public subscription) plus three-hundred acres adjoining a ritzy new suburb called Highland Park. Bordered by cotton fields on the west and woodsy waterways on the east, Highland Park was advertised in those days as a bucolic alternative to urban living, a place "beyond the city smoke and dust." It had been laid out six years earlier by landscape architect William David Cook, whose credits included California's Beverly Hills. In time Highland Park would become the address of choice for Dallas's wealthiest and most prominent citizens.

On the following day the Methodists traveled by train to Fort Worth, where they were greeted with a spectacular display of civic boosterism. A fleet of automobiles (so exotic then that the Fort Worth committee had had to make a public appeal in order to round up enough "machines") transported the delegates on their tour of the city. Businesses shut down, schools closed, and everywhere citizens lined the streets to wave flags and offer greetings. The best of the various Fort Worth offers featured one hundred acres in the new Arlington Heights section, a partial interest in an additional fifteen hundred acres and $400,000 cash.

Dallas's leading citizens were momentarily stunned by the unexpectedly fierce competition from Fort Worth. It was not until after the deadline for new bids had expired that Frank McNeny, a local realtor, was able to convince W. W. Caruth, who owned seven thousand acres north of Highland Park, to sweeten the pot on Dallas's behalf. McNeny tracked down Caruth at the farmer's market, where he was selling chickens, and delivered him to the place where the Methodists were meeting. Caruth promised to donate a half interest in an additional 725 acres adjoining the proposed Highland Park campus. When representatives from Fort Worth objected to Dallas's late bid, the Methodists politely gave them an opportunity to make a counteroffer, which they passed up.

After two days of intense deliberations, the Methodist educational commission voted 14–4 in favor of the site near Highland Park. Dallas, as usual, had got what it wanted.

SOUTHERN METHODIST UNIVERSITY was chartered in 1911 and opened its doors in 1915. There was an element of affectation in SMU's calling itself a university right off the bat. The modern American university—which combines instruction in the liberal arts with professional training, scholarly research, and graduate study—is the product of centuries of development in Europe and the United States. Most major independent American universities—Harvard and Yale, for example—began their institutional lives as small colleges and gradually expanded to fill larger roles. SMU's founding fathers were impatient. They wanted "a great university" instantly, with all the trappings. Others have succeeded at this but SMU fell short. According to Mary Martha Hosford Thomas, author of *Southern Methodist University: Founding and Early Years*, "What the Methodists really established in 1915 was a small liberal arts college with a theological seminary and a music school attached to it."

Since part of what defined a great university in 1915 was football, SMU had to have a football team. In the broad sweep of history, the idea that institutions of higher learning should somehow be connected in an organized way with athletics is relatively new, though by the latter part of the nineteenth century such was the rule, at least in England and the United States.

Historians trace the origins of football to a bloody spectacle played out in medieval England, whereby the citizens of one town would conspire to deposit an inflated pig's bladder in the center of the next town by whatever means at their disposal. In 1314 King Edward II put a stop to it, proclaiming, "there is a great noise in the city caused by hustling over large balls ... from which many evils might arise, which God forbid, we command ... on pain of imprisonment, such game [not] to be used in the city." Two hundred years later, King James I, recognizing that football was no longer so dangerously uninhibited (played now within defined boundaries with the object being to kick the ball across a goal line), revoked the ban. Richard Mulcaster a sixteenth-century British schoolmaster, is believed to be the first scholar to have suggested that football might play a role in the overall development of young boys. "Football strengtheneth and brawneth the whole body," Mulcaster opined. From there it was but a short leap to making sports a part of the formal curriculum, first taken in 1838 by Dr. Thomas Arnold, headmaster of the Rugby School in England. "Dr. Arnold's decision is most significant", writes Jack Falla in *NCAA, the Voice of College Sports*. "From this time on, football (and, later, many other sports) will have its fortunes tied directly not to clubs or towns or government or the military or any of the myriad social institutions that might have supported it, but instead to schools."

Legend has it that the first game of American football was played on November 6, 1869, in New Brunswick, New Jersey, between Princeton and Rutgers. The circumstances of this meeting are fact, although the game that was played that long-ago Saturday afternoon would hardly be recognized today as football; there were twenty-five men to a side and the rules prohibited touching the ball with the hands. Football at this stage of its development had recently undergone a split into two very different games, one allowing the ball to be carried and one not, and for a while it looked as if the soccer-style game would predominate. Harvard, though, favored a game more closely resembling rugby. On November 13, 1875, Harvard played Yale in New Haven under what were known as "concessionary rules" (Yale did most of the conceding) and the modern game was born.

In the forty years between the first Harvard-Yale game and the founding of SMU, football grew up. What had begun as a club sport organized and managed by undergraduates for their own amusement was now a public entertainment, coached by professionals, staged in grand arenas, and chronicled in the sporting pages of newspapers. Somewhere along the line football had become a source of revenue (though hardly dependable). A winning team was understood to build school spirit and promote positive public relations. Already, abuses were common; among them, paid athletes and "tramps" (players who kept showing up on different rosters, often in the same season). Partly in response to such abuses but mainly in order to stem the increasing violence of football, the Intercollegiate Athletic Association of the United States was organized in 1906. Four years later its name was changed to the National Collegiate Athletic Association.

In 1914, at the behest of the University of Texas, representatives from several prominent institutions in the Southwest met at the Oriental Hotel in Dallas to discuss the formation of a new athletic conference, one that would outlaw tramp athletes and otherwise seek to discourage professionalism. At this meeting was formed the Southwest Conference. The original eight members were Texas, Texas A&M, Oklahoma, Oklahoma A&M, Southwestern, Arkansas, Baylor, and Rice. The SWC was evidently serious about reform. It stripped Baylor of the first conference title in 1915 after it was discovered that Tom Stonerod, a quarterback, had previously enrolled at a college back east. Throughout the twenties and thirties the Southwest Conference made repeated attempts to stem the creeping tide of commercialism in college football. As late as 1932 Dr. D. A. Penick, president of the SWC, would attempt (unsuccessfully) to legislate against paid coaches.

SMU was not a party to the formation of the SWC, nor did it immediately join. Instead, SMU started out in 1915 as a member of the old Texas Intercollegiate Athletic Association. (Part of the motivation for organizing the SWC had been to eliminate the many abuses that flourished unchecked in the TIAA, which had no rules against athletes who transferred from other schools and no restrictions on freshmen eligibility.) Ray Morrison, SMU's first coach, arrived in Dallas the summer before classes were to begin. He is said to have been the fourth instructor, in any discipline, engaged by

SMU. Upon his arrival, SMU president Hyer (formerly of South-western) personally escorted him on a tour of the grounds. There were at this time only two permanent structures on campus: Dallas Hall, a grand, columned Georgian edifice styled after the Rotunda on the campus of the University of Virginia; and the Woman's Build-ing, a dormitory of similar though less imposing design. A double dirt road (Bishop Boulevard) ran south half a mile from the steps of Dallas Hall through a meadow of Johnson grass past a scattering of scraggly trees to Mockingbird Lane. There at the foot of campus, east of the dirt road, was the section designated for athletics. Mor-rison had vision, energy, and a sum of $1,500 raised by downtown Dallas businessmen to help start football at SMU. He immediately set about grading, shaping, and sodding a playing field.

The early years of SMU football were uninspiring. Morrison won only two games in two years and was fired in 1916. His replacement, Burton Rix, turned in three straight winning seasons, though only by the barest of margins. When the team fell to 3-5-2 in 1920, certain elements in the Dallas business community began to press for change. They found an ally in Hiram Abiff Boaz, SMU's second president, who had been chosen in part because of his fund-raising ability and downtown connections.

"Since the university was on a sound financial basis," Boaz wrote in his memoirs, *Eighty-four Golden Years*, "and the spiritual atmo-sphere on the campus had been greatly improved, and since the faculty was doing most excellent work in the classroom it seemed to me that we ought to lay some emphasis on securing a winning football team.... In keeping with the practice of other universities, scouts were looking for good players and the usual inducements offered to them in order to have them registered in SMU."

The "scouts" brought in an outstanding freshman class in 1921. Included were nine of the players who would one day be known as the Immortal Ten. Because SMU had joined the Southwest Con-ference in 1917 (after paying an entrance fee of $7.50), the new recruits came under conference rules barring freshmen from com-peting on the varsity. As a result, that year the junior varsity under Coach Ray Morrison (recently rehired) went undefeated, unscored upon, and unblemished by even one opposition first down. SMU fans began to like their chances in '22.

Not everybody on the Hilltop, as the campus is known (it sits at a modest elevation with respect to downtown), agreed that all the attention being paid to athletics was a good idea. Faculty leaders wondered where the money came from to support football at a time when they lacked adequate funds for instruction. Students satirized the Boaz administration's preoccupation with sports in an April Fool's edition of the school newspaper. The situation was complicated in the spring of 1922 when the Southwest Conference passed a new set of rules governing recruiting, rules that were extraordinarily strict by today's standards. Never mind the "usual inducements." Simple *persuasion*, whether by letter or in person, was outlawed. Scholarships granted purely on the basis of athletic ability were eliminated. Even training tables were banned. In short, it looked like everything SMU had done to gather and preserve the makings of a championship team was now illegal under the new rules.

Despite grumblings on campus and ominous rumblings coming from the SWC office, Coach Morrison and the recruiting class of '21 were called up to the varsity in the fall of '22 and they performed as expected. After having won only one game the year before, the new, improved Mustangs finished with a record of 6-3-1, their best ever. Since most of the star players were sophomores, the future looked even brighter.

In December representatives from around the conference gathered for their annual meeting in Dallas. There an investigative committee, chaired by a delegate from Texas A&M, delivered a report unfavorable to SMU. According to contemporary news accounts, the committee determined that SMU was "shot through and through with questionable athletics." It recommended that SMU be suspended from the conference and that three players—including Blink Bedford, the star end in Morrison's Aerial Circus—be banned. The vote was 4–3 in favor of the committee's recommendation, one short of the required two-thirds majority. SMU was spared only by the vote of its own representative.

Meanwhile, on campus the storm swirling around SMU athletics grew more intense. In an effort to quell the controversy, the board of trustees directed the university athletic committee, which had nominal control of athletics, to conduct an internal investigation. Far from calming the storm, exactly the opposite was achieved. In interviews with players, students, coaches, and faculty members, a true picture of athletics at SMU emerged, and it was not pretty.

The introduction to the committee's majority report, which sets out the aims of the investigation, reads like the last-gasp manifesto of a dying cause. "Football is becoming a huge and highly specialized business," the committee members wrote in February 1923, "and the amateur element characteristic of college athletics is in danger of disappearing from it. The function of a University so far as football is concerned is not to provide a spectacle for the entertainment of outside crowds, but to interest as many of its students as possible in healthful outdoor sports. If football is essential for purposes of entertainment, it should be professionalized outside of the university. . . . The advertising value of football is undoubted, but it brings in its train some harmful effects, and it should never be allowed to take precedence over the physical, moral and intellectual needs of the student body."

Almost all of the earlier findings of the conference were confirmed by the majority report. (The minority report, signed by Coach Morrison, absolved all parties of wrongdoing.) Some players had been accepted as transfer students without proper transcripts. Others had received cash gifts from university officials under the guise of loans, which in any case were illegal under SWC rules. (Money for some of the loans was provided by one R. H. Shuttles, wholesale jeweler and prominent member of the board of trustees.) Campus jobs were given athletes at wages as high as $1.75 an hour, the equivalent of almost $12.00 an hour today. ("In some cases the work was conscientiously done, and in others very little was done.") Of the eighteen so-called "student activity scholarships" awarded for the year 1921–22, all were awarded to football players; and while most other scholarships, including those given to the sons and daughters of Methodist ministers, paid $105, the student activity scholarships paid $200. Other seamy details emerged unexpectedly from the testimony, including the charge that R. N. Blackwell, the business manager of athletics and a poker-playing buddy of Knute Rockne, was providing football players with strychnine tablets (a stimulant) and hosting card games in his hotel room on road trips. A number of players were admonished for violating Methodist strictures by playing baseball on Sundays. Two players, Glen Huff and Elvin Smith, were declared ineligible.

"It has . . . been proven beyond any doubt," the majority report of the committee concluded, "that favors have been given to athletes and this in a number of cases in which the recipient has shown no qualifications meriting such favors except athletic ability; and for this attitude on the part of certain officials the University owes an apology to the Conference."

THE SMU FACULTY approved the majority report by a vote of 44–21. Certain lay members of the board of trustees—including the chairman, Judge Joseph E. Cockrell, and the jeweler Shuttles—were furious. In their eyes the decision to declare Huff and Smith ineligible amounted to groveling before the SWC. Judge Cockrell took it upon himself to publish a biting eighty-four-page pamphlet entitled *A Review of the Athletic Situation and the Case of Huff and Smith*, which he addressed to "Friends and Enemies of Southern Methodist University within and without." The pamphlet was distributed to every student. Shuttles ordered five hundred copies for himself.

When April 1, 1923, rolled around and the student newspaper again published its satirical edition, called *The Dinkey*, the lead story naturally addressed itself to the most divisive issue of the day. "Like a seething, growling Vesuvius," the anonymous undergraduate commentator wrote, "ever restless, ever threatening, now bursting forth in flames of red fury, to the accompaniment of frightful thunders and deluge of hissing ashes mixed with pelting, molten missives that smite and blind and batter, now subsiding to an angry, heaving calm, whose continued vaporings betray the undying fires upon which it feeds, the athletic situation in Southern Methodist University has been a regular little rascal of a volcano."

At the heart of the football scandal lay a larger question, one that would persist unresolved for half a century and resurface in later conflicts. For what really mattered to Cockrell, Shuttles, and other lay members of the board—beyond the plight of Huff and Smith—was power. Who would control SMU? Would it be the faculty? Or would it be the business leaders of Dallas?

BEFORE SMU EVEN HAD a science building, it built a half-million-dollar auditorium, described by President C. C. Selecman as necessary "for us to get our entire group together and develop a college spirit of loyalty, reverence, and enthusiasm." Thirteen years before

SMU had a library, it built a football stadium. Ownby Stadium—named for Jordan Ownby, an alumnus who contributed $10,000 toward its construction—was built in 1926 near the place where Coach Morrison had laid out the original football field in 1915. With space in Ownby to accommodate seventeen thousand spectators, it was assumed that gate receipts would be sufficient to retire the stadium's ten-year, $175,000 debt. The mortgage called for payments of $10,000 per year with the balance due in a lump sum ten years down the road.

During the period that SMU was making payments on the stadium, Ray Morrison's Aerial Circus was winning thrillingly and often, capturing SWC titles in 1926, 1931, and 1935. Nevertheless, the notion that the stadium would somehow pay for itself turned out to be wishful thinking. By 1931 President Selecman had to tell the board of trustees, "The general impression that college athletics are quite profitable financially has not been substantiated by our experience at Southern Methodist University. Since 1923, our athletics have produced a debit balance every year with the exception of 1925."

The Depression only made things worse. In 1931 the total university debt passed $600,000, more than $100,000 of which was interest due on the stadium and other buildings. The year before, Coach Morrison had signed a five-year contract with an annual salary of $12,000; this at a time when the president was earning $10,000 and a full professor only $3,500. The growing financial crisis prompted a 20-percent across-the-board pay cut in 1932 and a further three-month 50-percent cut in 1933, neither of which applied to Morrison because he was under long-term contract. After the second round of cuts, Morrison was earning 60 percent more than the president and roughly five times the salary of even the highest-paid professors.

In 1935 SMU won its first and only national championship. The Mustangs shut out eight of twelve opponents, scored 288 points, allowed only 39. There were magnificent victories in faraway places: 35–6 over Washington University in St. Louis, 21–0 over UCLA in Los Angeles. Three players—Truman Spain, J. C. Wetsel, and Bobby Wilson—were honored as all-Americans. The climax of the season—not just in Texas but around the country—was the epic showdown between SMU and TCU for the right to play in the Rose

Bowl. This was that most famous of games: the one that SMU stole in the closing minutes on a fourth-down, thirty-nine-yard touch-down pass from Bob Finley to Wilson; that was eulogized by Grant-land Rice; and that was carried live coast to coast by NBC radio.

Wetsel said later, it was "the greatest, most thrilling game I ever played in or have seen." The crowd, wrote Rice, was "tense, keyed-up." And yet few realized at the time just how important this game really was. For had the Mustangs lost, *had Wilson dropped the pass,* SMU would have come face-to-face with the prospect of financial ruin.

Bishop John Moore, the chairman of the SMU board of trustees, did not attend the game in Fort Worth that day; "physical indis-position" kept him at home. He had a radio, though, and as he listened, his thoughts were never far from SMU's monumental debt. The stadium had ended up costing $225,000. Alumni and friends had contributed about $50,000. Mortgage payments to date had eliminated another $90,000. That left $85,000 due, the long-awaited balloon payment, and SMU didn't have it. Recently, Moore had returned from a trip to St. Louis where he had succeeded in per-suading the Bennett Mortgage Company to hold off until January. He had reason to hope for a miracle.

"I never had two such nervous hours," Moore recalled in his memoir, *Life and I.* "I will not say that I prayed for victory, but I cannot say that I did not. We won! We went to the Rose Bowl. By feasting and folly we lost that game; but our receipts were $90,000! The stadium was cleared by the 'windfall' and our credit was pre-served."

8 A GATHERING STORM

THE BIG NEWS AT the NCAA meeting in New Orleans in April 1958 was that Auburn University, the Associated Press national champion, was going on probation. An alumnus, it seems, had offered "a prospective football player illicit financial aid for the benefit of himself and his family." Auburn's penalty—a three-year ban on television appearances and bowl games—was among the most severe ever levied under the NCAA's new enforcement program. Walter Byers, the NCAA's executive director, compared it to the one-year suspension imposed on the Kentucky basketball program during the 1952–53 season. Adding to the drama of the day was the announcement that the University of Seattle, which just that spring had lost to Kentucky in the finals of the NCAA basketball tournament, would be hit with two years' probation because two prospective players had been offered "financial aid and inducements" by the coach. John Castellani, athletic director and head coach at Seattle, stepped down two hours after the announcement, insisting he had not been forced to quit but had planned to give up coaching at the end of the year anyway.

With all the excitement over Auburn and Seattle, the fact that Southern Methodist was also put on probation hardly seemed worth mentioning. Byers correctly termed the Mustangs' punishment (one year, no sanctions) "not major," and neither, evidently, was the crime. It involved, naturally, a booster. His name was Harlan Ray. *The Dallas Morning News*, in an article about a later SMU probation in 1964, identified Ray as a "Dallas oil man who has been SMU's No. 1 football fan and benefactor since he played tackle on the Rose

Bowl team of 1936." Ray was an oil man all right, and there is no doubt he was a big booster—his picture appeared in the 1948 *Life* magazine article about Doak Walker, next to a sidebar entitled, "The Mustang Club Corrals Prospects"—but the rest is fiction. As much as he liked to talk about the '35 national championship team, which went on to play in the Rose Bowl, Ray was never a part of it. He earned his only letter in 1932. Like many strident boosters, he was a second-stringer in his playing days. His teammates called him "Ducky" because he was bowlegged.

The player involved was Glynn Gregory, a high-school all-American from Abilene, Texas, who of course had been highly recruited. Gregory signed with SMU and went to work that summer for Ray's oil company while continuing to live at home. "I traveled all over West Texas going to these various oil rig sites and getting information for his office," says Gregory, now an insurance executive in Dallas. "They wanted to see what was going on in certain areas of West Texas as far as oil and gas drilling, where they were completed, if so, how far down they were, etcetera, etcetera."

This was not a case of a recruit being paid for work he did not perform. "Quite a few of the drillers and tool pushers and roustabouts and roughnecks authenticated that I had been there, etcetera ...," says Gregory. And the NCAA was satisfied that Gregory had not been paid while away from the job at summer all-star games in Dallas, Wichita Falls, and Memphis, Tennessee. Nor was it a matter of his receiving an exorbitant fee for his services; $300 a month was thought to be about right. What the NCAA did conclude was that the job appeared to be "tailor-made" for Gregory, that in any case he lacked the proper qualifications, and therefore it amounted to special treatment of an athlete.

"Flat ridiculous," said Coach Bill Meek when he heard about the charges. "If we're on probation, then every other school I know of ought to be on probation."

SIX YEARS LATER on May 9, 1964, the day SMU learned it had been slapped with a two-year ban on postseason play by the Southwest Conference (later upheld by the NCAA), *The Dallas Morning News* sportswriter Bob St. John dropped by the mess hall at Letterman's Dormitory to gauge the mood of the team. "Saturday at Southern Methodist was a dark, gray day full of whispers and faces which looked as if they'd just been smacked with a wet towel," St. John reported. There weren't a lot of players around but St. John was able to talk to a Mrs. Kline. " 'I guess they're just not coming in today,' said Mrs. Kline very sadly. She runs the lunchroom. 'I guess they're just too sick to eat, poor things. Or maybe they've gone home for Mother's Day.' "

Strange that Mrs. Kline should mention mothers. In fact, one of the violations that had brought this sad day on SMU was a free plane ride to Harlingen, Texas, provided by SMU booster Johnny Clement (in his private Cessna 310) for SMU player Max Derden, Jr., which, according to Max's dad, was so that Max could visit his mom, who was sick. In another violation cited by the SWC, a coach lent his automobile to a player so that he could visit his grandmother in Waco. The grandmother had raised the boy and was said to have recently suffered a heart attack.

The more serious violations involved promises allegedly made to Randy Behringer, an all-state fullback from Waco who ultimately signed with Baylor. Because players rarely say anything against their schools, it has always been true that the best place to go for information is to players who were recruited by the school in question but signed with somebody else. This the investigators did. Behringer told them he had been promised help in obtaining a car if he signed with SMU. The offer, he said, came from a well-known SMU booster—none other than Harlan Ray. Reportedly, it was Ray's renewed involvement in shady dealings only six years after his previous run-in with the NCAA that led to SMU's receiving such a harsh penalty.

"It's a great miscarriage of justice," Ray told the *Morning News*. "If we committed any infractions whatsoever, they're so minor that every other school in the conference is guilty, too. If they're to be that technical, every other school should be on probation right along with us."

ONE OF THE FIRST decisions Paul Hardin had to make after he became president of SMU eight years later in 1972 was what to do about the football coach. The Mustangs' record that fall was 7–4, only their third winning season in eleven years under Hayden Fry. But wins and losses were not the issue, cheating was. Fry had been at SMU since 1962 and so shared responsibility for SMU's last probationary term in 1964. When a faculty athletic committee uncovered evidence of new violations and presented it to Hardin, Fry was fired. (Fry later became head coach at the University of Iowa; in 1982 Fry's Hawkeyes became the first Big-Ten team other than Michigan or Ohio State to go to the Rose Bowl in thirteen years.)

Within a year Hardin was faced with another crisis in athletics. It was brought on, apparently, by John Moseley of Missouri. Moseley returned a punt seventy-four yards for a touchdown in the fourth quarter of the fourth game of the 1973 season. SMU had a new coach then, Dave Smith, who afterward came up with a novel incentive plan designed to make sure SMU never got burned again. From then on, any player who made a tackle on punt coverage received $10 cash from Coach Smith. Later, Smith livened up practice by offering to pay $20 to any scout-team player who could block a field goal or an extra point. That wasn't all. Rather than have players sell their complimentary game tickets directly to boosters, Smith and some members of his staff offered to buy the tickets themselves.

Hardin found out what Smith was doing in late November 1973. He immediately relieved Smith of his duties as athletic director and placed Smith and an assistant coach, Pug Gabrel, on institutional probation. Then, at the December SWC meeting in Dallas, Hardin spilled the whole story and placed SMU at the mercy of the conference.

Hardin did what he was supposed to do. The enforcement process in college athletics is not like the enforcement process in the real world. The conferences and the NCAA are voluntary associations. What authority they possess is derived solely from their members. Nothing in any of their rule books has the force of law. No one has ever gone to prison for paying players. Their investigators can't *make* anybody talk, they can't subpoena documents, and they can't petition a judge for a search warrant. Without someone like Paul Hardin—a responsible individual who shares what he knows when he has learned of violations at his own institution—the NCAA is often hard pressed to uncover the truth.

The conference heard Hardin's report with gratitude and placed SMU on one-year probation without sanctions, essentially a slap on the wrist. It was understood that without Hardin's cooperation, the penalties would have been more severe. But that summer a follow-up investigation by the NCAA uncovered more violations, some of them going back to Hayden Fry's day. Rather than simply endorse the SWC's findings, the NCAA slapped SMU with its harshest penalty to date: a two-year television blackout and a ban on postseason play. It was SMU's third probationary term in sixteen years. The Mustangs were beginning to acquire a reputation as the bad boys of college football.

HARDIN WASN'T AROUND to learn of SMU's fate. On June 17, 1973, two of the richest and most powerful men in Dallas—C. A. Tatum, Jr., president of Dallas Power and Light Company and chairman of the SMU board of trustees, and Edwin L. Cox of Cox Oil, chairman of the SMU board of governors—had walked into Hardin's office on the second floor of Perkins administration building and demanded his resignation. Hardin was stunned. Only six weeks earlier, at the annual spring meeting of the full board of trustees, he had been reappointed by acclamation to a new term. Hardin asked for a meeting of the full board of governors. Cox said that would not be necessary, that he had already polled each of the governors individually and that they agreed overwhelmingly on the need for change. Two days later, convinced that he had no other option, Hardin resigned.

On that day, June 19, Tatum mailed ballots to all eighty-three members of the board of trustees asking that they accept Hardin's resignation and ratify Willis Tate as SMU's new president. (Tate, president for eighteen years before Hardin, was vacationing in Mexico; he was returned to Dallas by private plane.) In a letter accompanying the ballot, Tatum strongly implied that Hardin's resignation was voluntary ("It is with sincere regret that I announce that Dr. Paul Hardin has resigned . . ."), and the trustees obligingly voted their approval.

Later, of course, there was an uproar. "A storm is gathering here as the truth unravels concerning the resignation of Dr. Paul Hardin as President of Southern Methodist University," began a story in the *Texas Methodist/United Methodist Reporter*, the denomination's national weekly newspaper. "Dr. Hardin's resignation was not voluntary as originally reported, nor was it sought by the school's Board of Trustees. Rather, it was engineered by a small group of Dallas businessmen on the school's 21-member Board of Governors, and then represented as an act initiated by Dr. Hardin and accepted by the Board of Governors on the Board of Trustees' behalf."

Once the trustees found out they had been hoodwinked, some of them tried to change their vote. Faculty members who had been away on summer vacation held angry meetings upon their return and demanded to know why they had not been consulted. Students bemoaned the loss of a popular president. And then it died down. Hardin was out, Tate was in (pending selection of a permanent replacement), and that was that.

What happened? What had Hardin done that cost him the backing of the board of governors? How could a president who enjoyed the broad support of students, faculty members, and trustees be ousted by "a small group of Dallas businessmen"? What did it mean for the future of SMU?

THE LEADER OF THE successful campaign to bring the Texas Centennial to Dallas in 1936 was Robert Lee Thornton, a self-made businessman from Hilco, Texas, who built Mercantile National Bank into the third largest bank in Dallas. (Its descendent, MBank, was the last of the big banks in Dallas to go bust in 1988.) After sitting through endless committee meetings, Thornton grew tired of dealing with what he called "maybe" men, underlings who couldn't make a decision without asking the boss. Dallas was on the move. Things were happening fast. What the times demanded, Thornton decided, was a committee of "yes and no" men. Say, one hundred chief executives of the leading Dallas firms. After the centennial, Thornton's dream became a permanent institution. Being a direct man, Thornton thought it should be called the Yes and No Council. Accurate yes, politic no. The name ultimately chosen was the Dallas Citizens Council.

For years, before the times caught up with it, the Citizens Council acted as a shadow government in Dallas, abrogating for itself ultimate authority in all matters of civic import. It's accomplishments have become legend in Dallas. In 1948 Chance-Vought Aircraft (now LTV) of Bridgeport, Connecticut, was set to move its plant and headquarters to an abandoned Dallas airfield when the company president decided at the last minute that he had to have longer runways. So Rex Beisel of Chance-Vought telephoned "Deck" Hulcey of the Citizens Council and explained his problem. Three hours and forty minutes later, Hulcey called back with good news. The Dallas City Council, meeting in an emergency session, had appropriated $256,000 to extend the runways two thousand feet. Work would begin immediately. Today, LTV Corp. is Dallas's largest manufacturing company with fifteen thousand local employees and over $7 billion in annual sales.

By the early 1950s Dallas had need of a new luxury hotel, something to give the convention business a boost. The Citizens Council put together a package of incentives and invited Arthur Douglas of Statler Corporation to Dallas to talk things over. One night after a Citizens Council dinner, Douglas drove around town with (then mayor) Robert Lee Thornton and Stanley Marcus of Neiman-Marcus, looking for a place to build. Douglas chose his site, Thornton and Marcus made sure it was available, and Dallas got a 1,001-room Statler Hilton Hotel, the first big new hotel to be built in the Southwest after the war.

For decades not much happened in Dallas unless the Citizen's Council wanted it to happen, whether it was a new expressway or a new airport, an art museum or a zoo, a crime commission or school integration. Although pointedly nonpolitical, the Citizens Council influenced city elections through an organization known as the Citizens Charter Association, which always endorsed a pro-business slate. It was a cozy arrangement, made even cozier by the fact that until 1975—when a federal judge carved Dallas into eight single-member districts—the entire city government was elected at large.

"Perhaps not since the great cities of Renaissance Italy has there been such a striking example of oligarchy in action," wrote Holland McCombs in *Fortune* in 1949. "Like them, it has been a mercantile oligarchy, for it is the bankers and the merchants who largely run Dallas."

Whether, as *Fortune* concludes, they have always "run it well, with self effacement, and not for private gain," or whether Dallas as a whole might have benefited from a more pluralistic system is the kind of question that has more than one answer. For example, when it came to race relations in the late 1950s, business leaders in Dallas were not necessarily more enlightened than business leaders in other Southern cities. Far from it. (The Citizens Council, according to the *Dallas Times Herald*, once proposed to black leaders that it would build an all-black city on the outskirts of town—complete with churches, schools, and shopping centers—if blacks would agree to move out of Dallas; the idea, not surprisingly, "went over with a dull thud.") Yet on July 26, 1961, word went out from the Citizens Council that Dallas would be from this day forward an integrated city, and so it was. Dallas gave in, quickly and peacefully, largely because Dallas business leaders thought it best; they certainly wanted no part of riots and demonstrations.

Dallas has been widely praised for sidestepping the violence that accompanied integration in other Southern cities. Yet some black leaders see it as a mixed blessing. They wonder whether the black community in Dallas might not be better off today had blacks not obtained so much without a struggle. "Blacks in Dallas had no hands-on involvement in the changes that took place all across the South, so the black leadership here is unskilled," Peter Johnson, Dallas director of the Southern Christian Leadership Conference, told the *Herald*. "Dallas is 20 years behind the rest of the urban South in race relations."

EVER SINCE THE DAYS of R. H. Shuttles—jeweler, booster, benefactor, and chairman of the SMU board of trustees (1927–32)—Dallas businessmen have played a huge role in the affairs of SMU. They fought hard to have SMU built in their city (even in the very neighborhood where many of them lived). They supported it with their money. They sent their sons and daughters there to be educated and hired them when they graduated. They nurtured it and helped it grow. Yet for the first half century of SMU's existence, their influence was kept within bounds by the authority of the Methodist Church. With the adoption of the *Master Plan for Southern Methodist University* in 1963, those boundaries were erased.

The *Master Plan* came out of the fiftieth anniversary of SMU's founding. Its stated purpose was to prepare "this university to meet its second half-century with a sound self-knowledge of its basic nature, its distinguishing goals, and its essential motivation." What the *Plan* boiled down to was a renewed commitment to the goal SMU has always had (and still hopes to achieve): to be more than a church school, more than a regional college; to become "a great university," one that combines liberal education with distinguished professional training and research on the frontiers of knowledge.

Toward this end, the *Master Plan* spelled out changes in the way the university would be governed. Previously, the board of trustees was made up of the several standing bishops of the South Central Jurisdiction of the Methodist Church, plus fifty-six additional members, forty-eight of whom were church leaders selected by church conferences. In 1967 the nonbishop membership of the board was expanded to seventy-five, *all* of whom were chosen by the board and subject only to approval by the church. As a result, the reigns of power at SMU were taken out of the hands of church leaders and transferred to a self-perpetuating body dominated by lay persons.

This is not necessarily a bad thing. In fact, creation of a larger board drawn from the community at large might have had the effect of opening up the leadership at SMU had it not been for the role assumed by the new board of governors. At first, few saw the board as something radically new. "The Board of Governors will continue to be appointed by the Board of Trustees, report to the trustees, and derive its authority from the Board of Trustees," the *Master Plan* stated. "This is consistent with the function of the former Executive Committee; the only change is one in name." Yet in time the power of the board of governors grew beyond all expectations, to the point where its twenty-one members ran SMU almost by themselves, with wide-ranging authority over the faculty, the administration (including the president), and the board of trustees. More precisely, it was those *several individual members* among the leadership of the board of governors who possessed real power. They left their mark on SMU in ways deserving of both praise and condemnation, presiding over two decades of growth—in enrollment, endowment, and academic stature—but ultimately resigning under a cloud of scandal.

Between 1967 and 1987, only three men served as chairman of the SMU board of governors: Bill Clements, cofounder of SEDCO, an international drilling and pipeline construction company and a two-term governor of Texas; Bobby Stewart, chairman of the board of First National Bank (later Inter First Corp.), one of the original Big Three banks in Dallas; and Ed Cox, an independent Texas oil man recently described in *Forbes* as "perceived as being richer than God." It may seem strange that a plutocracy should dictate affairs in anything so fractionalized and unwieldy as a university. But what is bizarre in academe makes perfect sense in Dallas.

AS IT HAPPENS the man who led the campaign for school desegregation in Dallas while serving as president of the Citizens Council was C. A. Tatum, the same man who thirteen years later joined Ed Cox in removing SMU President Paul Hardin from office. Years at the helm of successful businesses, together with long experience as star players on the Citizens Council, had taught Tatum and Cox a thing or two about the way things worked in Dallas. These were lessons that Hardin, a newcomer, had failed to grasp.

Hardin's first wrong move was firing Hayden Fry. Coach Fry was generally well liked by supporters of the football program and there were plenty of those on the board of governors. Hardin probably made an even bigger mistake when he voluntarily turned in SMU for violating NCAA rules. Press reports at the time described Willis Tate—Hardin's predecessor and a former SMU all-American—as "livid" when he heard about it. Hardin later disputed this ("he backed my actions 100 percent") but acknowledged that the decision had been made on short notice, before there was time to consult with the board of governors. All in all, when it came to sports, Hardin never fit in with prevailing mores in Dallas. "I'm not properly worshipful of the great god football," Hardin once said. "We must be a community of scholars, not a farm club for professional football and basketball."

In the end it was not just football that cost Hardin his job. His fumbles there were only part of a larger pattern of independence that the board leadership found disturbing and ultimately unacceptable. For one, Hardin set himself against the board when he tried to strengthen the liberal arts at SMU even at the expense of the professional schools (law, business, engineering) that were so precious to the Dallas business establishment. What sealed his fate may have been a letter he mailed to Cox soon after his reappointment by the board of trustees in May. In it, Hardin outlined his plans to open up decision making at SMU, in part by bringing new blood to the board of governors. Hardin never found out for sure what Cox thought of that idea because Cox never even wrote back.

After the predictable uproar died down, Hardin was forgotten. Why dwell on the past when the present was filled with so much success? Hardin's permanent replacement (Willis Tate served one year as interim president) was James Zumberge, an imposing, silver-haired administrator who was the former chancellor of the University of Nebraska. During Zumberge's four-and-a-half-year term—which closed out the 1970s—he doubled the endowment, balanced the budget, saw applications for admission rise by almost half, and fanned the flames of Mustang Mania. It was hard to avoid the conclusion that the board leadership had done right by SMU after all.

It was only much later, after the monumental crisis that led to SMU facing the NCAA death penalty, that the Hardin affair was reexamined. On second look, it was like watching the pilot that previews the television series. All the familiar plot elements were there: a powerful board of governors, an acquiescent church, a handcuffed administration, a strident but impotent faculty, and a football scandal to set it all in motion. The most obvious difference was the outcome. In 1974 the board was able to contain the crisis. In 1987 it was not.

PART III

9 GETTING AWAY WITH MURDER

ON FEBRUARY 11, 1981, a Wednesday, Ron Meyer stopped in at the Mustang Barber for his usual haircut and a shine. The old Mustang was located within a bomb's toss of Ownby Stadium, across the street from the SMU practice fields. Although it has since moved to a shopping center half a mile from campus, longtime customers still feel at home among the vintage furnishings, which were transferred intact: the tubular-chrome chairs with deep-padded, gray vinyl upholstery, the pedestaled ashtrays, the black-and-white photographs of SMU football players, and the massive wooden shoeshine throne.

Meyer had in his hand an envelope. One of the barbers (wise, perhaps, or else just a wise guy) saw an opening. "Hey, coach," he said. "What have you got there? Automobile titles?"

Meyer didn't laugh. He didn't say anything. He just turned around and walked out and never went back to the Mustang Barber again. The men left holding the scissors were puzzled. "What's with him?" they asked each other.

Later that afternoon there was a press conference. That's when the public learned what Chris Rentzel had learned from Meyer after the Texas game. SMU was being investigated again by the NCAA.

IN 1976, AS SMU'S LAST probationary term (the result of Coach Dave Smith paying players to make tackles) was expiring, the NCAA had announced a one-year extension through January 1977. It was SMU's fourth football-related penalty. Again, the violations were not considered serious: Smith had handed out thirty-one football scholarships, one more than the limit, in what was apparently an administrative oversight; and assistant coach Julius Glosson, among other things, had given "a small amount of cash" to a football prospect and submitted a false affidavit to university officials. Glosson was fired, SMU lost one scholarship, and the case was closed.

Since then SMU had managed to keep out of trouble for four years. Now the NCAA was back. This time the arrival had the feel of something inevitable, like waking up on a winter morning after dreaming of the tropics. SMU supporters were crushed. There had been so many thrills in the season just completed, beginning with SMU's first defeat of Texas in fourteen years, followed by a 27–0 shutout of Texas A&M and later a 31–7 annihilation of Arkansas. Not since 1948 had the Mustangs beaten all three of the SWC's big state-supported schools in one season. Afterward, there had been a week-long party in San Diego leading up to the Holiday Bowl, SMU's first bowl appearance since 1968. What a game *that* was. SMU had Brigham Young University down by twenty points with four minutes left to play before quarterback Jim McMahon led a furious comeback, ending with a forty-one-yard touchdown pass to Clay Brown as time expired. Final score: BYU 46, SMU 45.

As hard as it was to go home a loser, most SMU fans were content to look ahead. The Mustangs had closed out the season ranked number twenty in the nation, a sure sign that they were back in the big show. The Holiday Bowl was over; time now to start thinking about the one that really mattered, the Cotton Bowl.

Yet SMU fans, chastened by long and bitter experience with the NCAA, were definitely worried—not just the ones making payments to players, but everybody. It is part of the gospel at SMU that little schools like theirs don't stand a chance in the long run. If you begin with the assumption that *everybody* cheats—"Give me a map and a dart and I'll show you a college that cheats," is a common way of expressing this view—then you ask, Why is it that some schools get caught and others don't? The answer is complicated. There are levels of understanding, stages of comprehension. Some blame the aggressive, highly competitive Dallas media. Others say SMU is not a major television drawing card and so the NCAA isn't afraid to put them on probation. Still others say SMU is victimized by influential graduates from other schools (usually Texas) who control the media, the networks, and the NCAA.

"It's always poor little old SMU," says booster George Owen. "They get the hammer dropped on their ass every time. As long as Texas and A&M and Arkansas are winning, that's fine. Let SMU win but once every twenty years, that way it'll be all right, but then let's keep them in their place. I've been here a long, long time. I've watched this thing grow up from its infancy and we've not been treated fairly, I *guarantee*. I'm not a screamer. Hell, if you're gonna dance, you gotta pay the fiddler, I understand that. But I just can't understand those people getting away with things that we couldn't get away with."

Many SMU alumni, even those who would not ordinarily ally themselves with a character like George Owen, can appreciate his point. They could see that Meyer was asking for trouble. Maybe he had brought SMU too far, too fast—engendering the ill will of powerful opponents with his hotshot demeanor and flashy dress; upsetting complacent competitors with his penchant for hard work; shocking the establishment with his success in recruiting. Now that Meyer was actually starting to win games, they figured, something had to happen. A lot of people were angry when it did. Few would say they were surprised.

"You can't tell me Ron Meyer wasn't strung up by a posse of those Southwest Conference and regional head coaches and assistants who don't like him or his recruiters," wrote *The Dallas Morning News* columnist Skip Bayless in June 1981, after the penalties were announced. "I've heard too many side-of-the-mouth remarks. Too many don't like the Super Bowl ring from his Cowboy scouting days or the way Meyer flashes the thing. Too many think the SMU football coach 'big-dogs' it. Too many think he's too cocky, too arrogant, too Las Vegas, too much a media favorite.... Meyer was an outsider who'd grown too big for his tailored slacks. He had to be stopped."

The biggest surprise to many, when the NCAA announced SMU's fifth probation on June 10, 1981, was how little the investigators were able to dig up on Meyer. "It was concluded," Meyer says, "that I supposedly—and I'd underline supposedly—led two prospects to believe that they could sell their tickets for more than face value. That was the only thing that I was directly linked to."

Meyer is not being absolutely truthful but he's not far off. The NCAA actually found four players who said that Meyer led them "reasonably to understand" (the NCAA's term) that they could sell their tickets "for an amount substantially in excess of their face value." In another violation, one that was counted in the NCAA's official tally but did not show up in any public report, Meyer was called for "questionable practice" when he "displayed a $100 bill . . . an act that could have been misinterpreted as an offer of improper financial benefits." This, apparently, was one of those times when Meyer used a greenback as a calling card. Meyer's own explanation is that he happened to be cleaning his fingernails with a combination nail file and money clip when he gestured innocently toward a bulletin board filled with other coaches' cards. "That gesture got embellished into tacking one-hundred-dollar bills on the bulletin board," Meyer says. "The more you tell it, the more it grows."

Whatever the truth about that particular incident, the fact is that while the NCAA investigated some eighty violations, it could make only twenty-nine stick. These ran the gamut of what are known in the profession as parking tickets (as opposed to murder): nine separate counts of coaches (including Meyer) making extra visits to recruits beyond the three allowed by the NCAA; one count of a coach playing racquetball with a recruit, regarded as an illegal workout; a couple of free dinners; free lodging for relatives during a prospect's campus visit; one case of a prospect receiving $10 to entertain himself on a campus visit; and one instance where Steve Sidwell, an assistant coach, contacted two players to find out what information they had reported about him to the NCAA, "an action that could have led (them) to conclude that Sidwell was encouraging them to report false information." The NCAA also had a problem with all those souvenir photographs that had been taken of prospects with Meyer under the scoreboard at Texas Stadium, which were interpreted as illegal benefits.

Nowhere in any of the publicly released documents, nor in the NCAA's own confidential report, is any mention made of a slush fund, or payments to players and their families, or motor-home excursions between Houston and Dallas, or any of the other serious violations that were later found to have been committed. On all of that the NCAA came up empty-handed. The NCAA also investigated charges involving board of governors chairman Robert Stewart— the bank president who had been funneling cash to Houston businessman Robin Buddecke from his office at First National—but was unable to find anything conclusive.

The NCAA infractions committee, which hears all cases involving rules violations and determines what penalties to impose, was chaired then by Charles Alan Wright, a University of Texas law professor. In his public statement on SMU, Wright noted that "the committee was particularly concerned that this case represents the third time in the last seven years that the Southern Methodist University football program has been found to be in violation of significant NCAA rules." The NCAA placed SMU on two years' probation, including a one-year ban on bowl games and television appearances.

New SMU president Donald Shields could have fired Ron Meyer for his role in the violations; a clause in Meyer's contract gave Shields that right. But Shields chose to stick by Meyer, saying, "it's a judgment matter and in this particular case I felt the actions of Meyer were not such that it merited a severe penalty. Obviously I believe Ron Meyer or the clause would be used."

Reaction to the NCAA findings was predictably mixed. SMU fans, of course, were devastated; the ban on bowl games and television came the summer before what many hoped would be a championship season. Now, even if the Mustangs won the SWC title, they would not be permitted to play in the Cotton Bowl. Around the conference, rival coaches and boosters who had long suspected Meyer of getting away with murder were generally satisfied with the penalties, even if all the NCAA had found were the parking violations. Many compared it to the way, once upon a time, the Feds nailed Al Capone for tax evasion.

EACH YEAR UNDER Ron Meyer the Mustangs had played a little better. They started with three wins in 1976, then four wins in 1977, four wins and a tie in 1978, five wins in 1979, and eight wins in 1980. Then in 1981, Meyer's sixth season as head coach, SMU won ten games and lost only one. It was the best record by any SMU football team since the long-ago national championship of 1935. Ten SMU starters were wire-service all-conference selections: quarterback Lance McIlhenny, running backs Craig James and Eric Dickerson, offensive guard Perry Hartnett, defensive tackle Harvey

Armstrong, linebackers Gary Moten and Eric Ferguson, defensive backs Russell Carter and James Mobley, and kicker Eddie Garcia. This was the team that finally, undeniably, transformed SMU from the patsy of the Southwest Conference into a national powerhouse, ranked number five by the Associated Press.

The other poll—conducted by United Press International—ignored SMU, as it does any team that is on NCAA probation. Partly for this reason, Meyer's '81 Mustangs have been called the Best Team Nobody Saw. They were forbidden to appear on television and they weren't allowed to go to a bowl game. Surprisingly few bothered even to watch them play at Texas Stadium; SMU's average attendance for seven home games in 1981 was only 33,325, a post–Mustang Mania low.

The season ended on a cool, hard-shadowed November afternoon in Fayetteville, Arkansas. The Mustangs needed a win to clinch their first SWC title since 1966. So far their only loss had been to Texas, 9–7, and Texas had been thoroughly embarrassed by this same Arkansas team, 42–11. The Razorbacks were fired up, too. A win today, combined with a loss by Texas, would put Arkansas in the Cotton Bowl. Men in green blazers—Cotton Bowl scouts—were in attendance.

For most of three quarters it was close. Arkansas, with the help of key turnovers, built an 18–12 lead. Then the SMU defense stiffened and the Pony Express kicked into high gear, and when it was over, SMU had won, 32–18. For the sixth time that season, both Dickerson and James rushed for more than one hundred yards in the same game.

Not many SMU fans had bothered to make the four-hour drive through the Boston Mountains to Fayetteville that day. Those who did watched with mixed emotions as Ron Meyer was lifted onto the shoulders of his players and carried from the field. They knew there would be no bowl game for SMU this year, no national recognition. Their season was over.

What they did not yet know was that Ron Meyer had just coached his last game at SMU.

MEYER'S RESIGNATION, when it came, was the end of an era at SMU. He was the last of the key figures credited with the revival of Mustang football to move on. James Zumberge—the lean, dignified, ex–polar explorer who had hired Meyer and athletic director Russ Potts and led SMU confidently into the eighties—had resigned in May 1980 to become president of the University of Southern California. He had been replaced by Dr. L. Donald Shields, a former chemistry professor and president of Cal State Fullerton.

In 1971, at age thirty-four, Shields had become the youngest state-university president in the country. By the time he arrived at SMU, he was an overweight, boisterous, red-faced man with a receding hairline who favored three-piece suits, long Cadillacs, and flashy jewelry. Next to Zumberge, says one booster, he looked like a "high-school principal." Kathy Costello—the former SMU vice president for university relations who was recruited by Shields from Vanderbilt—was so worried by his appearance that when he offered her a job, she inquired after his health. Costello was being practical. She was excited about coming to SMU, but she was not about to quit her job and move her family to Dallas until she had some reassurance from her new boss that he was likely to survive.

Although he was fond of sports, Shields was not a natural athlete. He played golf and tennis, neither with distinction. He loved football though. Within days of his being named president in October 1980, Shields attended the SMU-Baylor game in Waco. The Mustangs were undefeated after four games. They took an early 28–0 lead, but in the second half Baylor stormed back and won, 38–28. Afterward—as would be his custom as long as he was president—Shields visited the locker room. The players were banged up, worn out, angry, and in no mood for a pep talk from someone in a suit they didn't even know. "You could see them shaking their heads," says a former SMU assistant coach, " 'Who is this jerk?' "

Throughout his six-year term at SMU, Shields was often seen on the sidelines during football games. He taunted newspaper columnists who failed to sing the Mustangs' praises. He took what some academic administrators regarded as an unusual step by naming the athletic director to the president's executive council. "At every meeting," says a former member of the council, "the first thing the president wanted to know was how recruiting was coming along."

And yet despite Shields's obvious passion for athletics, the jocks generally despised him. "We were up in Minneapolis for the NCAA hearings," says one, "and at the end of the day Shields says, 'I'm gonna go take a nap, come get me when they're done.' We went and knocked on his door—Meyer and me and somebody else—and Shields stumbles to the door and opens it and he has taken a nap *but he took his nap with his vest still buttoned.* He said, 'I'll be with you in just a second.' Meyer went, 'Only Don Shields would take a nap without untying his tie, with his vest buttoned!' It was perfect."

Costello, who worked closely with Shields for more than four years, describes him as a man who was "easily caricatured" by members of the coaching staff.

"Those guys who are in that funny little fraternity, they sniff each other out," says Costello. "And, you know, it has as much to do with hormones and genes as real ability. But what I saw in Don was a really kind man who loved the limelight, who wanted to be tough and powerful and all those things but who wasn't a man's man, there's no doubt about it. He looked fairly macho but he had a real tender side. He loved the theater, he loved his wife and family. He often behaved sort of imperiously. He enjoyed the trappings of office. That's why he enjoyed the role of going in the locker room after the game, something that we on the academic side criticized him for. I'm sure he wanted to be on the field running the ball, as do many of the boosters."

LESS THAN A YEAR after Zumberge resigned, Potts also quit. The day he announced he was leaving to accept a job as marketing vice president for the Chicago White Sox—February 11, 1981—was the same day the latest NCAA investigation was made public. Potts swore up and down that he wasn't running away from the NCAA. He produced a telegram from a friend urging him to take the baseball job, dated January 17, to prove this was no sudden development. But according to Ronnie Horowitz, a friend and prominent SMU booster, Potts "just thought the posse was too close. He said, 'When the posse's a couple of hundred miles away, you don't have nothing to worry about. When you can hear 'em breathing on you, that's the time.' "

Bob Hitch, the new athletic director, was as different from Ron Meyer or Russ Potts as a parish priest from a revival-circuit preacher. Hitch grew up on a cotton farm close by the Tallahatchie River in northwest Mississippi. He played guard on the football team in high school and won a scholarship to Mississippi State, but a concussion suffered in his last high-school game ended his playing career. He became a student trainer and worked his way through college. He had spent the better part of his career before he came to SMU as a football coach and athletic administrator at various colleges in the South—Mississippi State, Southern Mississippi, and Louisville. Despite an outwardly gentle, Southern manner, Hitch was no pushover. He seemed determined to run things his way. Already he had taken steps aimed at distancing certain powerful alumni from the football program. It didn't seem to make any difference to Hitch that some of these undesirable alumni were also Meyer's friends.

WHEN RON MEYER left a sure thing in Dallas to accept a job as head coach of the New England Patriots, a lot of people wondered why. After all, probation was expiring, Dickerson and James had a year of eligibility remaining, and it was taken for granted by just about everybody that Meyer had the horses to make a run at a national championship in 1982. Meyer complained loud and often about the cold bed he had inherited at SMU. Well, the bed was warm now. In fact, it was hot. Why leave it for a cold one in New England, where the Patriots were coming off a record of 2–14?

This wasn't the first attractive offer Meyer had received. The University of Wisconsin had shown an interest as early as 1977, at which point SMU signed him to a two-year extension on his contract. (Dick Davis, the SMU athletic director at the time, says he stopped worrying about the possibility of losing Meyer to Wisconsin after he reminded Meyer that "you can't wear suede shoes in the snow.") Florida called, too, before settling on Charley Pell. One year, Meyer says, he was offered every available coaching job in the Big Eight Conference. And after SMU president James Zumberge resigned, there were persistent rumors that Meyer would become coach of the USC Trojans as soon as John Robinson ascended to the NFL. Surely there would be other offers. The way things were going at SMU, Meyer was close to being in a position where he could pick and choose. He was only forty years old. So why not wait?

For one, Meyer wasn't happy at the prospect of continued close scrutiny by the NCAA. As hard as it had been to accept the penalties in 1981, Meyer had to know that he was also lucky, that it could have been much worse. Maybe Meyer thought now was the time.

There were other considerations: the drudgery of recruiting; the frustration of always playing before small crowds in a city where the Cowboys enjoyed a near monopoly on fan support; the departures of Zumberge and Potts, with whom Meyer had developed close working relationships. But Meyer could have lived with all that. He had recently signed a new four-year contract with options that extended even further, and he spoke hopefully at the time about his future with the program. "I love it here in Dallas," he had said. "I love it at SMU."

In the end what really made Meyer decide to leave was probably simple: ambition. Ever since he had been a scout in the Cowboys organization, he had been priming himself for an eventual return to the NFL. It was where he longed to be and probably where he belonged. He had established his credentials at SMU—probation was no blot on *his* résumé, not as far as the NFL was concerned— and he was ready for the next step. "Once I had tasted the NFL," Meyer says, "there was nothing that even compared to it. It was like flying a Cessna 172 compared to an F-16."

Whenever the subject of Meyer leaving SMU had come up, as it often did during recruiting, Meyer made no secret of his ambition. "He always told us players that he would never leave us for another college football team," says Eric Dickerson, "but he would leave us for a pro team. He wanted to coach pro."

On the day he resigned from SMU, Meyer told the *Dallas Times Herald*, "The NFL has a singleness of purpose, and that's football, and I like that."

RON MEYER'S DEPARTURE closed the book on one of the most exciting chapters in SMU history. Later there would be championships and Cotton Bowl appearances and a shot at number one in the country. But for many SMU alumni, the most exciting time would always be the early years, under Ron Meyer, when the Mustangs were on the way up.

"We got it going," says a Dallas lawyer who was an active SMU booster, "and it was really exciting. You cannot imagine. It was, without a doubt, the high-water mark in my mind of SMU football. It wasn't the championships that came in the eighties, it was the excitement of being associated with the building in the seventies

under Meyer. Mustang Mania and all that, big crowds, enthusiasm, being competitive. You could *feel* that we were gonna get there."

They did, of course, but by then everything was different. "We were the winningest team in the eighties," says the lawyer, "and it kind of got to the point . . . it wasn't that it seemed tainted, as much as it just seemed like there was an anvil right above our heads. We were probably at that point an accident waiting to happen, and basically it took all the wind out of my sails. It was, in its own way, a very depressing time."

10 BLOWIN' AND GOIN'

ANY WAY YOU LOOK AT IT, 1982 was a good year for Dallas. Take real estate, the bellwether industry. Maybe 1982 was not quite the peak of the Dallas real-estate market—figures indicated continued growth over the next two years—but it may well have been the year when *confidence* peaked, the year when *nobody went bankrupt*. In 1982 institutional lending for the purchase of Dallas commercial property, buildings and land, surpassed $2 billion, a sevenfold increase in five years; total sales more than doubled; and foreclosures, which had declined steadily year by year, bottomed out at zero.

A barrel of West Texas crude still sold for more than $30 in 1982. Unemployment in Texas was two and a half points *below* the national average in 1982. More people moved *to* Texas than *from* Texas in 1982—429,032, to be exact—after which the decline in net in-migration began. The Dallas Cowboys—America's team—played San Francisco for the NFC championship in January 1982 (they lost, yet it was the fifteenth time in sixteen years that the Cowboys had appeared in a postseason game). "Dallas" was the most popular show on television in the 1981–82 season. Bill Clements, a Dallas Republican, SMU graduate, and former chairman of the SMU board of governors, was living in the governor's mansion in Austin in 1982.

The real-estate men have a term for what was happening in Dallas in 1982. Everywhere you looked, things were "blowin' and goin'."

SHERWOOD E. BLOUNT, Jr., grew up in a working-class neighborhood of East Dallas. His father was a fireman. In the late 1960s he turned down offers to play professional baseball in favor of a football scholarship to SMU. Like Ron Meyer, he was neither the biggest nor the fastest member of the team, only the most determined. He became the starting middle linebacker in his sophomore year and eventually was named co-captain. Meyer remembers Blount as one of two SMU players he scouted (and rejected) for the Cowboys in 1971. "He was a rolling ball of butcher knives," Meyer recalls.

After college, head coach Hayden Fry offered Blount a position on his staff, but Blount was more interested in making money. He gravitated naturally into real estate. "I know of no other business," he would later write to Rick Fambro, a former SMU quarterback who became his first employee, "where a young man willing to work can attain greatness as quickly as in real estate."

Blount was willing to work. By brokering deals and later through investments of his own, he amassed a fortune that business associates say reached $30–$50 million before the bust in 1985. More than the Cadillacs, the summer home on Lake Texoma, and the winter hideaway at Steamboat Springs, Blount's new wealth brought him prestige. He sits on the board of Lovers Lane United Methodist Church, in his words, "the third largest Methodist Church in the world." His name is carved in stone together with those of the other benefactors of a new park in the Lakewood section of Dallas, near where he grew up. The Sherwood E. Blount, Jr., family (he is twice divorced) is listed in the Dallas Symphony Orchestra program among the wealthy individuals and corporations who have endowed an annual concert in the symphony's youth series.

Blount's turf is far-north Dallas. In 1841, when John Neely Bryan came down from the Red River to stake his claim at the future site of Dallas, he followed an old Indian trail along the route of today's Preston Road. Bryan was traveling south, but the direction development has taken in Dallas is north, back up Preston Road. Today a drive up Preston Road from downtown Dallas takes you past the Highland Park mansion belonging to oil magnate Ed Cox, along the eleventh fairway of the Dallas Country Club, across Mockingbird Lane (eight blocks west of the SMU campus), by the dignified older homes and leafy side streets of University Park, through a long stretch of shopping centers and fancy brick houses with two-story atriums and crescent driveways (North Dallas), over the eight-lane LBJ Freeway, and finally into far-north Dallas, a nouveau world of shopping malls, country clubs, apartment complexes, and ritzy sub-divisions extending as far, it seems, as the Oklahoma border.

Sherwood Blount owns an expensive home in far-north Dallas in a country-club community known as Bent Tree (developed by a former SMU football star and Dallas mayor Bobby Folsom). He runs his real-estate business out of an office on North Dallas Parkway, the western boundary of the so-called magic corridor, bounded on the east by Preston Road. It was here in the 1970s that Blount and others like him transformed fields of maize into canyons of glass and built a power base to rival the old money of Highland Park.

In 1979 Nicholas Lemann described this new power base in a cover story for *Texas Monthly* entitled "Sherwood Blount's First Million," about a twenty-nine-year-old real-estate tycoon who was already worth over $2 million. "Most of the people Sherwood knows in Dallas share certain attributes," Lemann wrote. "They have a marked affection for SMU, particularly its athletic programs, and for sports generally, particularly football. Most of them have personally dedicated their lives to the service of Jesus Christ. On the subjects of SMU, sports, the free enterprise system, and religion, they are serious to the point of piety; on everything else, tough and ironic. They work in the business world, give money to good nonpolitical causes, are usually married. What distinguishes them from most Americans, besides having a lot more money, is the extent to which their lives are defined by deals. They spend their days discussing deals over their car phones, having deal-oriented breakfast meetings, doing deals in each other's offices; they live in houses that were good deals themselves when purchased."

In a town where big egos are taken for granted, Blount's is legendary. A former SMU teammate describes him as "the brashest, most personally arrogant guy in the world. It's the way he is. He just reeks it." Another SMU booster compares dealing with Blount to swallowing a shot of tequila: "You don't like that shit but you go ahead and drink it anyway."

Mike Harvey, the SMU business-school professor, calls Blount a "little rooster": "He's the young, aggressive, good-looking kid that snuck into real estate, did a couple of deals, and all of a sudden, 'I'm smarter than everybody else.' This is a guy that was making—I heard estimates—a million dollars a month. You begin to start thinking you're smart if you can do that. There were a lot of guys in Dallas who got into that syndrome and he was right there on the cutting edge of it—and it suited his personality."

Whenever Sherwood Blount negotiated a deal—whether it was for a piece of property up in Collin County or for an offensive lineman in Pittsburgh—he put himself on the line. Every deal was a big deal, another test for the tough guy from East Dallas who tried hard to prove himself to everyone he met.

"Sherwood was a real shaker and baker, a deal maker," says Barney Giles, one of a handful of Dallas realtors who were making as much money as Blount during the boom. "I think he's pretty smart, I think he's aggressive. I think he understands the real-estate business. He picked up the buzzwords and all the different tools it takes to be successful. And he worked hard. I never perceived Sherwood as dishonest or anything like that. He's just very competitive. And he always had something to prove—that he was better than everybody else—and, boy, would he fight."

As Blount's role in SMU recruiting became widely known in Dallas—and was trumpeted all over town in newspaper articles and on television—he went on the offensive, writing angry letters to reporters and threatening lawsuits at every turn. "I'm a crook and a hoodlum and a cheat and a liar," Blount says. "What else have they said about me? All that's true, every bit of it, write it. Go put it in your damn book, I dare you."

RON MEYER FOUND a soul mate in Sherwood Blount. Each had risen from modest beginnings to prominence in his profession. Neither was afraid of hard work. They shared a liking for expensive clothes, long cars, and big cigars. They were useful to one another. Meyer gave Blount the status of being a part of the Mustangs' inner circle; now Blount could go to games and tell his friends before the kickoff, "Ron told me the first play." And Blount helped Meyer build his organization—by contributing cash, introducing Meyer around, and using the strength of his personality to build support. He gave Meyer a powerful weapon in recruiting. Seventeen-year-old high-school kids who visited SMU tended to be impressed when the alumnus who met them in a Cadillac at the airport was a young, fast-talking millionaire who took calls on his car phone on the ride into Dallas and kept pointing out tall buildings and shopping centers as if he owned them. But Sherwood really showed what he was made of when it came time to nail down a commitment. "If you wanted to hotbox a recruit," says another SMU booster, "give him a real lip quiver, a real Jimmy Swaggert, he was a closer."

RON MEYER'S RESIGNATION was announced on Friday, January 15, 1982, the same day that seventeen top recruits were scheduled to arrive in Dallas for their official paid visit to SMU. Following a strategy that had worked for SMU in the past, the most sought-after players had been scheduled to visit at the end of the recruiting period, so that SMU would have the last shot. National signing day was less than a month away. Athletic Director Bob Hitch had to act fast—or risk losing any chance SMU had of salvaging a decent class. He promised to announce a replacement for Meyer by Monday.

Hitch said he was working on three possibilities, two college head coaches and one NFL assistant. Speculation in the local press quickly settled on Tom Osborne of Nebraska, Emory Bellard of Mississippi State, and John Mackovic, an assistant with the Cowboys.

There was one other candidate for the job, Steve Endicott. As Meyer's top assistant, Endicott was the first choice of many SMU alumni. Sherwood Blount told columnist Skip Bayless that he had written a check for $50,000 that "will pay Steve's salary if he's hired." Several days before Meyer officially resigned, Hitch had entertained a delegation of prominent Mustang Club members who argued in Endicott's favor.

"Hitch shot it down just as fast as you can imagine," says one of the Mustang Club members who was there. Ostensibly, Hitch's main objection to Endicott was that he was single and, like Meyer, ran with a fast crowd. Once, after a loss to Texas, Endicott had been seen by President Shields in the stadium club with a woman on either side and empty beer cans on the table.

"Who is it going to be," President Shields reportedly asked Hitch when they had discussed the possibility of hiring Endicott, "you or me that's going to have to pull our coach out of the clubs on Greenville Avenue?" The Mustang Club members thought that was a cheap shot. Endicott was young, only thirty-one, but they knew him to be hardworking and responsible. If Shields could not forgive Endicott's behavior after a hard loss, then Shields just didn't understand football.

Of course there were other factors. Endicott was one of Meyer's best friends; Hitch would naturally have preferred to bring in his own man. Maybe, too, he saw an opportunity. Over the years SMU had repeatedly failed whenever it tried to hire a big-name coach, someone who would bring the Mustangs national recognition (and maybe even fill Texas Stadium). This time around, SMU had a lot to offer. Probation was expiring. The Mustangs had finished 10-1 and were champions of the Southwest Conference. Fourteen starters were coming back for another year, including Dickerson and James—the now-famous Pony Express. It wasn't just a job SMU was offering; it was a national championship.

In fact, Hitch told the visiting delegation of Mustang Club members, some *very* big names were interested in SMU. He mentioned Osborne. "The engine's running on the airplane," Hitch reportedly said, "we are ready to fly, we're gonna have us a coach."

"If you go in there talking about Endicott," says the Mustang Club member, "and walk out thinking, 'We're gonna get Tom Osborne,' you can handle the disappointment."

But it didn't work out that way. Osborne may never have been serious about leaving Nebraska in the first place; as soon as he found out he was still loved in Lincoln, he kissed SMU good-bye. Mackovic—a hot property who had recently left Wake Forest for an assistant's job with the Cowboys—pursued SMU but later changed his mind and formally withdrew his name on Saturday morning; conversations with Tex Schramm and Gil Brandt apparently convinced Mackovic that if he ever wanted to become an NFL head coach, he was better off staying in pro ball. Bellard, Hitch's third candidate, simply was not ready to leave Mississippi State.

As late as 10:00 on Saturday morning, Hitch had no coach, no candidates, and a Monday deadline.

MONDAY MORNING, JANUARY 18, Thurman L. Collins, Jr.—who goes by Bobby—parted the curtains in a room at the Hilton Hotel near the SMU campus and looked down on the traffic clogging North Central Expressway.

North Central is a Dallas institution, a prominent feature of the urban landscape that, like the subways in New York, is absolutely necessary, universally despised, and the only unassailable excuse for being late to work. The ten miles of North Central Expressway connecting downtown Dallas with the LBJ Freeway and North Dallas are said to be the most congested stretch of road in Texas (which, by the way, has more than a quarter-million miles of road, more than any state and most countries; travel it all and you'll have traveled the distance to the moon). North Central's lone virtue is that it is relatively safe. Cars and trucks rarely get up enough speed while traveling on it to cause serious harm when they collide.

Collins, it would later be whispered in SMU booster circles, was badly shaken by the sight of a big-city traffic jam on a typical Monday morning. He is a soft-spoken, unassuming man with thick, silvery hair (he was forty-eight at the time), parted boyishly on one side and combed high over his forehead. He was born and raised in the pine-belt town of Laurel, Mississippi, and played his college ball at Mississippi State in Starkville. For eighteen years prior to moving to Dallas in 1982, he had been living and coaching in Blacksburg, Virginia; Chapel Hill, North Carolina; and Hattiesburg, Mississippi.

Collins had spent two decades toiling as an assistant before Southern Mississippi offered him his first opportunity as a head coach in 1975. At the time the Golden Eagles were a little-known regional independent, overshadowed in their own state by Ole Miss and Mississippi State. Collins made them a national power. In each of the last two seasons Collins's Golden Eagles had won nine games and wound up playing in a bowl. In 1981 they had finished the season ranked number eighteen by the Associated Press. While the long-suffering boosters of the Big Gold club in Hattiesburg were pleased to have their team receive national recognition, what tickled them the most—and helped earn Collins a $46,000 bonus in 1981—was his 10-3 cumulative record against Southeast Conference big shots Ole Miss and Mississippi State. Ole Miss was so embarrassed that it dropped Southern Miss from its schedule.

Collins would have been more than happy to finish his career in Hattiesburg, half an hour's drive from the town where he grew up, among friends he had known all his life. Then just thirty-six hours ago, Bob Hitch, himself a friend of fifteen years, had telephoned. On Sunday, Hitch had flown with President Shields to Hattiesburg and offered Collins a five-year contract at $90,000 per year—plus perks, a TV show, and commercial opportunities in Dallas—to take over a team that had lost only one game in 1981 (by two points!) and boasted a lineup dominated by underclassmen.

"There is an awful lot of talent coming back here next year,"

Collins would tell reporters after he arrived in Dallas. "That would look mighty good to any coach."

But right now—several hours before the scheduled press conference—Collins was looking down at all the cars on North Central and having serious second thoughts about life in the big city. "We almost didn't have a coach," a former SMU official later recalled. Bobby and his wife, Lynn, came *that* close to packing their bags and going back home to Mississippi. Later, perhaps, he would wish that he had.

SIGNING DAY was fast approaching. It was important that Collins and his new staff begin work immediately if they were going to contain the inevitable damage that occurs whenever a head coach suddenly resigns. As it happened, Collins was slow to take charge in Dallas. There was a brief period during the transition when a power vacuum existed. It was during that time that Sherwood Blount was seen in Ron Meyer's office at Ownby Stadium—his feet on Meyer's desk, his hand in Meyer's box of cigars—giving every appearance of running the show.

IN LATE FEBRUARY, Robin Buddecke flew from Houston to Dallas for a summit meeting with Bobby Stewart. In the past Buddecke had called on Stewart—then chairman and chief executive of InterFirst Corp.—whenever he needed to make a withdrawal from the secret recruiting fund. Stewart was semiretired now, though still active in the bank's affairs. He remained chairman of the SMU board of governors. Besides Buddecke, also present were Sherwood Blount and George Owen, representing the Dallas terminus of the I-45 axis.

While Blount—through his friendship with Meyer and by temperament—was the most visible of the Dallas-based SMU recruiters, George Washington Owen, Jr., may have played an even more important role. Owen was raised in East Dallas and attended SMU on an athletic scholarship, twenty-five years before Blount followed the same route. His years on the Hilltop were dominated by basketball and parties. "It was just like Mardi Gras every day," he once told *The Dallas Morning News*. "Great school. Great fun." After college (Owen never graduated) he helped start a maintenance-supply business called Mustang Chemical, the first stop in an eclectic career that included a stint as general manager of the New

Orleans Saints and, by the 1970s, had him involved in scores of North Dallas real-estate development projects. Owen prospered, and today he, like Blount, has an expensive home in Bent Tree.

But Owen's résumé does not begin to tell the whole story of the jowly-faced man in his midsixties—bushy eyebrows, lively eyes, crooked smile—who brags of knowing "every pimp, every whore, every gambler, and every banker" in Dallas. In 1957 Owen was in the apartment of Dallas stripper Candy Barr when police arrested her on charges of possession of marijuana. According to witnesses, Owen was spared when Barr told police, "If you let him go, I'll give you what you came for," and then reached between her bosoms and pulled out the stash; Owen walked away and Barr received a seventeen-year prison sentence. In 1974 Owen was questioned by a federal grand jury investigating gambling operations in Dallas. Among his former wives are Diane Wisdom, a Dallas nightclub singer, and Maureen "Mo" Kane, who later married White House counsel John Dean and became one of the most recognizable faces in America during the Watergate hearings. Among his closest friends are former pro-football players Billy Kilmer and Paul Hornung. He was for many years closely associated with Clint Murchison, Jr., the late founder of the Dallas Cowboys. He knew Jack Ruby.

"George is impervious to ridicule or criticism," says a fellow SMU booster. "His life has been led so much on the other side of the tracks that it doesn't matter to him. It adds to his allure. He's like a rock star, he doesn't care."

Owen originally became involved in SMU recruiting through Blount. In turn, he helped enlist Murchison, a graduate of Duke and MIT who became a passionate SMU booster. Because Owen knew almost everybody in Dallas—and could ask for almost anything without blushing—he was a valuable asset to the recruiting fund. Together with Buddecke, Blount, Ronnie Horowitz, Jack Ryan (a Corpus Christi rancher), Ken Grantham (Dallas car dealer), W. O. Bankston (Dallas car dealer), and perhaps a dozen others, Owen was part of the inner circle of boosters at SMU, one of those referred to by the players—only half jokingly—as a "team owner." He hobnobbed with Meyer and the staff, had a seat on the team plane, watched games from the sidelines. He probably could have run back punts if he had thought to ask.

In October 1980 Mike Harvey, in his role as chairman of the

faculty athletic committee, had briefed new president Donald Shields on the state of SMU athletics. Harvey told Shields about the NCAA investigation and named several boosters—including Blount, Horowitz, and Owen—who he said were making payments to players. Shields responded by ordering his own investigation of Owen in April 1981. The findings were reported to trustees Bobby Stewart and Ed Cox in May, at which time Shields recommended that Owen be disassociated from SMU athletics. Stewart could not have read much in Shields's report that was news to him. When he objected to SMU's taking action against Owen, the matter was dropped.

Now, nine months later, Stewart, Owen, Blount, and Buddecke were meeting for lunch high atop the First International Building in downtown Dallas. Ron Meyer, whose authority in all matters related to recruiting was unquestioned as long as he he had been the coach at SMU, was out of the picture now. Bobby Collins, his successor, had yet to assert himself. And so it was left to these four men—the chairman of the board of governors, two former SMU athletes, and a Houston businessman—to map out a course for the future of SMU's football program. "Okay, guys, what's the deal?" Buddecke quotes Stewart as saying. "Where do we go from here?"

The first item on the agenda concerned those players who were already being paid—the small group of stars with deals in the $500-per-month range, plus those who were getting lesser amounts on an as-needed basis. "Everybody was in agreement," says Buddecke. "We stay with our commitments. There was no way we were just gonna tell those kids, 'Forget it, we aren't helping anymore.' Then Stewart says, 'Okay, but what do we do after that?'"

According to Buddecke, Meyer had always disliked paying players. Like many coaches, he regarded it as a necessary evil, perhaps the only way to revive a dead program. But once the team started winning, the negatives far outweighed any possible benefits. Paying players was expensive, risky, and it undermined the authority of the coaching staff.

"We're where we want to be," Buddecke argued. "This is where Ron was trying to get when he came here. We can get all the players in the world we want if we just sit back and do a good job, play hard, you know, and take care of them when they get here—do the standard, normal thing. But we don't need a lot of money to recruit now."

If Meyer and Buddecke really believed that a day would come when SMU could simply stop paying players, they were naive. More likely, Meyer, if not Buddecke, knew better, which may have had something to do with why he left SMU when he did. Meyer had built a winner, enhanced his own reputation, and survived one NCAA investigation already; maybe he saw only more trouble ahead. In any case, as Buddecke recalls, Blount and Owen nearly leapt out of their chairs at the suggestion of cutting back on the payments now.

"They contradicted me completely," Buddecke says. They said, 'Baloney. We got 'em on the run, we got 'em where we want 'em. We need to bury them. We need to *increase* [the money]. We need to go after the very best players in the country.' "

Part of what worried Blount and Owen may have been the threatening noises they heard coming from the Horned Frogs over at TCU. Now that the SMU program had finally improved to the point where it was attractive to local players, it suddenly had to contend with a resurgent TCU program under head coach F. A. Dry. Within the last couple of weeks TCU had bested SMU for the services of two prep all-Americans right out of Dallas South Oak Cliff—Gerald Taylor and Egypt Allen. Fresh from the trenches of that losing battle, Blount and Owen knew full well what the public would not find out about for another three years: that TCU was spending thousands of dollars of its own on illegal recruiting.

The day would come when Blount would approach Dick Lowe—a Fort Worth oil man and Blount's equal among the Horned Frogs—with the extraordinary proposal that they conduct their own secret draft of local high-school talent and be done with all this foolish (and expensive) bidding for players. As it was, Blount still had sufficient faith in the free-enterprise system and his own skill at manipulating it that he preferred to keep up the fight.

Blount had other reasons for wanting to continue the payment program. Friends say he has a deep affection for his alma mater, which is partly gratitude to SMU for starting him out in his career and opening doors that would otherwise have been closed to the son of a fireman from East Dallas. By doing his part for the football team, Blount was saying thank-you in terms most Texans can appreciate.

Pride was also a factor. "I would not say he was doing it just for his own aggrandizement," says an SMU alumnus who has observed him for many years, "but there's certainly a large portion of that. I can remember him running down the aisle at a Mustang Club meeting, 'Well, here's ten thousand dollars, let's go buy those trophy cases.' He loved that kind of stuff, being the center of attention." As the front man in the payment program, Blount had the satisfaction of knowing that he was regarded, at least by some, as primarily responsible for the turnaround in SMU's fortunes. Saturdays at Texas Stadium, when the Mustangs were winning and the fans were having fun, Blount must have felt the way a hostess does when she knows her party is the social event of the season.

But there was an obvious economic motive, too. Robin Buddecke had been quick to appreciate the benefits to him as a stockbroker that came out of his involvement with SMU recruiting. "It was good for my business," Buddecke says. "You get your name in front of people, you get to meet certain people that you might not be able to meet otherwise. I mean, I could never have been buddies with Ed Cox, going fishing on his lakes or flying around in his private plane. How the hell could I have possibly gotten that kind of entrée if I wasn't involved in recruiting? It was the smartest thing I ever did." For Blount, as a realtor, the same benefits applied. Time spent recruiting in the company of other wealthy alumni was a good way to keep up with friends and meet new clients, like having lunch at the club or playing golf.

But Blount may already have been looking ahead, beyond real estate, to potential profits in a new business, one that depended for its success on continuing the payments to top-flight athletes.

"He knew that if you were giving them cash," says Buddecke, "then you had the hook in them. Simple as that. I don't know how else to put it."

CRAIG JAMES HAD first met Sherwood Blount while he was being recruited by SMU in the fall of 1978. "I really looked up to him and admired him for his personal accomplishments in the business world," James says. "I had always heard about the guys that had gone out and made a million bucks but I never really knew one." After James enrolled at SMU, Blount took him under his wing, becoming what James describes as a "big brother." "My relationship with Sherwood was very, very close," says James. "I was as close to him as anybody else."

At the time, James was still a junior at SMU, one year away from completing his eligibility. When it came time to choose an agent to negotiate his multimillion contract with the Washington Federals of the United States Football League, James would choose Sherwood Blount. After that first successful contract, Blount would found Athletic Associates, and run it out of the same office together with his real-estate company on North Dallas Parkway. His original partners in the venture would be Ron Meyer (after he was fired by the New England Patriots in 1984) and Steve Endicott. Later, fellow booster Ronnie Horowitz—who represents Michael Carter of the 49ers and Ricky Bolden of the Browns but does not collect a fee—also would become affiliated with Athletic Associates. Clients of the firm would include at least eleven former SMU football players, among them, Harvey Armstrong (Eagles, Colts), Russell Carter (Jets), Reggie Dupard (Patriots), and Ronald Morris (Bears). Once he became an agent, every dollar Blount spent on players who eventually enrolled at SMU would work two ways—to build a winning team *and* to help ensure a steady stream of future clients for Athletic Associates. "Sherwood," says an SMU professor who has followed the athletic situation closely for many years, "is an example of someone whose school spirit and entrepreneurial instincts coincided."

By the time the summit meeting broke up, the decision had been made—SMU would continue the payment program indefinitely.

11 GOOD OL' BOYS

FOR ATHLETES RAISED on Ron Meyer's cool, urban, hands-off approach to coaching ("just be ready by Saturday"), the slow-talking, slack-jawed crew from Mississippi spelled trouble. Black players thought some of the new coaches threw the word *boy* around a little too carelessly, and not all white players were impressed by the "y'all" way of talking that came naturally to Collins and his Mississippi mafia. Most of the new staff were steeped in the Southern school of football—disciplinarians, rah-rah types, college coaches who treated their players like college boys. Their arrival signaled the end of the professional atmosphere that had existed under Meyer (even for those players who continued to collect their pay).

"Ron had got to the point where he had his team," says Joe Beard, an all-SWC lineman who was recruited by Meyer and played one year under Collins. "By the time we were juniors, he knew what the players could do. There wasn't a lot of heavy contact during practices. It was more preparation, getting everything sharper. I remember the first time Collins got us out there, he was trying to get everybody clapping. And everybody was standing around [thinking], 'We don't clap. This is spring ball. We don't play any games until next September. Why should we be out here clapping?' "

On the day before his first game as head coach in 1982, Collins was "visibly disturbed," players recall, by their apparent lack of enthusiasm. "If you don't get serious," he told them at a tense meeting after practice on Friday afternoon, "you're gonna get yourselves beat tomorrow."

The final score of the game that Saturday was SMU 51, Tulane 7. "On the sidelines Collins was like a kid in a candy shop," remembers Beard. "He couldn't believe how the team all of a sudden just went out and really turned it on, both offensively and defensively. You could tell he was amazed at the transition that took place. After that he never questioned us again. He let the team's personality come out."

THE 1982 MUSTANGS were the only undefeated major-college team in the country. They beat Texas and Texas A&M on consecutive weekends by a combined score of 77–26. Only a 17–17 tie with Arkansas in a nationally televised game on the last day of the season prevented SMU from winning the national championship. Eric Dickerson and Craig James—the Pony Express—closed out their college careers having rushed for more yards (8,990) than any pair of teammates in the history of college football. As SWC champions, the Mustangs were invited to play in the Cotton Bowl for the first time since 1966, and only the second time since Doak Walker was a senior in 1949. "Believe me," says a young SMU Booster, "we were just giddy."

SMU's opponent in the Cotton Bowl game was the University of Pittsburgh, led by quarterback Dan Marino. It was a matchup that promised plenty of scoring. Yet January 1, 1983, was a cold, wet, windy day—the floor of the Cotton Bowl resembled a melted skating rink more than a playing field—and both teams struggled to get on track. The only touchdown of the day came in the fourth quarter, when Lance McIlhenny scooted in from nine yards out on a quarterback keeper. Pitt, meanwhile, could do no better than a field goal. Final score: SMU 7, Pitt 3.

After the euphoria of the moment had subsided, longtime SMU boosters turned their attention to the future. They hoped that 1982 would be remembered as a watershed year in the history of SMU football. Important goals had been met: a conference championship untainted by NCAA probation; victory in a major bowl; and national recognition by virtue of being ranked number two in both wire-service polls. Now they were ready for the next step.

When Ron Meyer first came to Dallas in 1976, he had shared with members of his staff and close friends a vision of the future of SMU football. Meyer knew that the University of Texas—the biggest, richest, and most glamorous of the state universities in the Southwest Conference—held an irresistible attraction for certain of the state's best high-school athletes. This was a given. It meant that UT probably always would be in a position to challenge for the conference title. Meyer could live with that, as long as there was room at the top for SMU, too.

His model was Southern Cal. Located in a major city (Los Angeles), USC is a small, private college with an attractive campus, relatively high academic standards, and a reputation for placing graduates among the local business elite. USC uses these advantages to compete successfully over the long run with UCLA in the Pac Ten Conference. Meyer saw no reason why SMU, which has the same advantages, should not be able to compete consistently with Texas. He believed SMU could be *the* private-school alternative in the Southwest Conference, a USC on the North Texas plains.

Boosters who shared Meyer's vision felt strongly that with SMU's success in 1982, the football program had reached a critical stage in its development. "Yes, it was a great experience to have gotten there," says an active SMU booster, "but you would hope that if you can climb the mountain, you can stay on it—like Georgetown did [in basketball]; it climbed up it once and then stayed there. We didn't want to crest and go over the other side of the mountain."

The first crucial test of SMU's staying power would be the 1983 recruiting season, just heating up now that all the bowl games were over. Collins and his staff seemed to understand what was expected of them. "We win this game," Bootsie Larsen, the new SMU recruiting coordinator had said during the week before the Cotton Bowl, "and we're going to be able to sign everybody. *Everybody.*"

"FIVE OR SIX WEEKS later," says an SMU booster, "it doesn't take Einstein to see that these guys are just giving it more or less a lick and a promise as far as their recruiting effort. Instead of us basically picking through the best players in America to determine which ones we're going to annoint, guys were committing elsewhere."

Some hard-line SMU boosters thought Collins was in over his head. They had accepted Meyer as one of their own—aggressive, ambitious, never one to miss an opportunity or fail to capitalize on an advantage. He had built up the SMU football program the same way many boosters had built up their businesses. But no one knew what to make of Collins. "It's like they opened the back door and let all these guys from Mississippi in," says the booster. "I don't mean to be regionally bigoted, but honest to God, if you take your best banker from Laurel, Mississippi, and throw him down here in Dallas, he's gonna be eaten alive. He's gonna be absolutely picked like a chicken. These guys didn't know what it took. They *just really did not seem to want it.* The irony of it is, had they come into town six or seven years before, when it wasn't quite as hell-bent-for-leather, maybe they would have fit in better. But Ron had changed the equation. Ron had taken the damn thermostat and turned it up about fifteen degrees."

As the deadline approached, some boosters were panicky: "We're sitting here two or three weeks before signing day and this land-office haul that we're supposed to get is just evaporating."

But there was one booster who was not going to leave the future in the hands of the good ol' boys. Around town, Sherwood Blount was telling anyone who asked not to worry about the recruiting problem this year. "I'm about to take care of it," he said.

In the weeks that followed, Blount traveled all over Texas—in effect, doing Bobby Collins's job. There were reports of Blount sightings in Bryan, Texas, where he was pursuing tight end Rod Bernstine and linebacker Todd Howard; in Temple, where he was talking to wide receiver Albert Reese (a future client of Athletic Associates); and in Belton, home of all-American quarterback Bret Stafford, where he was seen sitting in the bleachers in the school gym next to two of Collins's counterparts—Freddie Akers of Texas and Jackie Sherrill of Texas A&M.

THE SMU RECRUITING class of '83 was believed at the time to be the equal of the class of '79, which had both Dickerson and James. It contained many of the best-known high-school seniors in Texas, including Ronald Morris (now with the Chicago Bears), Jeffrey Jacobs, and Marquis Pleasant. But what attracted national attention to the class of '83 was the fact that SMU also signed *four Parade* magazine all-Americans: Jeff Atkins, a running back from Fort Worth Eastern Hills; Albert Reese, a tight end from Temple; David Stanley, a linebacker from Angleton; and Terence Mann, a defensive tackle from Cooley High in Detroit, Michigan. These were athletes who could have gone to any college in America and chose SMU. By doing so they helped certify a growing conviction among those closely associated with the program that SMU had finally arrived.

Ironically, it was the class of '83 that also contained the agent of SMU's destruction. In time it would be revealed that eight of the twenty-two players who signed that year—including Mann, Reese, and Stanley—did so after they were promised monthly salaries. Mann and Reese would have successful careers at SMU, but Stanley turned out to be a bust. He would see limited action as a linebacker for two years, then succumb to an addiction to cocaine and eventually drop out of school. A year later, looking bloated and sullen, David Stanley would go before a television camera to say that he had been paid $25,000 up-front and $750 a month by SMU recruiting coordinator Bootsie Larsen and later his successor, Henry Lee Parker, to play football for SMU.

And that would be the end of SMU's short stay on the mountaintop.

12 NO LIMITS

ON MARCH 10, 1983, vice president for university relations Kathy Costello received a surprise phone call from a producer at WFAA-TV in Dallas. The producer told Costello that his station was planning to report that evening that SMU had received official notification from the NCAA of a preliminary inquiry, the first step in a full-scale investigation. Did the university wish to comment?

Costello was furious. SMU president Donald Shields had said nothing to her about any new problems with the NCAA. She went looking for her boss.

"Look here, Don," she said. "One of the things we agreed is you're not going to keep me in the dark. What's going on here?"

Shields was stunned. "What?"

Somehow, producer John Sparks of Channel 8, the ABC affiliate in Dallas, had learned of the contents of the NCAA's letter to SMU on the same day it was received by the university. Not for the last time was Shields caught knowing less than the local media about a major development in his own athletic department.

The NCAA now had six months to decide whether a full investigation was warranted. President Shields retained Dallas attorney John McElhaney, who had represented SMU in matters regarding the NCAA since 1975, and asked him to begin an internal investigation.

"I'm terribly disappointed," athletic director Bob Hitch told the *Dallas Times Herald*. "We have all worked awfully hard the two years I've been here to run a straight ship, and I believe we are. At this point I don't think anybody should get excited."

But Sherwood Blount was already hot. "I'm more than a little upset," he said. "I'm perturbed."

AS REPORTED BY Channel 8, the initial focus of the NCAA investigation was the recruitment of Ronald Morris, who would be enrolling at SMU in the fall. Suspicion was said to center on two unnamed members of the Mustang Club: one a lawyer, the other a banker, both from Dallas. Within days, Danny Robbins of the *Times Herald* was quoting anonymous sources who said that Morris had been promised $4000 to sign with SMU and $400 for each month he was enrolled. Morris denied the allegations.

Over the next several months, *Times Herald* reporters Robbins, Jack Sheppard, and Mark Hyman turned up new evidence of cheating involving other players, too. On March 17 Rice University assistant Tony Sexton was quoted, saying that Marquis Pleasant had told him he had been offered a Camaro Z28 to sign with SMU. Pleasant, who was driving a 1980 Camaro at the time, said the car had been bought for him by his mother. On March 23 an uncle of James Lott, a highly recruited defensive back from Refugio who ultimately signed with Texas, told the *Times Herald* he had been given a yard job by an SMU booster one week before signing day, apparently in the hope that he could influence his nephew's decision. On June 24 another Texas-bound recruit, running back Edwin Simmons from Hawkins, told Robbins, "Nobody tried to buy me, except SMU. I'm not saying that the coaches did it. But things happened." And on July 14 Robert Smith, a running back from Dallas Spruce High bound for the University of Iowa in the fall, said he had received cash from a man involved in SMU recruiting.

Meanwhile, NCAA investigators were vigorously pursuing the same leads. Throughout the spring and summer of 1983, Dan Beebe ventured out from NCAA headquarters in Mission, Kansas, to talk with players, boosters, high-school coaches, recruiters, and anyone else who had information to share about SMU. As a result, tension among supporters of rival SWC schools—already high in the wake of the most competitive recruiting season in recent memory—increased. Some vocal SMU boosters were convinced that the root cause of their problem with the NCAA was simple jealousy, born of SMU's two-straight conference championships and recent victory in the Cotton Bowl. "It seems like every time you get to beating people," said Jack Ryan, a cattle rancher from Corpus Christi, "they all get to hollering."

When Sherwood Blount heard that Beebe had visited Austin, he told Mark Hyman of the *Times Herald,* "Based on the facts I have . . . the only reason it's gotten this far is because somebody like Fred [Akers, head coach of Texas] turned us in. . . . And the only reason Fred turned us in is because a kid committed to him and then changed his mind because he didn't want to play for Fred. A lot of kids don't. And you can quote me on that."

The first five weeks following the announcement of the new NCAA investigation happened to coincide with the annual Mustang Club Fund Drive. On Monday, May 16, university officials announced that a total of $2,828,189 had been pledged to the SMU athletic department, exceeding the goal by 13 percent. It was the most successful Mustang Club Fund Drive in school history.

ANGLETON, TEXAS, the seat of Brazoria Country, is about forty miles south of Houston and fifteen miles north of the Gulf of Mexico. The country all around is lush and low, a place where cotton was once grown and antebellum plantation buildings can still be found. To-day, Angleton, population 15,174, is what guidebooks describe as a "tranquil" community, although a visitor might choose an adjective like "forlorn."

During the spring of 1983, reporters from Dallas traipsed all over tiny Angleton—stopping at the courthouse, the high school, and at a little bar called Daniel's Place—trying to uncover the particulars of one of the most farcical skirmishes ever to come to light in the annual Texas recruiting wars. This is the story:

Dawn and Harley Stanley used to lease the coffee-shop conces-sion on the first floor of the courthouse in Angleton, which is how district judge Neil Caldwell, whose chambers are in the same build-ing, came to know their son, David. David Stanley was one of those boys who had always been bigger and stronger than the rest of his classmates. He is described by those who knew him in high school as a loner, someone who had few obvious friends, boys or girls. His attitude toward adults was respectful but distant; if they spoke to him, he listened—he might say, "Yessir"—but he avoided looking straight at them.

Once on the football field, though, David was transformed. "He was put in the category that he was a very physical, very tough person," says Dan Gandy, his former high-school coach. "He accepted that challenge and got tougher and tougher and meaner and meaner. He played three years for us and, gosh, the last two were just unbelievable—the threshold of pain that he had and the pain that he put on the running backs. He had that rattlesnake strike—just before he got to a person, he unloaded. It wasn't a fun game for him, it was a deadly game."

David was the lone linebacker in Angleton's unusual 6-1 defensive alignment, which Gandy had designed specifically to take advantage of his homing instinct for the ball carrier. In retrospect, Gandy thinks the recruiters should have seen that his raw, undisciplined talent might not translate well to college, where he would be expected to play a defined role in a structured defense; Gandy knew it was not like David to accept limits. But David made five hundred tackles during his high-school career and was named to seven all-American teams, including *Parade* magazine. Everybody wanted him.

Judge Caldwell, a loyal Longhorn who earned both his undergraduate degree and his law degree from the University of Texas, naturally took an interest in David's college plans. He once went so far as to offer to arrange a tour of the sacrosanct Burnt Orange Room for David on his next visit to Austin.

In mid-January of his senior year, David was unaccountably absent from school for several days. Later it was learned that he had flown to Lake Tahoe, Nevada, where he won almost $2,000 at the gaming tables. David's companion on the trip was an older man named Ken Corley, a used-car dealer from nearby Texas City. It so happens that Ken Corley has a brother, Jim, who supplied coffee to the Texas athletic department. Evidently, whatever loyalty Jim felt to his brother was superseded by loyalty to his customers; Jim told UT recruiting coordinator Ken Dabbs that he thought his brother's trip to Lake Tahoe with David Stanley probably had something to do with SMU. Dabbs, who had begun to despair of ever making David Stanley a Longhorn, passed this morsel of intelligence on to Caroll Kelly, a booster from Freer, Texas. Kelly called up Judge Caldwell in Angleton and asked him to look into it. If a link could be found between Corley and SMU, then the trip to Lake Tahoe would have been a violation of NCAA rules.

Caldwell says he had never heard of Ken Corley before he heard from Kelly. But when he started asking around, he learned some things he decided the Stanleys ought to know. Several days before the signing deadline, Caldwell called Harley Stanley and told him that Ken Corley was, at best, an inappropriate travel companion for their teenaged son; in fact, Caldwell said, Corley was suspected of dealing drugs and transporting cars illegally into Mexico.

It was not long before an irate Ken Corley called up Judge Caldwell. He had heard what Caldwell said about him to the Stanleys and demanded an apology. If Caldwell would not give him one, well, Corley let him know that he had been in touch with his attorney.

Caldwell just laughed. "Sue me," he said. Then he hung up the phone. Ken Corley had walked right into Caldwell's trap.

Up to now Caldwell still had no proof of a link between Corley and SMU; evidently, Corley had never even graduated from high school. But now Caldwell had been threatened—or so he believed—with a lawsuit, and in Texas a person who has reason to fear he is about to be sued can instigate sworn depositions. Corley had unwittingly given Caldwell the right to compel testimony from him and view relevant documents, phone records, for example. Caldwell walked down the hall to the office of Judge J. Ray Gayle —friend, colleague on the bench, and fellow Longhorn—and filed his petition.

Once Corley saw what was happening, he backed off. "I have no intentions of suing Neil Caldwell," he told Judge Gayle in Brazoria County Court on March 23. "All I ever wanted was an apology. I have two children and I'm raising them here. That's it. I don't want to sue nobody.... I work seven straight days buying and selling cars. I don't need this."

Corley chose to represent himself that day in Judge Gayle's courtroom. Caldwell, though, had help. He brought along an attorney, Joe Jamail—otherwise known as the "King of Torts"—the famous trial lawyer from Houston who represented Pennzoil in the multibillion dollar lawsuit against Texaco over the purchase of Getty Oil, and who won the largest civil judgment in history. Jamail, it happens, is a Longhorn and friendly with former Texas coach Darrell Royal.

In the end Judge Gayle ruled there was "sufficient testimony to indicate that Mr. Corley has discussed a pending lawsuit." He ordered Corley to return to court on April 13 and to provide Caldwell with his telephone records from January 1 through March 31. "Mr Corley," said Judge Gayle in closing, "I would suggest you get . . . your attorney to represent you at this point when the deposition is taken."

The next time Corley came before Judge Gayle, he did bring a lawyer—Hugh Hackney, a partner in the prominent Houston firm of Fulbright and Jaworski, who, as it happens, has two degrees from SMU and is a member of the Mustang Club. By now, though, Judge Gayle had decided that since he, too, had once discussed college plans with David Stanley, he was compelled to disqualify himself from the case.

On April 28 the contesting parties met at the Harris County civil courts building in Houston. The new judge in the case was Wyatt Heard, a Baylor graduate and active football booster himself, who could be counted on to be impartial because Baylor had dropped out of the running for David Stanley very early in the game. The deposition took place in an empty jury room and lasted only twenty minutes before a recess was called pending examination of the phone records Caldwell had requested. Afterward, Corley and his attorney pressed quickly through the group of waiting reporters, refusing to comment. Caldwell and Jamail, on the other hand, were acting as if they had just gotten away with something so clever that they just had to talk about it.

"I got the distinct impression he wanted to be somewhere else," Caldwell said, describing Corley's attitude while the deposition was being taken to a reporter from the *Dallas Times Herald*.

"He acted like he had a boil on his butt," said Jamail.

As far as Caldwell was concerned, he already had everything he needed. The headline in the newspaper the next day was, "NCAA will talk to judge about SMU." And subsequent examination of Corley's phone records—which Caldwell gladly shared with the NCAA—turned up several calls to the Dallas phone number of George Owen, the SMU booster who had worked with assistant coach Bootsie Larsen on signing David Stanley. It was the link Caldwell was searching for all along.

By then other evidence had already come to light. On May 8 it was reported that an Angleton lawyer named Jerry Farrer, a friend of both Caldwell and Corley, had stopped in at a bar called Daniel's Place one day in early February and found Corley there. "I said, 'I understand that you've got some problems with Judge Caldwell, and he's gonna try to protect himself (from a possible slander suit),'" Farrer told the *Times Herald*. " 'And I understand somebody said that you had taken the boy to Lake Tahoe.' I don't remember anything in the conversation at that point. He didn't say anything (about) what he'd done or hadn't done. But when he turned around to walk off, he said, 'Well, I did get the boy for SMU.'"

"Just both of us in a bar drinking," Corley countered when he was asked about Farrer's story. "I was roaring drunk and I don't think I did (make the SMU comment). I don't know what was said."

THE REVELATION OF the phone records was the last the public would hear about David Stanley for more than three years. After a short and disappointing career at SMU, Stanley would drop out of school in December 1985 after having sought treatment for his addiction to cocaine. But those who knew Stanley when he first arrived on campus describe a teenager who was already deeply troubled.

"He threatened everybody," says a teammate from the recruiting class of '83. "He didn't want anybody around him. He threw all his roommate's furniture and belongings out of the dorm room and told him to get out. And the guy he threw out was the biggest freshman recruited that year, Dan Betterton, weighed over three hundred pounds. He was always talking about the 357 Magnum that he had in his car. David had a Toronado, brand new. He wrecked that car. The whole front bumper was missing. It always had the spare tire on, you know, the little bitty one? Next thing you know he was driving a Nissan 300 ZX, brand new. He had the best stereo system I've ever seen. I always told my friends, 'You're stereo's nothing, wait till you see this guy's at school.' After he kicked Betterton out of his room, he'd crank it up as loud as it could go. Nobody was going to say nothing to him about turning it down."

ON JUNE 9, 1983, the probationary term SMU had received two years before when Ron Meyer was still coach formally expired. This was small consolation to SMU people, who were consumed now by the new investigation. They were looking ahead to September, six months after SMU first heard from the NCAA, when the preliminary inquiry would either be extended for another six months, upgraded to a formal investigation, or dropped.

Uncertainty hung over the upcoming season like a storm cloud. High hopes of a third straight SWC title were tempered by fear of probation, which would likely mean having to sit out the Cotton Bowl again. In July athletic director Bob Hitch told *The Dallas Morning News*, "Our people in our department are very bitter. We are having a tremendous morale problem." President Shields publicly raised the possibility of a lawsuit against the NCAA, presumably on grounds of harassment.

On September 6, three days after SMU began the 1983 season with a convincing 24–6 win over Louisville, the NCAA formally announced that it was continuing its preliminary inquiry. The investigation was just getting started.

13 STAY OUT OF IT

AFTER HEARING FROM THE NCAA, Bob Hitch and the SMU administration took steps to try and control the situation themselves. Hitch began a series of meetings with key boosters that would continue for the next seventeen months. On September 26 he banned all boosters from team flights and from locker rooms after the game, a move that earned him few new friends. For those boosters who still thought of Hitch and Coach Collins as interlopers from Mississippi who had taken over their team, this was the final indignity.

But for Hitch it was a logical next step in a development in his thinking that had begun soon after he arrived at SMU in 1981. That first year, he had come across a two-thirds page listing in the game program, thanking—on behalf of the Mustang Club, athletic director Russ Potts, and head coach Ron Meyer—those who had "given tremendous support . . . for the SMU football program." When Hitch checked the more than one hundred names on the list against official records of contributors to SMU athletics, he found that less than half the names matched. Obviously, the kind of support some boosters were providing was not showing up in the books.

Also in the fall of 1983, at the urging of President Shields, SMU attorneys began a series of interviews with SMU players who had been recruited by other schools. The purpose of these interviews was not to discover which players had accepted illegal incentives from SMU, but rather what they had been offered by other schools. It wasn't long before the internal investigation yielded unwanted results.

On November 1, 1983, two SMU players, Darrin Boone and Doug

Hollie, told John McElhaney, the SMU attorney, that they and others on the team were currently receiving regular cash payments. They gave McElhaney the names of boosters who were funding the payments and told him which coaches were actually delivering the cash to the players. This was troubling news, the first concrete evidence from SMU players themselves that the NCAA investigation was more than simple harassment.

McElhaney and his associate, Mike Moore, did not record the interview with Boone and Hollie, but immediately after it was over, they dictated their recollections into a tape recorder. Later they played the tape for Donald Shields. Shields hit the roof, expressing what was later described as "shock and outrage." He immediately called in Hitch, and later head coach Bobby Collins, and confronted them with what he had learned. Both denied any knowledge of an ongoing system of payments to players. Shields also called Ed Cox, chairman of the board of trustees, and requested an urgent meeting.

On November 8 Shields and Cox met, not in the president's office on campus but at Cox's spectacular Highland Park mansion on the corner of Beverly Drive and Preston Road. Shields told Cox about Boone and Hollie and also mentioned someone else—described only as a "highly respected former SMU football player"—who had contacted McElhaney independently and provided information consistent with what the lawyer had been told by Boone and Hollie. Cox suggested they discuss the matter with the incoming chairman of the board of governors, Bill Clements.

Earlier that spring, Bobby Stewart had signaled his intention to step down as chairman of the board of governors, a position he had held since 1976. Paul Corley (no relation to Ken Corley of Angleton), a former oil-company executive, had been fingered by Cox to replace Stewart. At one point, while Corley was considering whether or not to accept, he had been invited by Cox and Stewart to attend a meeting with SMU's two most prominent boosters, Sherwood Blount and George Owen. The subject of the meeting has never been disclosed, although it seems reasonable to assume that had Corley attended, he would have been brought up to date on illegal recruiting at SMU. Corley, though, had chosen not to attend the meeting and later declined Cox's offer to become chairman of the board of governors. At that point the board leadership had turned to Bill Clements.

Clements is the grandson of a Texas mule skinner and the son of a ranch manager. He grew up in a small house on Normandy Avenue in Highland Park, a poor kid in a rich neighborhood. In his youth he was an achiever, an Eagle Scout at age thirteen, a high-school fraternity president, and class president and editor of the yearbook at Highland Park High. He could have had a football scholarship to SMU in 1934, but with the Depression aggravating the always uncertain financial situation at home, he set off for the South Texas oil fields to make money. Eighteen months later he came back to Dallas and enrolled at SMU. By then, though, he was independent and itchy to make his own way. He lasted barely two and a half years in the classroom before deciding to resume his education in the oil fields.

After the war, Clements and a partner, Ike Larue, went into the contract drilling business with financial backing from Toddie Lee Wynne, a wealthy Dallas oil man closely associated with Clint Murchison, Sr. The Southeastern Drilling Company (their first contracts were in Mississippi), later shortened to SEDCO, grew and prospered, helping pioneer the new technology of offshore drilling and later entering foreign markets in South America and Asia. Clements took the company public in 1965 and made himself and a small group of associates very rich.

In 1964 Clements donated $100,000 to the losing senate campaign of George Bush and personally headed up his fund-raising effort. He served his first term as chairman of the SMU board of governors from 1967 to 1973, before moving to Washington, where he served three years as deputy secretary of defense under Presidents Nixon and Ford. In 1978 he became the first Republican in more than a century to be elected governor of Texas. His campaign was financed partly through funds raised by many of his wealthy Highland Park neighbors and fellow SMU board members, notably finance committee members Ed Cox and Bobby Stewart, who was also raising funds in the late seventies for SMU football. Cox and Clements both served on the board of Stewart's bank, InterFirst. Clements's organized effort to get out the vote in 1978 is credited with providing the margin of victory for another fellow member of the SMU board of governors, Senator John Tower.

Clements brought a new style of management to state government in Austin—the Dallas way, forged in the tradition of the Dallas

Citizens Council. His advisers were mostly wealthy businessmen like himself, and he created what *Texas Monthly* called a "government by entrepreneur." Just as membership in the Citizen's Council was restricted to successful businessmen, so was access to power in Clements's administration. Lawyers were generally looked down on as a breed of men who never took risks.

Journalists who observed Clements during his first term as governor of Texas were quick to note those traits that would surface later during the crisis at SMU. "Clements thinks in straight lines," wrote George Rodriguez in *D* magazine. "Getting things done and damn the torpedos."

"Clements has two tactics that are interesting," noted Dave McNeely, also in *D* magazine. "One is the appearance of consensus. He will say he talked something over with other officials, 'and they agreed with me.' Checking with those officials may show that they haven't agreed with him at all, but he has put them in the position of having to appear to be disagreeable.... The second tactic is denial of the obvious, followed by attacking anyone who questions him about it. It reminds me of a friend who vows if his wife ever catches him with another woman, he will flatly deny it. 'That's not a woman,' he will say. 'You're imagining this.' "

In 1982 Clements was defeated in his bid for reelection by Mark White. He returned to his home on Preston Road in Highland Park and his office at SEDCO headquarters in the historic Cumberland Hill School Building on Akard Street, which Clements had renovated in the 1970s. In the late summer of 1983, after Corley refused to become chairman of the board of governors, Clements agreed to return to SMU. He said at the time that he had no intention of remaining for very long and that it would be his primary goal to identify a suitable successor.

OVER THE NEXT two days following President Shields emotional meeting with Cox, the chairman of the board of trustees huddled privately with Clements and Bobby Stewart. On November 11 the board leadership returned to campus for a breakfast meeting with Shields at the student center. Stewart, no longer formally connected with SMU except as an ordinary trustee, did not attend, but Cox and Clements were both there, along with Shields and the attorney McElhaney.

Shields took the opportunity at the outset to express, once again, his outrage at what he had learned about the nature of SMU recruiting. Clements and Cox heard him out, but they had no stomach for his moral indignation. They accused him of being naive.

"Do you think all the nationally recruited football players found their way to SMU by accident," Clements said sarcastically, "or did they choose SMU instead of UCLA or Oklahoma because they liked SMU's school colors?"

Clements assured Shields that he and Cox were well aware of the payments to athletes and were taking appropriate measures through discreet channels.

"We'll take care of it," Clements told Shields. "You stay out of it. Go run the university."

This put Shields in an impossible situation. Each year the NCAA required that Shields and Hitch—as president of the university and athletic director—sign statements certifying that they are in compliance with NCAA rules. The exercise serves to reinforce the theoretical control of athletics by the president and faculty of the university. But Clements and Cox were telling Shields that athletics were none of his affair, and that he ought to mind his own business. Like Paul Hardin twenty years earlier, Shields was learning the limits of his authority the hard way.

Before the meeting broke up, Cox and Clements ordered McElhaney to henceforth keep his nose out of what was happening in the SMU athletic department and concentrate instead on finding out what was happening at other schools.

Later that day, Clements and Cox continued their discussion with Shields in the president's office in Perkins Hall. Clements told Shields that he and Cox had met with persons who had described to them the existence of a fund, which he said totaled roughly $400,000 and had about sixty contributors. Shields reaffirmed that this was news to him, and furthermore that it was news to Hitch, too. But Clements refused to believe that Hitch was ignorant. "Hitch is a professional," Clements told Shields. "It is his job to know."

In fact, Hitch reported later that day to Shields that his inquiries over the last few days had turned up conclusive evidence that a fund existed for paying players. Hitch said he had spoken to a member of the SMU athletic staff who had told him that Sherwood

Blount, George Owen, and Bobby Stewart were involved, with Owen serving as "coordinator/administrator" of the fund.

THE LAST EVENT on Clements's calendar that day was the semi-annual meeting of the board of trustees, where he was introduced by Cox as the new chairman of the board of governors. Clements made a point of assuring the trustees that there would be no further rules violations in the SMU athletic program, either by SMU officials or by outside supporters.

WHAT SPOILED THE 1983 season for SMU was a showdown with Texas in Dallas on October 22, before a national television audience. The game was decided in the fourth quarter when SMU scored on fourth and one to make the score 13–12, then chose to go for two. Lance McIlhenny rolled right, found Reggie Dupard running toward the flag, but had to throw off balance. The pass fell incomplete. Texas added a safety with one minute to play to ice the game, 15–12. It was SMU's first defeat since losing to Texas in 1981 and ended the nation's longest running winning streak at twenty-one games.

With Texas unbeaten and playing in the Cotton Bowl, SMU accepted an invitation from the Sun Bowl. Christmas in El Paso was not anybody's idea of excitement and many of the players would have preferred not to go. Game day was cold and snowy. SMU's unranked opponent, the University of Alabama, got off to a fast start and buried SMU early, 28–0 at halftime. According to a former player, the team's morale was so low that players almost refused to take the field for the second half. Final score: Alabama 28, SMU 7. The Mustangs dropped from number six in the polls to number eleven.

NOTWITHSTANDING CLEMENTS'S assurances to the board of trustees, recruitment in 1984 proceeded along familiar lines. Had SMU backed off after 1983, as soon as they learned they were under investigation again, it is possible that the NCAA would have been forced to give up for lack of evidence. But certain boosters connected with SMU had no intention of slowing down; either they did not believe they would be caught or else they didn't care. Early in 1984 SMU made a big push to sign Sean Stopperich.

Stopperich lived in Muse, Pennsylvania, a small town south of

Pittsburgh. He was six four, 272 pounds, an offensive lineman who looked like a candidate for a beefcake pinup in *Playgirl* magazine. Sean's dad, Carl, had been working in a steel company but had recently been laid off and was beginning to fall behind in his bills. During his senior year, Sean made all the high-school all-American lists and attracted the attention of SMU. The assistant in charge of recruiting Stopperich was Tony Marciano, only twenty-eight years old, unusual on Bobby Collins staff for his youth and because he was from the North, where he had played college football at Indiana University in western Pennsylvania.

According to NCAA documents, on February 5, 1984, a booster—later identified as Sherwood Blount—checked into a hotel near the Stopperich family's home on February 5. He must have cut an impressive figure—brash, smartly dressed, bearing the promise of a new life in the Sunbelt for a family defeated by hard times up North. According to NCAA documents, a representative of the university's athletic interests (Blount) gave a prospect (Sean Stopperich) and his family $5,000 cash. Blount promised Sean's dad, Carl, assistance in finding a job in Dallas, a rent-free apartment, and a $300 monthly allowance for Sean during his enrollment at SMU. All Blount asked in return was for each of their signatures on a post-dated National Letter of Intent. Until then Sean Stopperich had been planning on signing with Pitt. He changed his mind.

In April, 1984, Carl Stopperich would visit Dallas to scout for a job before the rest of the family moved down. At that time an unnamed booster gave him $2,000 for living expenses and provided him with what the NCAA called "lodging, entertainment . . . and the use of an automobile. . . ."

SMU'S PROBLEMS with the NCAA were not going unnoticed by other schools. Evidently, someone saw an opportunity to take advantage of the fear recruits have of signing on with a program that may end up on probation. On the day before national signing day in February 1984 two SMU recruits received a semiliterate letter on SMU stationary with the addresser and addressee's names blocked out, purporting to be news about the pending SMU investigation. "I have been in contact with my colleagues in the NCAA and have finally been informed as to the nature of the penalties to be assessed against SMU," the letter began, before outlining what it said would be a penalty of three years' probation, including a three-year ban on television and bowl games. Both players who received the letters—Highland Park lineman David Richards, the *Parade* magazine high-school player of the year, and Bobby Waters, a quarterback from Garland High School—disregarded the warning and signed with SMU.

IN EARLY MARCH, one full year after SMU received its first indication that the NCAA was considering a formal investigation, Donald Shields learned that the NCAA investigation would continue indefinitely.

ON MARCH 30 a student drawing of two pigs mating was removed from a student art exhibit by an SMU administrator. The charcoal drawing by senior art major Kathy Galloway entitled "Two Magicians" was ordered removed by Eugene Bonelli, dean of the Meadows School of the Arts after the opening night of the exhibit. "I don't really feel angry," Galloway told *The Dallas Morning News*. "I'm just amazed. It's not the sort of thing you would expect to happen in a university in the twentieth century."

DAN BEEBE AND Ron Watson, two NCAA investigators, visited SMU for three days in April in order to conduct further interviews, and Beebe came back for a week in May. Shields was growing continually more concerned. In a meeting May 2 at Ed Cox's house, attended also by Bill Clements, Bob Hitch, and John McElhaney, he specifically asked Clements for assurances that the cheating had stopped. Clements backed off somewhat from the blanket assurance he had given the board of trustees in November. This time he said he could not vouch for the actions of boosters outside the control of the university. But he was encouraged by Hitch's reports of his ongoing conversations with various boosters. Both Clements and Cox reiterated to Shields that he should not concern himself with the football program or the progress of the SMU investigation.

"Stay out of it," Shields was told. "Go run the university."

By now President Shields must have been growing accustomed to being dismissed by the board leadership. On at least two occasions, colleagues recall, he had actually been told to shut up, either by Cox or by Clements. "In all the years I have been at universities and around business people," says a former administrator who witnessed one of the incidents, "I have never heard the lowest level employee talked to in that kind of voice. Period. I thought it was outrageous. Frankly, if they had done that to me, I would have resigned on the spot."

But Shields did not resign. He simply lowered his chin until it almost touched his chest, and he flushed bright red. "What could he do?" says the former administrator. "You can't fight an unequal foe. When you encounter someone in that kind of position who would be that rude, it tells you a lot about what you're up against in the university. It made me sick to my stomach."

ON JUNE 24th, 1984, the *Dallas Times Herald* published the results of an investigation by Danny Robbins, Jack Sheppard, and Harold Vieth into cars driven by SMU football athletes. The *Times Herald* found that over the last two years, at least fifteen SMU football and basketball players had bought cars from dealerships owned by W. O. Bankston, and that eight of the fifteen were Datsun 280ZXs or 300ZXs. The *Times Herald* turned up a variety of suspicious circumstances: Jeffrey Jacobs, a wide receiver, was driving a 1982 Datsun 280ZX secured with a lien in his cousin's name; tailback Reggie Dupard had driven two Datsuns purchased in his father's name from Bankston dealerships; Don King, ten days before the start of spring practice when he would be named number-one quarterback in place of graduating senior Lance McIlhenny, had begun driving a 1983 Nissan ZX, registered in his father's name. The *Herald*'s investigation had been underway for some time but was held until it was learned that the NCAA was also investigating cars driven by SMU athletes. Of the six football players with cars, four signed in 1982 or later, and two, Ricky Bolden and Russell Carter, came to SMU as freshmen in 1980, under Ron Meyer.

IN JUNE 1985 the Stopperich family moved into an apartment in Carrollton, a Dallas suburb. Over the next four months, according to NCAA findings, a booster arranged for $500 cash to be given to the family to pay each month's rent, for a total of $2,000, plus an additional $1,100 in living expenses. In August, Sean Stopperich reported for football practice driving a new car. One day, as he was pulling out of the parking lot by Ownby Stadium, he had an accident.

According to NCAA documents, a booster, later identified as John Appleton, gave $100 cash to the driver of the other car and "subsequently arranged to provide an envelope containing $800 in cash to the young man to pay the cost of repairing his automobile."

"I saw this massive young man standing by his car, almost breaking down in tears," Appleton later told *The Dallas Morning News.* "He said he came from a poor family and he was trying to save some money by not buying insurance. I wanted to help him. At the time I did not think anything was wrong."

Sean Stopperich never played a down for SMU. A knee injury, sustained prior to his senior year in high school while wrestling, failed to heal properly. He became disillusioned, and in September he and his family moved back to the Pittsburgh area. On November 30, a Friday before an off weekend for the Mustangs, it was reported that Sean Stopperich was talking to the NCAA. After more than a year and a half of inconclusive findings, the NCAA had found a witness who could hang SMU.

SMU FINISHED THE 1984 season tied for the best record in the SWC at 9–2, losing to Texas and Houston. The loss to the Cougars was the Mustangs' first to a conference opponent other than Texas since 1980. It was enough to prevent them from receiving the Cotton Bowl bid, which went to Houston. Instead, over the Christmas holidays, the SMU football team and a large group of supporters—including President Shields, most of his top administrators, and their spouses—flew to Hawaii for the Aloha Bowl. The Aloha Bowl, while not as prestigious as The New Year's Day bowls, is popular for obvious reasons. SMU won, 27–20 against Notre Dame, a fitting climax to the four-year period, starting under Ron Meyer and continuing under Bobby Collins, during which the Mustangs were the winningest major-college football team in the country.

Bowls are usually considered an important source of revenue for winning teams, but SMU chose to have fun at the Aloha Bowl instead. The team's share amounted to $400,000, of which only $16,699 remained by the time they returned to Dallas.

14 THE NAUGHTY NINE

UNTIL NOW SMU had pursued a two-part strategy in the face of the continuing NCAA investigation: one, deny publicly and in the strongest possible terms that there was any truth whatsoever to the charges; and two, search for evidence of cheating by other SWC schools, information which eventually could be used at the NCAA hearing to discredit SMU's accusers. But the news that the NCAA was talking to Sean Stopperich forced a reevaluation. If Stopperich had in fact told all, there would no point in SMU continuing to pretend it was innocent.

To the extent that board of governors chairman Bill Clements was ignorant of the exact circumstances surrounding the recruitment of Stopperich, he would have heard the whole story on January 2, 1985, when he had his first-ever face-to-face meeting with Sherwood Blount. Nothing of what was said in that meeting is known; only that Clements shared what he had learned with fellow board member Ed Cox and athletic director Bob Hitch two days later; and that he met privately with head coach Bobby Collins four days after that.

The current payment program at SMU had been set up by Ron Meyer. From the beginning it had depended for its success on the power and influence of fund raiser Bobby Stewart, then chairman of the SMU board of governors. While it is true that after Meyer left, Blount, George Owen, and various other boosters had assumed a more active role, they did so with the complicity of Bobby Stewart and the active participation of certain football staff members, among them, Bootsie Larsen. If Collins and Hitch were indeed unaware of the extent of the cheating, as they claimed, then they were guilty of negligence at the very least. And yet, Bill Clements began now to implement a new policy, whereby SMU would freely admit that violations had occurred while at the same time attempting to pin responsibility for such violations wholly on a handful of overzealous boosters. Sherwood Blount, in particular, was about to get squeezed.

In February 1985, after much prodding, Blount gave in to pressure from Clements and agreed to meet with the NCAA. He did so voluntarily; the NCAA has no authority to compel testimony from anyone, much less a businessman with no official connection to the university. There were two NCAA investigators present to hear Blount's story, along with SMU's lawyer, John McElhaney.

Blount, according to witnesses, was "absolutely unapologetic." He freely admitted his role in the recruitment of Sean Stopperich, telling the investigators, in effect, "I can damn well spend my money any way I damn well please." If the NCAA didn't understand that, then they were "a bunch of communists."

Any doubts the NCAA investigators may have had about the stridency of SMU boosters would have been erased after their meeting with Blount. If it had indeed been Clements's aim to demonstrate what kind of screwball boosters SMU had to contend with in its football program, Blount had played his role to perfection.

MARCH 26, 1985, was a warm, windy, overcast day. The air felt heavy and damp, a preview of the thunderstorm that would arrive later that evening and dump an inch of rain on Dallas. Exactly one month from this day, SMU attorney John McElhaney would open SMU's defense against charges of cheating in its football program before the NCAA infractions committee in Kansas City. Today, Bill Clements had brought all the interested parties together to discuss the future of the payment program.

They met on Clements's turf, at SEDCO headquarters, one of the few old buildings in a downtown that is otherwise a mix of empty lots, flat-topped glass towers, and elaborately ornamented skyscrapers faced with brick and stone.

The last time such a meeting had taken place to discuss the future of the payment program, Bobby Stewart had been the host. Today he was present largely as an observer and as support for Clements, his Highland Park neighbor. Clements and Stewart represented established power—both in Dallas and at SMU. Representing the North Dallas power base was Bobby Folsom, a teammate of Doak Walker's who went on to serve a term as mayor of Dallas and was now president of his own real-estate development firm, Folsom Investments Inc. It was Folsom who had developed Bent Tree, two of whose most notable residents were also in attendance: Sherwood Blount and George Owen. Bob Hitch, the athletic director, was also there. The rest were lawyers: McElhaney; his associate, Mike Moore; and James Drakeley and Jerry Hiersche, representing Blount. They sat around a conference table in Clements's office. Clements and Blount did most of the talking. Clements's message to Blount was simple: "For the good of the university, you need to get out of the program."

Blount, typically, was belligerent. Disgusted, perhaps, at the course of events but never one to act hurt or offended, he spoke for all of the other boosters in saying, in effect, "Fine, you want us out? We'll go."

But it wasn't as simple as that, a fact which Blount appreciated better than perhaps anyone else in the room. Promises had been made. Long-term arrangements had been entered into. It simply was not possible to pull the plug now, not unless SMU was prepared to deal with a lot of angry players who would feel betrayed. And so Blount dropped his bombshell.

"You've got a payroll to meet," he said. "Maybe you should consider adding a line item to the university budget."

Clement's reply was curt. "This isn't the time or the place to talk about that."

ON APRIL 24, on the eve of the NCAA hearings in Kansas City, Donald Shields signed letters formally disassociating nine boosters from the SMU football program. The so-called naughty nine received sanctions ranging from a two-year suspension on recruiting to a permanent ban on any involvement whatsoever with SMU athletics. The criteria by which the naughty nine were singled out appear arbitrary, at best. In some cases, these were boosters about whom the NCAA had hard evidence of cheating, even if—in the case of George Wilmot, for example, who stands accused of taking a recruit and his family to dinner *after* signing day—the violation was minor.

Sherwood Blount received a letter, of course, and George Owen.

So did Ronnie Horowitz, who, like Robin Buddecke (who was spared), had had little to do with SMU recruiting ever since Ron Meyer left for the New England Patriots. Horowitz was specifically cited for lending his automobile to a recruit for the afternoon. "I'm gonna tell you why I gave him the car," Horowitz explains. "Because after lunch he needed to be somewhere, and his body odor was so severe I said, look, you just take the car, drive it to your house, and I'll pick it up tonight."

Others who received letters were examples of boosters who, like Blount, disdained the rules of recruiting and were likely to embarrass SMU again in the future. Take Bill Stevens, for example, a Dallas banker whose activities were first reported in connection with the recruitment of Ronald Morris. Stevens is a small, wiry silver-haired man with eyes so blue they might as well be white. Stevens is perhaps the leading proponent of the theory that SMU's problems with the NCAA can be attributed exclusively to the University of Texas. "If you'll check back the records," says Stevens, "every key person that was involved [in reporting about SMU] was a University of Texas grad. Danny Robbins [*Dallas Times Herald*], John Sparks [WFAA-TV], every one of those cocksuckers was a University of Texas guy. . . . If you'll stretch it right back up the ladder, you'll find there's some very influential people in the Belo Corporation [owner of *The Dallas Morning News* and WFAA-TV] that are University of Texas big guys. And they loved it, the whole shootin' match."

According to Stevens, "The only reason that SMU ever got in this business of assisting athletes was strictly as a defense mechanism because the other schools were forcing us to do it. A player would come say, 'Well, I'd a hundred times rather go to SMU than the University of Texas, but they're offering to do one through ten.' So if we'd match one through ten, then the guy would come to SMU. Most guys would a lot rather live in Dallas than Austin, and you could say the same for Norman, Oklahoma; Fayetteville, Arkansas; or College Station. None of those places are worth a damn. Any damn fool would much prefer to live in Dallas than any of those damn places."

Jack Ryan, who received a five-year ban on recruiting, works out of the offices of the Ryan Land and Cattle Company, South Texas Real Estate Development, Rocky A. Ryan Homes Inc., and Rocking R Ranch, all under one roof on the fifth floor of the American Bank

Tower in downtown Corpus Christi. His office is decorated with statuettes of cattle and racehorses. On his walls are a distinguished alumnus award from 1968, a plaque commemorating his service on the Corpus Christi School Board in 1966, and citations from the Better Business Bureau, the Chamber of Commerce, and the Junior Jaycees. Another plaque identifies Ryan as "a special friend of SMU athletics," a sentiment backed up by the various football helmets and game balls—one of them inscribed to "Coach Ryan"—on display in his office. On the coffee table are two large picture books, *Tejas Vaqueros* and *Texas Women*. He drapes his suit coat over a saddle instead of a hook and sits at his desk facing the head of a Longhorn steer mounted on the opposite wall, a flagrant act of disloyalty to the Mustang mascot only Jack Ryan could get away with. He is a large man in his seventies, with pasty, liver-spotted skin, white hair, and gold-rimmed glasses. His secretary's name is Debbie.

"Hot coffee," he tells her.

"All right!" she says brightly, and disappears.

"They go around like this is a big deal," says Ryan. "Hell's bells, in the forty-two years I been recruiting there isn't anything new. Just the amount of dollars changed. Hah-hah! LSU is probably the worst of any of them. They just got trouble gettin' them to go down there 'cause they got a bad black problem, and who wants to live there, my God?"

So why did SMU get caught?

"Real simple," he says. "They had a stupid guy, the athletic director. Total idiot. And they had an idiot for president. You couldn'ta had two worse. They didn't know how to handle a two-bit donkey. Plus they got a big disadvantage in Dallas."

How so?

"[The NCAA investigators] can jump on a plane and be down there in an hour and fifteen minutes. And these guys, these young guns they got workin' for them, all like to go to the joints in Dallas. And they party there. Have a hell of a time. They love it. There's not another big city like it in the world. They go in there and chase girls, drink whiskey and have a big time. Why go to College Station [Texas A&M] when you can go there and have a big time? So it's happy hunting grounds. They just love it. I been out with 'em. The ones that were investigating me, too. I know the girls they were going with."

"I believe it!" says Debbie, who returned a while ago with Jack's coffee and is standing now behind his chair, massaging the palm of his upturned hands, first one, then the other.

The official reason why Jack Ryan was banned by SMU is for his role in the recruiting of James Lott, who later signed with Texas. It was Ryan who gave Lott's uncle a job. "His uncle worked for me for a year," says Ryan. "They tried to hang that on me. Hell's bells. He didn't go to work for me until after the kid had already signed with Texas. If there had been anything involved, you think I woulda put that gorilla on the payroll?"

Jack's son Reid, who runs the family funeral parlor in Corpus Christi, was suspended for two years; Ken Andrews, a businessman from Seagoville, near Dallas, was suspended for three years; John Appleton, the booster who paid for the damage to Sean Stopperich's car, was suspended for three years.

BY BANNING THE naughty nine, SMU sent a signal to the NCAA that it was prepared to deal severely with those who would commit violations on behalf of the university. It in no way solved the fundamental problems in SMU's athletic department. Rather, it appears to have been an attempt on the part of Bill Clements and the board leadership to isolate the blame on outsiders while protecting SMU and those coaches, administrators, and board members whose culpability was equal to, and in some cases greater than, that of the most wild-eyed booster.

One of the nine, Jack Ryan, had recently donated a large sum of money for construction of an academic support facility at Ownby Stadium. He says that the university waited for his check to clear before they mailed him his letter. Today a plaque affixed to the west wall of Ownby Stadium reads:

In Appreciation
of
Jack Ryan

For his long and continuing interest
in the SMU athletic program

and the academic aspirations
of all Mustang student athletes.
His generosity has made possible
this academic support and study facility.

The plaque is dated September 1985, five months after the date on Ryan's letter of disassociation.

15 THEN DO IT

TWO WEEKS BEFORE the start of the scheduled hearings, a delegation of SMU officials traveled to Kansas City to go over the list of allegations with the NCAA enforcement staff. It is a process similar to a pretrial hearing, in which the charges are discussed and some are dropped. There were over 125 alleged violations. SMU was able to eliminate about three dozen.

SMU officials returned to Kansas City for three days in late April 1985. The formal hearing took place at the Westin Crowne Center Hotel. Don Shields, as head of the SMU delegation, was ensconced in a suite where the group met often to plan strategy. Coach Collins was there, as were Tony Marciano, the assistant coach who had helped recruit Sean Stopperich, and Bootsie Larsen. The presence of both Larsen and Marciano was kept secret. Whenever their presence at a hearing was required, they were called in through the service entrance.

The major item on the list of alleged violations concerned the NCAA's so-called prospect no. 1 (as he would be identified in the official report), Sean Stopperich. SMU did not bother to contest that Sean Stopperich had been recruited illegally, that he had received a $5,000 payment in advance of signing or that he had received funds in response to emergencies that arose after he arrived in Dallas. What SMU did contest was the participation in or knowledge of illegal activities by Tony Marciano. The NCAA had phone records showing at least two conversations between Marciano and Sherwood Blount, but Marciano denied that either had anything to do with the recruitment of Stopperich.

SMU tried to characterize the illegal recruitment of Stopperich as something that occurred to Blount on his own, and which was carried out independently by him. According to a member of the official SMU party, Marciano, when he was confronted with the documentary evidence linking him to Blount, broke down and cried. "What do you want me to do? Confess to something that I didn't do?" When the NCAA issued its final report on SMU, it would cite an unnamed coach (Marciano) for failing to "conduct himself in accordance with the [NCAA] principles of ethical conduct ... [providing] false and misleading information concerning two telephone calls to an athletics representative [Blount] who was involved in certain of the violations."

On the final day of the hearings, William Clements appeared before the committee to discuss the involvement of boosters in recruiting, particularly Sherwood Blount. SMU had already announced its intention to ban Blount and the eight other boosters. Now Clements sought to assure the NCAA that he could control the actions of Blount in the future. "I've had some very heart-to-heart talks with this young man, again in my office," Clements told the NCAA, "and with John McElhaney present, and he's heard these discussions. ... Mr. Sherwood Blount is listening to me. ... We will not tolerate any misbehavior whatsoever in the future by any of the people in the administration, in the coach [sic] and athletic department, the coaching staff, or any of these alums, to the extent that we can."

"The whole point of Bill Clements's appearance before the infractions committee," says a member of the official SMU party, "was, 'Don't you think for a minute that I don't have the power to control this man.' I went away from that meeting being tremendously reassured ... because he had made it clear in so many words that he could shoot Sherwood Blount in the economic kneecaps."

After three days of testimony covering twenty-two hours, the SMU delegation returned to Dallas to await the verdict of the NCAA. Clearly, key people had failed to divulge what they knew. Clements, McElhaney, Moore, and Hitch were all aware of violations beyond those raised by the NCAA, and yet had failed to make them known in the voluntary way that the NCAA depends on.

* * *

ON MAY 29 the NCAA committee on infractions arrived at a final decision, finding SMU responsible for more than fifty violations, most of them involving four prospects. It was clear, however, that the bulk of the NCAA's case rested on what they had been able to discover about the recruitment of Sean Stopperich. Without Stopperich, SMU would not have been faced with penalties nearly as severe as those ultimately imposed.

Until now, the NCAA investigation had rarely been mentioned in the minutes of any meetings of the board of governors or the board of trustees. There is no discussion of the NCAA situation reported in the minutes of the board of governors meetings in February or March 1985, and no more than a cursory mention of the upcoming hearing in April. In May the board of governors did not meet. But on June 6 President Shields, the attorney McElhaney, and athletic director Hitch met with ten members of the board of governors to discuss the athletic situation. This was the first discussion of the topic by what could be called a representative sampling of the university leadership.

According to board minutes, there was a full discussion of the NCAA findings and penalties. Shields's recommendation was that SMU exercise its right of appeal. One board member, Cary McGuire, a Dallas oil man, thought SMU ought to sue the NCAA for selective enforcement.

Clements quickly pointed out the inherent danger in initiating a suit. He reminded the board members about the federal law of perjury, meaning that in a lawsuit of this kind, with SMU witnesses under oath, anything could come out in court. Clements's advice was heard with sympathy by the board, which rejected McGuire's proposal. The board then voted in favor of Shields's recommendation that SMU appeal the NCAA's findings. Shields announced SMU's appeal the very next day.

IN JULY, Bill Clements officially decided that he would run for governor again in 1986. Clements told board of trustees chairman Ed Cox and President Shields he wished to resign as chairman of the board of governors. He recommended Bill Hutchison, chairman of Texas Oil and Gas Co., as his successor. Both Cox and Shields prevailed on Clements not to resign right away, asking that he stick by SMU during this difficult period, at least until matters were settled with the NCAA. Clements agreed, consenting, in effect,. to do SMU a favor. His colleagues on the board would have cause to remember his favor in the months ahead.

ON AUGUST 14 McElhaney and Shields argued SMU's case for one hour and thirty-five minutes before the NCAA Council, the only avenue of appeal. Two days later, SMU's sixth football probation was announced. The loss of forty-five scholarships over two years was the most serious scholarship reduction ever imposed on a NCAA institution at that time. There would be no bowls in 1985 or 1986 and no TV in 1986. Assistant coach Bootsie Larsen was placed on probation and his salary cut 15 percent.

At the press conference following the announcement, Clements, Shields, Collins, and Hitch faced the local media. Each steadfastly maintained that the violations occurred as the result of individual initiative on the part of the boosters, that the one staff member who was found to have been a party to the violations had been punished, and that there was no reason to blame Hitch or Collins. Clements talked about the "compassion" he felt for the affected boosters, but said, "I think these people involved understand if they are involved again our sense of compassion will be overworked."

SMU HAD BEEN CAUGHT and punished by the NCAA. But while investigators turned up scores of minor violations, they could find only one player, later identified as Sean Stopperich, who was receiving regular payments. As it turned out, there were at least twelve other players on the payroll concurrently with Stopperich. The NCAA never knew who they were until a year and a half later when they read their names in the newspaper like everybody else. Once again there was a wide gap between what the NCAA could prove and what was really going on. Why can't the NCAA do a better job?

The NCAA, founded in 1905 as the Intercollegiate Athletic Association of the United States, was not intended as a police force for college athletics. Its purpose was to promulgate standardized rules of play and eliminate unsafe practices. One of the first acts of the nascent organization was to outlaw the hurdle play, which involved placing the ball in the hands of the smallest member of the team and then throwing the player downfield. The play

View of Dallas Hall looking north on Bishop Boulevard. (United Press International)

Ron Meyer, soon after he became head coach at SMU in 1976. (Southern Methodist University)

Steve Endicott, Meyer's top assistant charge of recruiting in Houston. (Southern Methodist University)

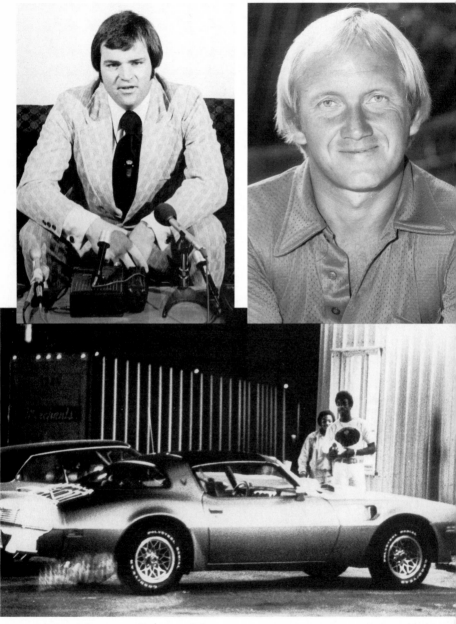

Eric Dickerson walks toward the new 1979 Pontiac Trans-Am he received shortly before announcing his intention to enroll at Texas A&M. Dickerson later changed his mind about A&M but kept the car and drove it for three of the four years he played at SMU. (World Wide Photos)

Dickerson *(left)* and Craig James, SMU's Pony Express. (Southern Methodist University)

Houston stockbroker Robin Buddecke helped recruit Dickerson in the fall of 1978. Throughout the late 1970s and early 1980s Buddecke made regular payments to the families of SMU players in Houston.

Booster George Owen, one of the naughty nine, was banned from any association with SMU athletics in 1985. *(The Dallas Morning News/*Clint Grant)

Sherwood Blount, in 1979, age twenty-nine, poses with his Cadillac and his second wife in a far-north Dallas maize field he brokered for $6 million. (Andy Vracin, copyright © 1979 by Texas Monthly)

Bobby Collins, the winningest coa[ch] in SMU history, at Texas Stadiu[m] (Southern Methodist University)

Donald Shields at the press conference announcing his appointment president of SMU in October 1980. Looking over his shoulder is Ed Co[x] chairman of the board of trustees. (Southern Methodist University)

Bob Hitch, SMU athletic director from 1981 to 1986. (Southern Methodist University)

Parade All-American Sean Stopperich, whose recruitment led directly to SMU's 1985 probation but who never played a down for the Mustangs. (Southern Methodist University)

David Stanley as a freshman in 1984. (Southern Methodist University)

Stanley as he appeared on television the night of November 12, 1986. (WFAA-TV/Dallas)

Bobby Collins examines SMU envelopes used to mail payments to the family of David Stanley. Henry Lee Parker *(left)* and Bob Hitch *(right)* look on. (WFAA-TV/Dallas)

Dallas banker Robert H. Stewart III, former chairman of the SMU board of governors, was a fund-raiser for the football slush fund. (*The Dallas Morning News*)

Oilman Edwin Cox, chairman of the SMU board of trustees, answers questions after a meeting of the board of governors. (*The Dallas Morning News*)

Lonnie Kliever (*left*), William Stallcup (*center*), and David Berst announce the death penalty to the national media at a press conference on the SMU campus. (*The Dallas Morning News*/John Sonnenmair)

Berst, NCAA director of enforcement, faints minutes after announcing that SMU had received the death penalty. (*The Dallas Morning News*/William Snyder)

Kliever, SMU faculty athletics representative and head of SMU's 1986–87 in-house investigation. (*The Chronicle of Higher Education*/John C. Phillips)

Forrest Gregg, SMU '56, was hired to rebuild the SMU football program. (Southern Methodist University)

Bill Clements announces his intention to seek a second term as governor of Texas on July 26, 1985. One month later, as chairman of the SMU board of governors, he would authorize the continuation of illegal payments to football players, an act that led directly to SMU receiving the death penalty. (United Press International) was usually good for a short gain until, predictably, defenses adjusted by throwing one of their own at the ball carrier. College football at the turn of the century was so out of control that without action by a national committee, it might have been banned. In 1909 thirty-three young men died while playing college football.

In 1929 the Carnegie Foundation produced a 383-page study entitled "American College Athletics," in which egregious abuses of the kind documented at SMU around the same time were found to be occurring regularly at colleges all over the United States. Still, it was not until the late 1950s that the NCAA saw fit for the first time to hire a full-time director of enforcement.

Even today, with the NCAA having become a far-flung bureaucracy with an annual budget of over $62 million, the department of compliance and enforcement remains a relatively minor division. Only $1.65 million was spent on tracking down cheaters in 1987, a fraction of the more than $1 billion spent annually by the Division I-A football powers to operate their athletic departments. At peak strength, the department employs fifteen full-time investigators.

"There's such a wide range of violators out there," admits Ron Watson, a former NCAA investigator who is now an assistant athletic director at the University of Oklahoma. "[The NCAA] doesn't have sufficient force to go out and put fear in the hearts of those who want to cheat. They're not doing what needs to be done."

Over the years the NCAA has repeatedly gone to court—and once before a congressional committee in Washington—to defend itself against charges that its investigative procedures are unfair. (Most recently, the Supreme Court found in favor of the NCAA in a case involving Jerry Tarkanian and the University of Nevada–Las Vegas. At issue was whether or not the NCAA had the authority to compel a member institution to enforce the mandated suspension of its coach.) It isn't hard to find a coach, such as one former assistant, who will say, "You know what the problem is? The NCAA has too much goddamn power."

Yet exactly the opposite is true. The NCAA is bound by an enforcement procedure that recalls the days when policing the membership was a routine business accomplished in a family way, often with a phone call. This despite competitive pressures that Walter Byers, former NCAA executive director, has said are "much more intense than they used to be." When confronted with an institution that has done wrong, knows it has done wrong, and is determined to defend itself, the NCAA is pitifully overmatched.

The enforcement department follows up on what it happens to pick up—from parents, athletes, coaches, boosters, and to a large extent, investigative reports by newspapers and television stations. "There are no undercover assignments in the NCAA," says Hale McMenamin, a twenty-six-year veteran of the FBI who worked part-time for the NCAA out of Denver. "There just isn't manpower and funds to stay with prospects for the whole recruiting season."

Nothing in the 440-page NCAA manual gives the enforcement department the right to place wiretaps, to subpoena documents, or to compel witnesses to testify. "The whole process is dependent for effectiveness on a large degree of institutional cooperation," says Frank J. Remington, professor of law at the University of Wisconsin and former chairman of the NCAA Committee on Infractions, which hears cases and metes out punishment.

After the NCAA completes an investigation, it presents a list of allegations—an official inquiry—to the university. At that point the university must conduct its own investigation. Then both parties appear before the Committee on Infractions.

The process, as in the case of SMU, has been known to take years, often delaying justice until long after the principals have departed. Until recently, all charges—everything from buying a prospect a soda pop to buying him a prostitute—had to be brought before the Committee on Infractions. Now "secondary" violations are treated separately in an effort to speed things along. "The process is as quick as the individuals involved in it are quick," says David Didion, the assistant director of enforcement. "If you've got a group that fights you at every turn, its going to be slow."

Enforcement procedure 12-(a)-(8) prohibits the use of tape recorders while interviewing sources or suspects. "With a lot of the people we deal with, electronic devices are intimidating," says Steve Morgan, former head of the enforcement division. Enforcement Procedure 12-(a)-(9) states that "individuals who have reported information to the enforcement staff should be given the opportunity to review the information set forth in the investigator's report of the interview and be provided the opportunity to make additions or corrections."

"You have to take handwritten notes," explains Dan Beebe, who headed the 1985 investigation of SMU. "Then all the notes have to be dictated into a memorandum, then the memorandum has to be confirmed by the source. At that point he can make changes. Many times he realizes what he said. Or he talks to somebody who says, 'My God, did you say that?' And that's the part he goes back and changes."

In some cases, sources may simply refuse to cooperate. The NCAA has no authority at all over boosters, who, says David Berst, assistant executive director in charge of compliance and enforcement, "represent a significant part of the problem in any serious case. They are the source of improper benefits and are ready and willing to cheat if the coach gives any signal that that's what's to occur."

Theoretically, coaches and players are bound by the NCAA constitution, which defines unethical conduct to include, "Refusal to furnish information relevant to an investigation of a possible violation of an NCAA regulation when requested to do so by the NCAA or the individual's institution."

"You can use that to affect a person's eligibility," says Morgan. "But in order to do that you really have to be able to prove he knew something that he didn't tell you. If he's really a bad actor and he knows that he's screwed up, he may choose not to have anything to do with you and just hope to hell you can't prove what he did."

During the inquiry into SMU, NCAA investigators were often stonewalled. "I did not feel that they were cooperative," says one investigator. "The [university] counsel in that case would do the law profession proud. But in NCAA work, that's not proper. You try to find out what went wrong as you would within a family and take care of it. I had misgivings about what their actual desires were."

"You come away thinking there's a whole lot more there than you know," says Morgan. "So what you do is prove what you can. If you can at least show willful and intentional violation in one instance, the consequences of that alone are going to be significant. We probably don't get even a substantial percentage of the violations that take place."

One of the serious problems continually facing the NCAA is a lack of experienced investigators. Many come to the NCAA straight out of law school. They start out earning far below the average starting salaries for lawyers in private firms or government jobs. Then, when investigators have been on the job long enough to become adequate at what they are doing, many move on.

"When they are developed to that point," Berst acknowledges, "they are very good targets for institutions that want a person who is knowledgeable about NCAA affairs and regulations. I would like for us not to be that vulnerable. If we can't keep the people we have now for a longer period of time, we have a problem."

An alarming number of investigators who leave the NCAA go on to midlevel jobs for more pay in university athletic departments, not unlike employees of government regulatory agencies who later become industry lobbyists. Butch Worley, who oversaw the 1987 SMU investigation, is today an assistant athletic director at the University of Texas. Ron Watson, who helped Dan Beebe on the 1983–85 SMU investigation, works now for the University of Oklahoma. While the enforcement department has so far managed to avoid serious accusations of a conflict of interest, such charges are inevitable.

"We have to always be alert so that our investigators, while they are here, are not compromised by anything that is available to them through a member institution," says Morgan. "We're still small enough where we really do all know each other and we're observing the cases that everybody is processing. We're alert to that and watch for it."

NCAA investigators tend to be hardworking idealistic types. Dan Beebe and Lou Onofrio both left the NCAA for jobs with universities —Wichita State and Boise State, respectively—only to return eventually to the NCAA. But as long as there is job movement of this kind, there will be the appearance of impropriety. Whether or not the NCAA is honest or corrupt, the fact remains that as they are presently organized, they lack the authority or the capacity to effectively police college athletics.

THE AUGUST 19, 1985, BOARD of governors meeting was a stormy affair. Paul Corley suggested that the athletic department be reorganized, starting with the firing of Bob Hitch, the director of athletics, and Bobby Collins, the head coach. Clements disagreed, as summarized by the minutes:

"Understand and sympathize with some of the comments; have met and talked with many, many people—lots of time spent—was not easy. Felt strongly that the sooner we lay this aside the better off we will be. We have problems in our athletic department and we are not going to be able to clear this situation up overnight."

Toward the end of the meeting, Bob Hitch was called in to face the board. Laura Blanton of Houston, one of only two women on the board of nineteen, pointed her finger at Hitch and asked, "Is this program now clean?"

"Yes," Hitch replied.

IN LATE AUGUST, after the board meeting, Bill Clements and Ed Cox came to campus for an important meeting with President Shields and athletic director Bob Hitch. By this time, there was agreement among all parties that no new payment obligations would be entered into with any players. The leadership knew this, so did the administration, the coaches, the boosters, and the NCAA. No new payments. But there was a sticky problem that had yet to be confronted, one that Clements had alluded to in the board meeting. The players were returning to campus after the summer vacation. Some would be expecting their regular payments. What do we do about them?

There was disagreement. Hitch and Clements argued against stopping the payments now. As far as Clements was concerned, that decision had been made in the spring, after the March 26 meeting at SEDCO headquarters when Sherwood Blount had announced, "You have a payroll to meet." Clements had followed up with Blount, George Owen, and Bill Stevens, and they had agreed that all current obligations would be met. Bootsie Larsen, the assistant coach primarily responsible for distributing funds to players, had been informed of their decision.

Clements acknowledged that the policy was risky, saying, in effect, "This could blow up at some time in the future. But if we stop the payments, it will blow up right now."

He did not have to remind anyone that as far as the public and the NCAA were concerned, Sean Stopperich was the only player to whom SMU had agreed to make continuing payments. Since Stopperich was no longer enrolled at SMU, theoretically they were now running a clean program. If they eliminated the payroll without warning, there would be some players angry enough to quit, and some who would talk to the press.

Clements knew that there were thirteen players currently on the payroll, all of whom would be gone after the 1987 season. All they had to do was "wind down" their commitments and in three years they would be free and clear.

"With that," Clements argued, "we would be able to see the light at the end of the tunnel."

Cox and Shields disagreed. Even if the decision had been made to continue the payments back in the spring, there was a new factor they had to consider now. At the NCAA's annual convention in June 1985, the membership had overwhelmingly approved new legislation designed to raise the stakes for repeat offenders. This was the so-called death penalty; SMU had been one of only six schools to vote against it. Under Section 7-(f)-(1) of the NCAA enforcement code, anyone caught cheating twice within a period of five years now risked losing the right to compete for up to two years. SMU already had strike one. The new rule was scheduled to take effect only a few days from now, on September 1, 1985. After that, if SMU was caught cheating again, the football program would be shut down.

After Clements had heard from Cox and Shields, he repeated his opinion that the payments ought to be continued. But he reminded them that the decision was theirs. He planned to step down as chairman of the board of governors as soon as a suitable replacement could be found and would abide by their decision.

By the time the meeting broke up, no definite agreement had been reached.

Clements and Hitch left the meeting together. Hitch walked Clements to his car, which was parked in a small lot south of Perkins Administration Building, used only by university officials. The entrance to the parking lot is on Hillcrest Avenue, a strip of convenience stores, bookshops, and restaurants on the western edge of campus. There is a quiet grove nearby that memorializes the SMU students who died in World War I. It is one of the few places on campus where the live oaks are arranged randomly, rather than in straight lines.

Here, Hitch and Clements paused. They talked for fifteen minutes. Recollections of the tone of their conversation vary with the retelling but the substance is clear. Both agreed that the payments had to continue, no matter what Cox and Shields said. The group had already discussed the fact that there was a booster willing to fund the payments on an exclusive basis. This was Sherwood Blount, who only a few months before had been banned officially by the university from any further involvement in SMU athletics.

There was a problem, though. Bootsie Larsen, who had handled the regular payments in the past, had recently been dismissed, ironically, for having contact with a banned booster (he had spent part of his summer vacation at the Wisconsin lake house belonging to John Appleton). They would have to find a new staff person who was willing to work with Blount and make the actual payments to the players.

"Can you take care of that?" Clements asked Hitch.

Hitch said he could.

"Then do it."

16 WINDING DOWN

ON AUGUST 26 Shields called a meeting of all members of the athletic department, something he did at the beginning of each year. He went over the rules. He said that there would be no more violations. Anyone who committed a violation of any kind would be fired immediately.

After Shields left the meeting, Bob Hitch addressed the same group. He told them not to worry about what Don Shields said, that there was only one boss at SMU and that was Bill Clements. He runs the university, not Don Shields.

On the evening of September 6, the night before the opening game of the 1985 season against the University of Texas–El Paso, Shields spoke again, this time at a pep rally on campus. He reminded the cheering crowd that the three-year ordeal with the NCAA was over. He told them that not one member of the current team had been found guilty of a single violation.

The next day, the Mustangs—ranked number three in the country in a preseason poll—rolled to an easy victory, 35–23, over the Miners from El Paso. SMU scored seven touchdowns. Two were two-yard runs by Reggie Dupard, who rushed for over one hundred yards. One was a forty-eight-yard touchdown catch by wide receiver Marquis Pleasant. Noseguard Jerry Ball led the defense with ten tackles and two sacks for minus eleven yards.

Dupard, Pleasant, and Ball were three of the thirteen players on the field that day who were receiving regular monthly payments funded by Sherwood Blount.

* * *

ON SEPTEMBER 28 SMU slaughtered a demoralized TCU team, 56–21, before a nationally televised audience and a sold-out stadium in Fort Worth. One week later, they went to Tucson, Arizona, ranked number six and holding the longest unbeaten streak in the nation, eight games. The Mustangs were taunted by the crowd—some of whom leaned over the tunnel and shook their car keys as the players were taking the field—and soundly defeated by the Wildcats, 28–6.

In retrospect, the loss to Arizona was a turning point. SMU's record the rest of the way would be four wins and four losses. The five losses in 1985 would be equal to the number of games lost in the four prior seasons combined. And SMU's final record of 6–5 would be its worst since 1979. Scandal, scholarship reductions, and a growing discontent among the coaching staff and team members had ended too soon the dream of building a college football dynasty in Dallas. By the end of the 1985 season, SMU's glory days were over.

IN SEPTEMBER 1985 Texas Christian University coach Jim Wacker abruptly ended a payment program that had been instituted under his predecessor, F. A. Dry. The subsequent NCAA investigation turned up seven players who were receiving regular cash payments from Horned Frog boosters. Others had received illegal gifts including cowboy boots, airline tickets, new tires, and beautiful women. The NCAA's "Student-Athlete No. 3," for example: "Approximately four days prior to the National Letter of Intent signing date in February 1981," according to the NCAA, "a representative of the university's athletic interests transported the young man from his home to a local motel where lodging was provided until the signing date, and the young man was entertained with meals and prostitutes."

In May 1986 TCU would receive three years' probation, including a three-year ban on bowl games and television appearances and a two-year ban on athletic scholarships; plus the university would have to forfeit $343,203 in previously collected bowl revenues. The scandal received major play in the local media and must have served as a frightening reminder to SMU officials of the consequences should their own payment program ever come to light.

There were other reminders, too. Teresa Hawthorne, an employee in the tutorial program for athletes, had been fired in the summer of 1985. After trying unsuccessfully to win reinstatement, Hawthorne threatened to sue SMU. Reportedly, she and her attorney were agreeable to a settlement of $8,000, which had been negotiated by SMU vice president for legal affairs, Leon Bennett. Hitch, though, was opposed to the settlement, as was John McElhaney, SMU's attorney on all matters pertaining to the NCAA. McElhaney recommended against any settlement unless Hawthorne followed through with her threatened suit.

In November 1985 Hawthorne's attorney drafted an official complaint. When McElhaney saw it, he may have wished that he had agreed to the proposed settlement. Hawthorne stated now that she had knowledge of rules violations in the SMU athletic department, including cash payments to athletes and rent-free apartments. Faced with the threat of public disclosure, university attorneys negotiated a new settlement. On January 10, 1986, Hawthorne received a check from Leon Bennett for $17,500.

On the same day, Hawthorne consented to a taped interview with McElhaney, during which she stated for the record that she in fact had no knowledge of any rules violations committed while she was an employee of the SMU athletic department. The tape was set aside for possible use in a future NCAA investigation.

WHAT IS REMARKABLE about the wind down of payments at SMU is that it was almost successful. The responsibility for actual delivery of the cash to players belonged to Henry Lee Parker, a Mississippi native who flew thirty-five bomber missions in World War II and came to SMU from a bank in Knoxville, Tennessee. After ten years as an assistant coach at Mississippi State, his alma mater, Parker had joined the New Orleans Saints as director of player personnel under general manager George Owen, the SMU booster. Parker joined the SMU staff in November 1983 with the title of administrative assistant to the athletic director, with primary responsibility for recruiting. Eventually, he succeeded Bootsie Larsen as paymaster.

Even before the fall of 1985, some SMU players had grown accustomed to speaking with Henry Lee Parker whenever they needed cash. There was apparently an effort made during the 1983–85 NCAA investigation to institutionalize the payment system and bring it under the control of the coaching staff. One former SMU player who graduated in 1984 says that toward the end of his playing career, he was instructed by the booster he ordinarily turned to for funds to make all future requests directly to Henry Lee Parker.

"You would call Henry Lee and say, 'This is how much I need, this is why I need it,' " says the player. "He never questioned you about it. There were maybe a couple of instances when you asked for a couple of hundred dollars and he'd give you one hundred seventy-five or something." According to the player, requests often took several days to fill, apparently the time it took Parker to obtain the funds from the boosters. Money was delivered in an envelope that bore the player's name. "Yup," says the player, "dumber than shit. It was pretty laid back."

According to figures later provided to the NCAA by Bob Hitch, Parker delivered a total of $47,000 to thirteen different players during the 1985–86 academic year and $14,000 to eight players from September through December 1986.

Besides Teresa Hawthorne's lawsuit, the only other time the SMU payment program came close to being exposed was in the early fall of 1986, when two unidentified players broke into Henry Lee Parker's desk drawer and stole a month's payroll. Both players were caught, but they refused to return the money, knowing full well that the coaching staff would not dare take any action against them. Ultimately, the staff had no alternative but to ask Sherwood Blount to replace the cash.

BY THE MIDDLE of David Stanley's junior year, life at SMU had become unbearable. Stanley had managed to earn varsity letters his first two years at SMU, without ever quite living up to the expectations others had for him. Early in the fall of 1985, he had undergone an emergency appendectomy, which knocked him out for the entire season. Then there was the continuing problem with drugs. Stanley has admitted that he started smoking marijuana and taking amphetamines while still in high school. His coach at Angleton High, Dan Gandy, says that Stanley played most of his senior year on painkillers to mask the symptoms of a shoulder injury. Stanley also admitted that by the time he arrived at SMU, he was using much of the $400 per month he received under his recruiting agreement (an additional $350 per month was sent directly to David's family) to buy drugs, mostly cocaine. And since then, in early 1985, Stanley had spent time in a hospital drug-treatment program at SMU's expense.

In November 1985 Lonnie Kliever, the SMU faculty athletics representative, heard from Bob Hitch that Stanley wished to transfer out of the SMU football program. Players who transfer between programs are normally required to sit out one year at their new school before they are eligible to compete again. The exceptions are upperclassmen who, because of NCAA probation, will not be able to play in a bowl game before they graduate. With SMU on probation Stanley was free to transfer without penalties. Kliever helped him straighten out his affairs and agreed to answer questions from schools that might be interested in signing him to a scholarship.

Then in July 1986 Kliever heard from Dawn Stanley, David's mother. David had been unable to find another school that would offer him a scholarship and so wished to reenroll at SMU. Kliever checked Stanley's academic standing and called the NCAA to check the applicable legislation before telling Mrs. Stanley that as far as he was concerned, there was no reason why David Stanley could not return to SMU in the fall. Collins, however, wasn't interested in having Stanley back. He told Kliever that since Stanley had abandoned the program when it was down, inviting him back would be unfair to the ones who had stayed.

A hostile act requires means, motive, and opportunity. Stanley already had the means to bring SMU to its knees: extensive knowledge of the violations. Now SMU had made him mad (motive) and forced him out of football (opportunity). The act would follow shortly.

BY THE LATE SUMMER OF 1986, anger and resentment on the part of SMU boosters toward President Shields was building. Sherwood Blount, in particular, was angry at Shields for acting as if all the problems in SMU's athletic department were entirely the fault of the boosters. He expressed these views in a letter to Clements on August 12, 1986, concerned, no doubt, that Clements would soon be leaving the board and that Blount would lose his best contact with the leadership. When he failed to receive a response, Blount wrote again on September 24, threatening to "take matters into his own hands" if Clements failed to respond. On October 20, with election day less than a month away, Clements met with Blount, his attorney James Drakeley, and SMU attorney John McElhaney in Clements's office at SEDCO to give Blount a chance to air his views.

What bothered Blount, after more than a year as the exclusive provider of funds for SMU football players, was President Shields's attitude, expressed in repeated public statements, blaming a small core of overzealous alumni for everything that was wrong with SMU. Of course, that was the strategy—isolate the boosters. At a certain level Blount must have understood that. But enough was enough.

Clements was understanding. He promised Blount that Shields was on his way out (the board leadership would soon agree secretly to replace Shields no later than May 1987). In the meantime, Clements would talk to Shields and ask him to tone down his remarks.

Blount reported to Clements that he was working closely with Henry Lee Parker, who was distributing the funds, and that the payment system was operating smoothly.

"We are getting things wound down," Blount told Clements. "It has been expensive but it is about wound down."

"Good," said Clements.

ON OCTOBER 21, a Tuesday, John McElhaney met with Bob Hitch to brief him on the meeting with Blount. Hitch was edgy. He did not want to talk about the payment program. At that point they had made it through six games of the 1986 season. Texas was coming up on Saturday, followed by Texas A&M and Notre Dame. SMU was halfway home to the point when—as Hitch liked to say—SMU would become the "cleanest program in North America." If they could make it through this year, there would be only three players remaining on the payroll in 1986–87.

On that same day, unbeknownst to anyone at SMU, NCAA investigator Butch Worley was meeting with David Stanley and his mother, Dawn. Stanley was telling everything he knew.

ON MONDAY AFTERNOON, October 27, WFAA-TV producer John Sparks, sportscaster Dale Hansen, and two cameramen came to campus for an interview with Hitch, Coach Collins, and Henry Lee Parker. SMU was facing a minor NCAA issue at the time—a request for additional scholarships beyond those allotted to the program under the terms of probation. SMU had lost a handful of players;

David Stanley had withdrawn and several others had been lost because of drug problems since SMU began testing players for drugs. When Sparks called, Hitch had made it clear that he would not discuss the request for additional scholarships. Sparks had agreed. He said he wanted to talk about recruiting.

The interview took place in a conference room at Moody Coliseum. With cameras rolling, Sparks and Hansen surprised the three SMU officials with questions about the recruitment of David Stanley. Sparks had gotten to Stanley ahead of NCAA investigator Butch Worley and had heard the whole story—about the $25,000 payment to sign with SMU, the continuing monthly payments of $750, the payment for the drug-treatment program, everything. But the critical piece of evidence that Sparks had obtained was an SMU envelope with the initials HLP scribbled in the upper left-hand corner. Dawn Stanley, David's mother, claimed that it was one of the envelopes in which she had received cash from Henry Lee Parker. The postmark on the envelope was dated October 4, 1985, thirty-four days after the NCAA's death penalty legislation took effect. If in fact the envelope had contained cash, and it came from Henry Lee Parker, the SMU football program's days were numbered.

LONNIE KLIEVER GOT a phone call that afternoon from Bob Hitch at the airport. Hitch was on his way to a convention of college athletic directors in Chicago. Hitch told Kliever that there had been an interview that afternoon with Channel 8, that some serious allegations had been raised, that they had handled the situation well, and that he would call him the following morning with all the details.

Kliever was raised in Fort Worth, went to college in Abilene, and later earned graduate degrees at Union Theological Seminary and Duke. Now, at age fifty-five, he was professor of religious studies at SMU. He looked the part, with his intelligent eyes, his scholarly beard, and his poorly concealed expression of perpetual irony. And yet, for all his lofty refinements, Kliever was still a Texan and therefore a football fan. He had become the university's faculty athletic representative just prior to the NCAA hearings in the spring of 1985 and since then had worked closely with Bob Hitch. More than colleagues, they were friends.

After Kliever and Hitch had had a chance to discuss more fully the charges raised in the interview, Kliever called NCAA director of enforcement David Berst on October 29 to give him the bad news. Berst listened without comment to Kliever's report.

When Kliever had finished, Berst said, "I appreciate more than you know your call." Then Berst told Kliever, "Not only do we already know this, but we know a lot more."

Kliever explained that the president of the university was not on campus and that he was not empowered to act in his stead. But Kliever assured Berst that SMU would make every effort to get at the truth.

Berst told Kliever that he hoped they would. Then he reminded Kliever that such charges were connected with the threat of the death penalty.

Berst and Kliever agreed to stay in touch.

Later that day, Hitch reported on his interview with Channel 8 to William Stallcup, acting president of SMU. Donald Shields, who was suffering from complications related to adult-onset diabetes, was on thirty-day medical leave in California.

ON THE DAY BEFORE Halloween, Hitch, Coach Collins, university counsel Leon Bennett, and Lonnie Kliever got together to discuss what had happened during the interview with Channel 8 and decide what truth there may have been to the charges. Hitch, confronted with the possibility that the entire payment program would be disclosed, along with his role in it, chose to lie. His lie had three parts:

First, he said he had no idea whether Sherwood Blount or Bootsie Larsen had made any payments to David Stanley prior to the last NCAA investigation—all that was ancient history, anyway.

Second, he insisted that Stanley had never received a dime from Henry Lee Parker.

And third, he stressed that no payments had been made to any player after August 1985, when SMU went on probation.

Hitch, supported by Collins, sought to convince the others that Stanley—portrayed as a drug addict and a lost soul—was lying, and that SMU had nothing to worry about. For the time being, Bennett and Kliever were convinced that Hitch was telling the truth.

Over the next few days, Kliever was in constant telephone contact with Butch Worley, the NCAA investigator assigned to the case.

Worley was telling Kliever that the NCAA's most immediate concern was David Stanley's drug rehabilitation, which had been paid for by SMU in violation of NCAA rules. During the NCAA hearings, SMU had repeatedly taken the position that all the illegal activity had been carried out by a band of renegade boosters. Yet the payment to Harris Hospital for Stanley's drug treatment had apparently been authorized by President Shields. This was the first hard evidence the NCAA had that SMU's attempt to blame the boosters had been a ploy.

On November 4 Bill Clements narrowly defeated Mark White, winning a second term as governor of Texas. One of the areas where White was vulnerable with the electorate was in his support for Texas's no pass/no play law, which requires high-school students to pass all their classes before they can participate in sports. Most football fans in Texas voted for Bill Clements.

AS THE DATE approached when Channel 8 would air their report on David Stanley, Lonnie Kliever, Bob Hitch, and others were busy planning the university's response. Hitch continued to insist that Stanley was lying, and Kliever believed him.

Kliever had been designated the university's official spokesman on NCAA matters. He was trying to anticipate possible questions from the media once the report aired. So he asked Hitch if he had questioned Henry Lee Parker yet about his alleged role in the payments. Did Henry Lee Parker absolutely deny having paid any money to Stanley? Hitch said he had not yet asked Parker that question—which struck Kliever as odd—but promised he would at the first opportunity. Evidently, Hitch did ask Parker that weekend on the team flight to South Bend, Indiana, for the game against Notre Dame. Later, he confirmed for Kliever that Parker still denied having paid Stanley or anyone.

On the afternoon of November 12, the day before the scheduled broadcast, Kliever decided he ought to go talk to Henry Lee Parker himself. Kliever visited Parker in his office at Ownby Stadium. Parker, predictably, denied everything. He told Kliever that the handwriting on the envelope adressed to the Stanleys—with the initials HLP in the upper left-hand corner—was not his. The proof, he told Kliever, is that he wrote cursive and the initials on the envelope were printed. But as Kliever was getting up to leave, he noticed a scratch pad on Parker's desk with printing on it. For the first time, Kliever thought to himself, "This man is lying."

Then, as Kliever was on his way out the door, Parker said something that Kliever thought was very strange.

He said, "It's a bum rap for SMU to be accused of cheating by a drug addict and an extortionist." Then he told Kliever that Stanley had allegedly demanded $150,000 from Sherwood Blount as his price for not talking.

Lonnie Kliever was left to wonder how Henry Lee Parker knew about a demand that allegedly had been made to a banned booster. Blount was not supposed to have any contact whatsoever with the SMU athletic department, much less an assistant athletic director like Henry Lee Parker

Kliever did not yet know what he was not being told, but he figured he was not being told the truth.

WEDNESDAY, NOVEMBER 12, 1986. Donald Shields had returned from California on Monday. Lonnie Kliever brought him up-to-date on developments since the interview with the Channel 8 reporters and shared with him his planned statement to the press, to be released following the broadcast. Shields invited Kliever, along with Bob Hitch, Leon Bennett, and presidential assistant Mark Sherouse, to his red-brick house on Potomac Avenue that evening to watch the show.

Hitch and Kliever were together at Moody Coliseum late that afternoon for a varsity-alumni basketball game. Outside, the fog had broken and it was raining. The temperature was on its way down to freezing. Hitch told Kliever that Channel 8 had called Henry Lee Parker to tell him they had administered lie-detector tests and a handwriting analysis since the interview and that the results backed up David Stanley's story. Parker had been asked, in light of those developments, if he wished to make any further comment. Parker had said no.

BY EIGHT O'CLOCK, ALL those who had been invited to President Shields's house were in the den, gathered around a large-screen television set. The broadcast was still two hours away. While they were waiting, someone took a phone call from a source who claimed to have inside information. The source claimed to know that the

Channel 8 report would focus on the university's role in David Stanley's drug treatment. This worried Donald Shields because it implicated him personally. However, the effect of this news on the rest of the group was to put them somewhat at ease. Paying for David Stanley's drug treatment, while technically a violation, was justifiable on humanitarian grounds. If that was the worst of it, then SMU was probably going to be okay.

From the opening frame of the ten o'clock news—a red Mustang against a field of blue—all five men in the room knew immediately that Channel 8 had much more than a story about one player's drug problem. David Stanley and his mother, Dawn, were shown in their living room at an undisclosed location "in the Rocky Mountains" (the family had moved from Angleton). Stanley wore blue jeans and a gray crew-neck sweater. He sat in a straight-back chair, his arms folded and resting on his ample stomach. He spoke in a low, deliberate monotone, occasionally letting his gaze fall to the floor but always returning to meet the eyes of his interviewer, John Sparks, who sat slightly to one side of the camera.

"I received $25,000 to attend SMU and Bootsie Larsen paid me," Stanley said. "And when he got fired, Henry Lee Parker picked up the payments."

As effective as David Stanley's testimony was, the most powerful segments of the forty-minute report came from the taped interview with Henry Lee Parker, Bobby Collins, and Bob Hitch. They sat next to one another on one side of an elongated-oval conference table, opposite Sparks, the Channel 8 producer, and Dale Hansen, the sports anchor.

Parker, a graying, almost professorial man who wore a cardigan sweater and a red tie during the interview, denied in response to a question from Hansen that he had ever had any contact with the Stanley family. Then Hansen confronted Parker with Stanley's allegations.

"He says you paid him."

"David Stanley says I did?"

"He says when Bootsie Larsen left you handed the money over to him."

Parker closed his eyes and shook his head. "No Dale, that is wrong. Entirely."

Then, as the camera stayed on Henry Lee Parker, who sat now

with his hand partially covering his mouth, John Sparks said, "He said that Bootsie Larsen made those payments on the first of the month in the football offices at SMU, and then he said that you continued to make the payments after Bootsie left."

"No," Parker said haltingly. "That's not correct. I think Bob [Hitch] explained it a little while ago. The primary reason I came here was to ... help us ... eliminate some of the things that, uh, that we ..."

"This isn't easy," Hansen broke in.

"Uh-huh."

Then Hansen handed Parker three envelopes. "Is that your letter?" he asked. "The one in the left hand, specifically, with your initials on the SMU stationery?"

Parker examined the envelopes, holding them at arms length, as if trying to focus his eyes. "That is mine, yes."

Sparks: "Did you write it?"

Parker examined the envelopes again. Then he tapped his chest, reached inside his sweater, and said, "Lemme get my glasses." He pulled out a pair of half-moon reading glasses and squinted at the envelopes for several beats. "No ... that's ... I ... this is printed ... uh ... on there ... and I do not ... Do you see that?" Parker showed the envelopes to Collins, who kept his hand over his mouth and barely glanced at the offending pieces of paper. Then he handed it to Hitch. "It's printed there," Parker said. Hitch looked at the envelopes and handed them back to Hansen.

"Are you saying you didn't do this?" Hansen asked Parker.

"Uh-huh," Parker said. The camera stayed on Hitch, who nodded in agreement.

"And the HLP, somebody else put that up there?"

"It seems to me, 'cause I don't write that way."

Never did three men look more guilty.

THE BROADCAST CONTINUED with testimony from a handwriting analyst, who compared the writing on the envelope with a known sample of Parker's handwriting and concluded that they matched, followed by shots of David Stanley and his mother strapped to lie-detector machines (they passed).

Near the end of broadcast, Bob Hitch, struggling visibly to control his anger, tried to take the offensive.

"The [1985] investigation showed that there were some things going on at SMU illegally," said Hitch, "paying and so forth. I guess the thing that bothers me is that people, and possibly you [Dale Hansen] and John [Sparks], would think that we had knowledge of those kids being paid and did not take appropriate action. That bothers me. Had we have had knowledge, had kids 've walked up to me and said, 'Mr. Hitch, I was paid,' for you to think that I would cover it up, you know, that, that bothers me."

SHIELDS, KLIEVER, Hitch, Bennett, and Sherouse sat in stony silence and watched the big-screen TV. After it was finally over, Hitch stood up.

"I obviously can't help you," he said, and walked out of the room.

Shields followed him to the door, then returned to the den, where the four remaining officials stayed to talk over the implications of what they had seen. Shields called Ed Cox to see if he had seen it. Cox had not. He called Paul Corley. He would have called Bill Clements but Clements was in Florence, Italy, vacationing after his election victory. Shields invited the rest of the board leadership to his house at 7:30 the next morning to view the tape of the broadcast and discuss strategy.

PART IV

17 DAMAGE CONTROL

ED COX WAS AT President Shields's house first thing in the morning, along with Paul Corley and Bill Hutchison. Hutchison, the chairman of the board of Texas Oil and Gas Corp. and a director, like Cox and Bill Clements, of InterFirst Corp., was set to assume Clements's role as chairman of the board of governors when Clements moved to Austin in January. Lonnie Kliever was there, too. Shields, who last night had appeared to be handling the situation well, looked like he had had a bad night. Adult-onset diabetes can cause even those who are not under stress to feel tired and run-down. Clearly, Shields was suffering.

They all watched the tape again. Shields was distraught. His plan, concocted during the night, was to appoint a blue-ribbon investigative committee. Cox was sympathetic but only to a point. He wanted a committee appointed by—and responsible to—the board of governors, chaired by Corley and Hutchison.

Lonnie Kliever was immediately skeptical. His only prior experience with Cox and Corley and the board leadership had come as a faculty representative on the committee that chose Donald Shields as president. Kliever had been shocked then by the strong-arm tactics employed by the board of governors and trustees to force through their choice. He told Cox that he thought a board-chaired committee would run into trouble with two groups of people—the NCAA and the faculty, both of whom had serious reservations about the impartiality of the board, and may even suspect that the board was part of the problem.

Kliever's view was summarily dismissed. The battle was between

Shields and Cox, both agreeing about the seriousness of the problem but disagreeing over who should control the investigative committee. Shields argued for decisive action on the part of the president; Cox argued for the same from the board. Shields grew more distressed with every passing minute. He rightly saw Cox's position as a challenge to his authority, which had been undermined so often in the past.

Finally Cox told Shields the board had to lead the investigation because Shields was part of the problem. Hadn't Stanley said on television that Shields knew about his drug problem and had authorized payment for his treatment? Shields then retreated to a fallback position; the board and the president would jointly appoint the committee and it would report to both. Cox rejected that, too.

Then Hutchison, Cox, and Corley retired to another room in order to confer in private, leaving Shields and Kliever alone in the den. When they returned, they announced that the investigative committee would have six members: Hutchison and Corley as the co-chairs, plus Kliever, one other faculty member, and two blue-ribbon outsiders, to be appointed by Shields. Then Cox, Corley, and Hutchison left Shields's house and continued their deliberations in private.

Later that afternoon, Bill Hutchison had lunch with Paul Paige, a member of the board of trustees. Paige told Hutchison that he had been told by Hitch on November 7 that there had in fact been continuing payments to David Stanley—and that Clements was the one who gave the go-ahead.

TWO DAYS LATER, on Saturday morning, Shields invited university counsel Leon Bennett, presidential assistant Mark Sherouse, and Lonnie Kliever to a meeting at his house. In just a few hours, a Southwest Airlines charter was scheduled to leave Love Field for Lubbock, Texas, where the Mustangs would play Texas Tech. Shields who ordinarily made every trip, would not be on the plane. Also missing would be tight end Albert Reese, who on Friday had been reported by *The Dallas Morning News* to be living rent-free in an apartment complex owned by booster George Owen. Reese had immediately been suspended by Bob Hitch, pending an investigation by the athletic department. (Later, as more serious violations came to light, the Reese investigation was dropped.)

Shields told his guests that he had invited board members Ed Cox, Paul Corley, and Bill Hutchison to come over later that afternoon; Shields was considering two alternate proposals he would make at that time and he wanted their input. He was torn between offering his immediate resignation to the board, or staying on but recommending that the football program be voluntarily suspended for two years.

To those who were with Shields that morning, the president appeared to be much worse, both physically and emotionally, than at any other point in the crisis. He was a beaten man, visibly worn-out, anxious, depressed. His advisers tried to help him clarify his options, rather than offer advice. Eventually, Shields decided on the second option—he would recommend to the board that the SMU football program be immediately suspended.

Later that afternoon, Shields presented his proposal to the board leadership. They rejected it. They also told him they were not yet ready to talk with him about early retirement. Shields was devastated.

ON SUNDAY NIGHT Bob Hitch and Lonnie Kliever flew to Kansas City to keep an old appointment with the NCAA regarding SMU's request that it be granted additional scholarships under the terms of the last probation. Events had altered the agenda. Now they wished to formally withdraw that request, and to present the NCAA with documentation regarding David Stanley's drug treatment. Hitch had gathered preliminary information on Albert Reese's rent-free apartment and was prepared to discuss that, too.

That weekend there happened to be a regular meeting of the NCAA Committee on Infractions. The entire NCAA enforcement staff was staying at the Westin Crowne Center Hotel. Investigator Butch Worley came by Kliever's room late Sunday night and picked up the report on Stanley's drug treatment. He was anxious to look it over and be prepared to report to enforcement director David Berst first thing Monday morning. At the moment that was still the most serious violation in the NCAA's eyes. Kliever had sent a videotape of the TV program up by express mail the day after it was broadcast, and by now they had all had a chance to view it.

Around lunchtime on Monday, November 17, Berst, Worley, and another investigator, Charles Smrt, came to Kliever's room along with Hitch to talk things over. Kliever, at this point, was feeling separated from the investigation. He had told Shields on Saturday that he would not be a part of any investigation as long as it was under the board's control. As Berst talked, it became evident what Kliever had predicted all along—that the NCAA would never be satisfied with an institutional investigation of the kind SMU had conducted in the past, one run by university lawyers from a defensive posture. The NCAA wanted a *cooperative* investigation. Of course the university was entitled to proceed as it saw fit, but Berst made it clear that an antagonistic approach would not sit well with the NCAA.

Afterward, Hitch and Kliever had lunch together in the coffee shop on the ground floor of the hotel. They understood then, perhaps for the first time, how serious the situation really was. Unbeknownst to Kliever, there were still secrets between them; yet they both saw clearly now that this was not something that was going to disappear on its own. They were beginning to realize also that there was only one SMU official capable of leading an investigation that the NCAA would accept as impartial.

"Well," Hitch told Kliever, "It's obvious there's only one person who holds the key to this business, and that's you."

Kliever didn't even want to think about it.

AFTER LUNCH, Kliever and Hitch left for the airport. They called Shields, who was anxious to know how the NCAA had responded to the acknowledgment that SMU had paid for David Stanley's drug treatment. Kliever told Shields that he thought the presentation went as well as could be expected under the circumstances. Then he briefly outlined some of the NCAA's concerns about the nature of the university's investigation.

On the plane back to Dallas, Kliever and Hitch kicked things around a few more times. Kliever had been thinking about what Berst said. He told Hitch he might be willing to be part of an investigation, but only if certain conditions were met. Kliever wrote them down on a cocktail napkin:

He wanted to head the investigation himself. He wanted to conduct the investigation in full cooperation with the NCAA. He wanted a full disclosure of all of SMU's problems, with nothing held back. He didn't want any lawyers involved. And he wanted personally to present SMU's case before the NCAA Committee on Infractions.

Kliever felt sure these were conditions the board leadership would never accept.

KLIEVER AND HITCH landed at Dallas/Fort Worth airport and drove back to campus, where Shields was waiting for them. Earlier on the phone, Shields had apologized for being so emotional and upset on Saturday. He said he felt better now, although as the evening progressed and he missed his mealtime, his condition appeared to worsen. He grew noticeably haggard and wane.

Kliever outlined the NCAA's concerns and the three discussed them at length. By this point Shields had decided that he would take the one crumb tossed his way by the board leadership—the right to select the two outside members of the investigative committee—and do the best he could with it. But Hitch explained to Shields that he felt sure the idea of a blue-ribbon committee would not fly with the NCAA, no matter who Shields chose to serve on it. He said that based on what he now knew of the NCAA concerns, he thought the one hope SMU had of avoiding the death penalty was if they could convince David Berst that they were genuinely interested in discovering the truth. And for that to happen, Hitch said, Kliever would have have to play a major role in the investigation.

Shields agreed. "We gotta get this message to Ed Cox," he said. He had a meeting scheduled with Cox in the morning—to give him his nominations for the committee—but he asked Hitch to go in his place and tell Cox what he had learned on his trip to Kansas City.

Hitch then turned to Kliever and asked him, "Can I tell Cox that you are willing to join the investigation, providing your demands are met?"

Kliever asked Hitch for time to think it over. He said he would call him later that night.

Later, when Kliever did talk to Hitch, he told him to go ahead and explain the situation to Cox. If Cox would agree—and Kliever still did not think that was likely—then he would head the investigation.

* * *

ON TUESDAY MORNING, November 18, Lonnie Kliever left Dallas on an 8:00 flight to Austin. He was planning to spend a couple of days at Southwestern University in Georgetown, where he was scheduled to deliver a lecture. After serving eight years as chairman of the religious studies department, Kliever was on his sabbatical. In planning out this year, he had set aside time for research and interspersed a few lectures and visits to other colleges to keep himself in the loop. After two days at Southwestern, he planned to travel to UNC–Greensboro. But he never made it to North Carolina. Tuesday afternoon, his wife called and left a message that Don Shields was trying urgently to get in touch with him. Kliever did not get the message until after midnight. When he called the next morning and tried to get through to Shields, he was told that the president was ill and in seclusion. Kliever canceled the rest of his trip and returned immediately to Dallas.

SHIELDS'S CONDITION had worsened considerably. If there was a final straw, something that irrevocably made Shields understand that he could not go on, it may have been when he learned that Cox, Corley, and Hutchison, having heard Hitch's report and learned that their plan for a blue-ribbon committee did not meet with NCAA approval, had decided they would go secretly to Kansas City themselves and try to work out some kind of a deal. Shields was not invited.

Over November 18 and 19, Cox, Corley, and Hutchison negotiated the terms of Shields's early retirement and reached an agreement. The last days for Shields were the worst. He called together his closest friends and advisers—Leon Bennett, Mark Sherouse, and Kathy Costello, his former vice president for university relations who had recently resigned her post at SMU. Costello, seeing Shields for the first time in more than a month, was shocked at how pale and thin he looked, and she expressed her sorrow at the course of recent events. Shields was overcome.

Bennett, Sherouse, and Costello spent Wednesday afternoon and Thursday with Shields, helping to reconcile him to the decision that had to be made. Shields was anxious that his resignation be understood as the result of medical complications related to his diabetes, and not a case of bowing to scandal. In truth, either cause by itself would have been sufficient to force Shields out of office. Even had he been healthy, it is doubtful whether he would have been able to long survive the board's crude undermining of his authority amidst the escalating scandal.

SHIELDS'S RESIGNATION was announced on Friday, November 21. That same day, John McElhaney met with Cox, Corley, and Hutchison at Cox's house and told them he could not continue to represent SMU in light of a possible conflict of interest with another client, the A. H. Belo Corp., which owns *The Dallas Morning News* and WFAA-TV. He did, however, have a few things to share with his former clients prior to withdrawing. He told them about Clements's meeting on October 20 with Sherwood Blount, during which the progress of the wind-down had been discussed. He also told them about the earlier meeting back in March 1985, at Clements's SEDCO office, when Blount had told them all they had "a payroll to meet."

Bill Hutchison already knew something about Clements's role in the payments, based on his conversation the week before with trustee Paul Paige. Ed Cox, of course, had been in on the discussion with Shields, Hitch, and Clements in August 1985, when he had argued for elimination of the payroll. But whatever the extent of the board leaders' previous knowledge, as of November 21, there was no longer any doubt in the minds of Cox, Hutchison, and Corley that Clements had been aware of the post-August 1985 payments, that David Stanley was not the only player involved, and that SMU was in serious danger of receiving the death penalty.

ON SATURDAY, NOVEMBER 22, governor-elect Clements returned from his vacation in Italy. He had previously been contacted by Ed Cox and so was aware of what was happening back home. Saturday was also the day of the last SMU football game, an embarrassing loss to Arkansas at Texas Stadium. Some students in the stands wore T-shirts with pictures of dead ponies on them.

On Sunday, Cox, Corley, and Hutchison met with Clements at his home in Highland Park. Clements confirmed then what the group had been told by John McElhaney. He added the detail that Sherwood Blount was the sole source of funds for the continuing payments, and told them that Bobby Stewart had been a contributor to the fund during his tenure as chairman of the board of governors.

Clements also said that he was planning to step down as chairman of the board of governors before his inauguration in January.

Then the board members decided that Bobby Collins and Bob Hitch would have to resign. Never before, whenever problems with the NCAA had come up, had the board considered taking the drastic step of firing staff members. In fact, one of the reasons for the downfall of former SMU president Paul Hardin had been his decision to fire Hayden Fry without prior approval from the board. Since then, Dave Smith, Ron Meyer, and Bobby Collins had each been through at least one NCAA investigation of his own and none had lost his job because of it.

In 1985, immediately prior to the NCAA hearing in Kansas City, the board had approved the decision to ban nine boosters, hoping to deflect responsibility for the violations away from the institution. Removing the boosters had helped, but only to a point. Now the board was confronted with a crisis of far graver dimensions. They were like passengers in a hot-air balloon that was losing altitude fast. When they looked around and asked themselves, who else is expendable? the answer was the head coach and the athletic director.

By the time the meeting broke up, the board members had decided that even one of their own, Bobby Stewart, would have to resign. Now the only ones left in the balloon were a handful of powerful Dallas businessmen, most notably, the governor-elect.

ON MONDAY the leadership of the board flew secretly to Kansas City to meet with the NCAA. Cox, anxious to lay the whole matter to rest, was ready with a dramatic proposal—SMU would admit its guilt, concede the charges made by David Stanley, and suspend its football program for a period of two years.

David Berst was not impressed. He insisted a thorough investigation was necessary to determine exactly what had happened and who was responsible—to find out whether Stanley's charges in fact were true. Cox said that if there was to be an investigation, then it would have to be concluded as soon as possible, within thirty days. The SMU delegation then explored with the NCAA whether they would be comfortable with Lonnie Kliever as head of the investigation. Cox told the NCAA that they were no longer represented by John McElhaney, and that the NCAA would have a veto over SMU's choice of an attorney to assist Kliever.

LONNIE KLIEVER had been out of touch with events for several days when, on the evening of Monday, November 24, he received a call from acting president William Stallcup, inviting him to a meeting the following morning at Ed Cox's house.

Kliever arrived at 9:00. It was his first visit to Cox's columned white mansion at the corner of Preston Road and Beverly Drive, perhaps the most prestigious address in Dallas. Kliever drove his compact Japanese car through the gate on Preston road, parked in the driveway, walked to the door, and rang the bell. Cox himself answered. He escorted Kliever through a library and a living room into a breakfast room that opens on to an indoor pool. Ed Cox, Paul Corley, William Hutchison, William Stallcup, and Mark Sherouse were already there, and had evidently been there for some time. There were breakfast plates and coffee cups scattered about. On a table were stacks of press releases and resolutions for the board of governors meeting scheduled for later that morning.

Kliever approached this gathering with little optimism. He fully expected to be asked to serve on and perhaps even chair an investigative committee, with conditions he could not accept, and he fully expected to say no. With quick dispatch, Cox presented his proposal to Kliever—that he chair the committee and that he do so with basically those five conditions that he had set out for Bob Hitch on the airplane coming back from Kansas City the week before: that he head the investigation himself; that it be conducted in cooperation with the NCAA; that there be full disclosure; that there be no lawyers involved; and that he personally present SMU's case before the NCAA Committee on Infractions.

Kliever was astounded. He pressed to make sure that what they were talking about was really a joint investigation. That made Bill Hutchison uncomfortable. It was decided that the term would be an investigation "in cooperation with" the NCAA, to avoid any possible disclosure of investigative files under open-records laws that do not apply to SMU as a private inbstitution but may apply to the NCAA. Perhaps this should have been a red flag for Kliever, but it wasn't. As long as the NCAA was in on the process, he was happy.

Kliever was also concerned when the board insisted that he work with a lawyer. At least the lawyer was not John McElhaney, whom Kliever could not have accepted. The board members gave him several names from which to choose. They made it clear that whoever he chose would be working for him, not the board. If at any time he was unhappy with the lawyer he had chosen, they would fire the lawyer and hire a new one.

There was also a small problem regarding the confidentiality issue. Despite assurances to Kliever that he could conduct an open investigation, there was talk that day of keeping some of the names secret. Kliever did not object, partly because he felt sure that the NCAA would never agree to anything short of a full disclosure of names, if not to the public then at least to them; and as long as the NCAA was assisting in the investigation, Kliever felt that his integrity and the integrity of the investigation were safeguarded.

What Kliever did not realize at the time was that confidentiality was the one issue on which the board had no intention of ever compromising. It was the key to concealing the role played by Clements and the only way to avoid the risk of disclosing the complicity of the board of governors.

LATER THAT MORNING, William Hutchison telephoned Robert Thomas, the attorney selected by Kliever, and asked him to assist Kliever in the university's investigation. Hutchison gave Thomas the straight dope, telling him substantially more than what the board had shared with Kliever. Specifically, he told Thomas that David Stanley was just one name on a payroll that numbered sixteen players in 1985–86 and ten players in 1986–87, and that would be three in 1987–88. (The actual number of players on the payroll was later determined by the NCAA to be thirteen, eight, and three.)

Following the gathering at Cox's house, most of the participants returned to campus for a special meeting of the board of governors. The board that day approved the new investigation to be conducted by Lonnie Kliever (a decision that drew some criticism from faculty members who were worried about Kliever's close association with university athletics over the years). The board also approved the appointment of a commission to conduct a thorough study into the state of athletics at SMU. Stallcup was approved as acting president in place of Donald Shields, and in his first executive order,

Stallcup announced an immediate end to special admissions for athletes. The impact of Stallcup's order can be measured by the results of a *Dallas Times Herald* report in January 1985, which found that nearly half the SMU athletes admitted between 1980 and 1984 would not have qualified for admission under the NCAA's new proposition 48, which requires a minimum combined SAT score of only 700.

Afterward, Clements said at a press conference that he was "tired of this monkey business, this Mickey Mouse business, going on in our . . . football program." He talked about abolishing football altogether, and said, "The university must bring into focus that our primary fundamental focus is academic. We are an educational institution."

The Dallas Morning News, in an editorial entitled "SMU Athletics: School leaders are facing up to problems," applauded the actions of the board and cited the governor-elect approvingly for his tough talk. "He seemed prepared to take tougher steps if warranted by the investigation, as he should [when] the university's credibility is on the line."

LONNIE KLIEVER and Bob Thomas met for the first time on the evening of November 26, at Kliever's house, where they compared notes on the upcoming investigation. Thomas did not tell Kliever what he had learned that day about the existence of a payroll for football players.

Despite having just been appointed to head the university's investigation, Kliever caught a plane to Washington the following day, where he would be attending an international scholarly conference. For the next several days—over Thanksgiving weekend and through to Monday, December 1—Kliever was gone.

On Friday, the day after Thanksgiving, Hitch and Clements talked on the telephone. Clements wanted Hitch to know that the board leadership had been fully briefed and Hitch was going to have to resign. Over Thanksgiving weekend, Hitch, Collins, and Henry Lee Parker were in constant contact. Together they agreed that, come what may, they would keep the governor-elect's name out of this.

On Monday, Bob Thomas, the new lawyer, met with John McElhaney, who brought him completely up-to-date on all details of the payment program as he understood them, including the full extent of Clements's involvement and everything he knew about payments to players other than David Stanley.

AT 3:00 ON MONDAY afternoon, Cox, Corley, Hutchison, President Stallcup, and Leon Bennett met at Cox's house in preparation for the arrival of Bob Hitch. Bennett, the university counsel, had been a close adviser to Donald Shields. He had not involved himself in any substantive discussions regarding the problems with the NCAA since soon after the taping of the Channel 8 report, at which time he had heard Bob Hitch deny that there was any truth at all to David Stanley's allegations. But by the end of the day, he would know as much of the truth as anyone.

Previously, the others had discussed what possible role Hitch might play in the investigation; they hoped he had enough information regarding the payment program to satisfy the NCAA without opening up a can of worms. Once Hitch arrived, though, Hutchison spoke harshly to him, criticizing him for his role in the payment program and strongly voicing his displeasure. This was strange, given what Hutchison knew about the role played by Clements. Hitch thought so, too.

"I was only doing what I was told," Hitch told Hutchison. He described the meeting with Clements in the parking lot outside Perkins Administration Building in August 1985. He made it clear that when Clements asked him if there was a booster willing to foot the bill, and Hitch had replied that there was, that Clements's response had been, "Then do it."

Hitch told the group that after talking to Clements, he had passed the order on to head coach Bobby Collins, and that Collins had directed Henry Lee Parker to take the necessary steps to see that it was carried out.

Hitch then told them that he did not have the information that they needed for their investigation but he could get it. He would not, though, until he received some assurance on the status of his employment contract. The meeting broke up with all parties agreeing to reconvene the following afternoon at 3:00.

THAT NIGHT, Hitch ran into Lonnie Kliever at a basketball game in Moody Coliseum. Kliever and Hitch appreciated each other for their differences. Kliever saw in Hitch an ex-jock who seemed to have come far in his career on wholesome country values and common sense. He was impressed that for Hitch, athletics did not appear to be the most important thing in his life, and that he so obviously cared for his family. Later, after Hitch was gone and rumors circulated that Hitch had perhaps abused the powers of his position—accepting perks and favors that were beyond those to which he was entitled—Kliever would prefer to give his friend the benefit of the doubt. Hitch, for his part, saw in Kliever a man of diminutive build and scholarly accomplishment, a faculty type who didn't hesitate to spice his conversation with mild profanities, a comfortable contact on the academic side of the university.

Hitch came in at halftime and Kliever went over to his seat to say hello. This was the first they had seen of each other since leaving Don Shields's office together two weeks ago. Kliever asked Hitch how he was making out.

"Well, I'm talking with the board," Hitch told Kliever. He said he was trying to work out details of his contract.

Hitch looked tired. "Is it gonna be okay for you?" Kliever asked him.

"Well," said Hitch, "They're beating up on me pretty bad, but if they show me a little respect and give me what I ask for, I think everything'll work out." And then Hitch said something that Kliever would not understand until later.

"I'm gonna make your investigation easy," he said. "I can't tell you what I'm talking about but you're gonna be able to keep your integrity and I'm gonna be able to make your investigation easy."

That was all he said, and Kliever was left to wonder what it meant for the rest of the game.

AT THE MEETING the next day, Hitch confirmed that he would not cooperate with any investigation unless he were permitted to resign with the understanding that his contract be honored in full. The same, he said, went for Coach Collins and Henry Lee Parker.

SMU ultimately agreed to pay all three the full amount remaining on their contracts. Henry Lee Parker was paid $60,299 through May 31, 1988. Bob Hitch received $246,442 through May 31, 1989, and Bobby Collins will receive a total of $556,272 through December 31, 1990. In return, they agreed to give up their university automobiles and some insurance benefits. Hitch and Collins would continue to earn mortage subsidies on their houses. Only Hitch and Parker agreed to cooperate in the investigation.

Afterward, many would wonder why the board of governors had agreed to such liberal terms, given the fact that all three had clauses in their contracts that would have allowed them to be terminated for violating NCAA rules. In Hitch's case, they needed his cooperation; satisfying his demands was the only way to get it. As for the others, there was the risk that they would sue on the grounds that they had only been following orders. Even if they were unsuccessful, a trial would inevitably lead to unwanted disclosures. The board members wanted Hitch, Collins, and Parker gone; they wanted to keep Clements's and other board members' names out of the investigation; and they wanted to placate the NCAA. Giving Hitch, Collins, and Parker everything they wanted was the only option they had.

Others in the SMU community were not pleased. As rumors of the deals leaked (the total cash settlement came to $863,01.[1]), resentment grew, especially among athletic department staff members in other sports. SMU was committing itself to nearly a million dollars in deferred payments stretching into the next decade. Athletics had never had much success breaking even in the past, and now it looked like the football program—generally a source of revenue—would be suspended for as long as two years. How could the deficit be made good? Many saw the likelihood of future cuts. They began to worry about their jobs.

WEDNESDAY AFTERNOON, Lonnie Kliever and William Stallcup were scheduled to appear before a meeting of the faculty senate. This was a regularly scheduled meeting in which Kliever, as faculty athletic rep, and Gerry Gurney, the athletic academic adviser, would report with the athletic director on the state of athletics at SMU. Kliever had been attending the annual Southwest Conference meetings that week at conference headquarters on Mockingbird Lane, near the SMU campus, and he stopped by President Stallcup's office to brief him on their progress. As Kliever was getting up to leave, Stallcup mentioned that he had spent the last couple of days learning more about what was happening in the SMU athletic department than he had ever cared to know. He told Kliever that there were about twelve or thirteen kids being paid, and then he mentioned —in a casual, offhand way—that Bob Hitch was involved.

This knocked Lonnie Kliever for a loop. He had thought Henry Lee Parker looked guilty on television, and he had begun to wonder whether David Stanley was really the only player on the payroll. But to learn that the friend he thought he knew so well had in fact been lying to him all along was a complete shock. Kliever was moved to tears.

AT THE FACULTY senate meeting, there was a report on the investigation, a report on the decision to waive the request for further scholarships, and a finance report. Newspaper reporters were present. Kliever, with his new knowledge, was struck by the way Hitch responded to questions. He made pointed use of the word *we*, as in "We were close to having the cleanest program in the country." He said he had inherited the dirtiest program in North America but that "We were within a year of having everybody out of the program who had been involved in cheating." Hitch, in effect, was admitting that other players had been paid, something that only a handful of individuals involved in the investigation knew at that time. But the remark seemed to fall on deaf ears.

After the meeting Kliever and Hitch spoke briefly. Kliever did not question Hitch then about what he had learned. He told Hitch only that he would be flying to Kansas City the next day.

"You'll get the full story on the way to Kansas City," Hitch said.

THIS PARTICULAR flight to Kansas City was different for Kliever than the others he had made over the years. He flew out of Love Field, not Dallas/Fort Worth, in Cox's private jet. The board members who had come along sat in facing seats around a worktable in the front of the plane. Midway through the flight, they came back to the tail section where Kliever was sitting with attorney Bob Thomas.

Though he was technically the head of the investigation, Kliever was undoubtedly the least well-informed passenger on the plane. Now they laid it out for him. They told him about the payroll, approximately how many players were involved, approximately how much they were paid, and that Hitch, Collins, and Parker were all involved. Clements's name was not mentioned. They explained that deals had been made to settle contracts with Hitch, Collins, and

Parker, and that Hitch was prepared to provide detailed information about the payments to Kliever and the NCAA. There was, however, a caveat: Ed Cox and Bill Hutchison insisted that the names not be disclosed, neither of the players who were paid nor of the boosters who paid them.

After he had heard all this, Kliever told the board members that he simply did not believe the NCAA would be willing to accept that. If it was only a question of not releasing the names to the public, that would be another matter entirely. In fact, that is what the NCAA ordinarily prefers. But he felt certain that David Berst and the rest of the enforcement staff would insist on knowing who they were dealing with.

"Well," said Hutchison, "we'll just have to find a way."

IN KANSAS CITY the party was met by limousine and driven to NCAA headquarters in suburban Mission, Kansas. Cox opened the meeting by stressing again how important it was that the entire matter be settled within thirty days. Cox and Hutchison told the NCAA that Hitch, Collins, and Parker were on their way out. They said further that they had sources who could provide detailed information on what they conceded had been continuing payments, a "hangover" problem. All payments, they said, had now ceased (a fact confirmed by athletic-department employees, who noted that when the word was passed that there would be no pay envelopes in December, at least ten football players had lined up in the hallway to apply for special student loans). They talked about the necessity for absolute confidentiality.

The NCAA indicated that to them the most important thing was that SMU discover its own problems, that it find out how many other David Stanleys were out there, what was the extent of booster involvement, and what was the extent of institutional knowledge and responsibility. If SMU could get all that, then the NCAA was not so much interested in public disclosure.

Although the meeting broke up somewhere short of a resolution of all differences, the consensus in both parties was that they were headed in the right direction. But whether by design or oversight, an important point had been left unsaid. No one in the SMU party had mentioned that the source who could provide the payroll information was in fact the SMU athletic director Bob Hitch; and certainly no one had said that Hitch not only had knowledge of the payments but had participated in the decision to go ahead with them. When Berst finally realized the full implications of this, it would come as a great shock.

On the flight back from Dallas, Cox called university attorney Leon Bennett and found out that Hitch had signed his separation agreement. The announcement would be made the following day.

LONNIE KLIEVER spent Friday morning at the Southwest Conference meetings in Dallas. Bob Hitch showed up at the lunch break; he had come to fetch senior associate athletic director Dudley Parker and bring him back to campus for the press conference. But since he was there, he sat down and had lunch.

Afterward, Kliever walked over to Hitch's table and joined him. They sat there alone with the dirty dishes and the soiled napkins. Hitch was still under the assumption that Kliever had first learned the truth about him on the plane to Kansas City. Now Kliever told him that he had heard part of the story the day before, from Stallcup.

Hitch laughed. "Well, he was not supposed to say anything," he said. Then he asked his friend how it had made him feel to learn that Hitch was involved.

"It hurt," Kliever said. "It was one of the most painful things that I have ever learned in my life."

Hitch was silent for a moment. "The hardest thing about this whole business was I having to lie to you," he said. "But I can't talk about this anymore. I'm gonna have a hard enough time making it through the news conference at four o'clock."

Before they parted, Kliever asked Hitch when he would be ready to talk to him and Butch Worley of the NCAA.

"Anytime you want to," Hitch said. They agreed to meet at the attorney Bob Thomas's office at one o'clock on Monday.

HITCH LEFT FOR the press conference. It lasted only thirty minutes. Both Hitch and Collins read from prepared statements, then answered a few questions. Coach Collins, typically, was the most visibly upset. Collins was leaving SMU with a record of 43-14-1, the best winning percentage, by far, of any head coach in SMU's long football history. His teams had won or shared two SWC championships and been to three bowl games. Hitch was stepping aside after presiding over a glorious era in SMU athletics that extended beyond nationally ranked football teams. During his six-year tenure, SMU had won three NCAA championships and eleven Southwest Conference titles, and placed thirty-two teams in the nation's top ten. Now both were stepping down in disgrace.

BEFORE THEIR scheduled session with the NCAA investigator Kliever and Hitch met for breakfast Monday morning at the Hilton Hotel on Mockingbird Lane. Their plan was to avoid discussing anything substantive; Kliever was determined that anything having to do with the investigation take place only with the NCAA present. Rather, they were meeting as two friends who had been through a crisis in their relationship. The conversation was strictly personal.

As they were leaving, though, Hitch asked Kliever again about his trip to Kansas City. Kliever summarized the impression he had received from the board of governors—that Hitch had been involved in the cheating all along, that he had known about it when he came to SMU, and that he had personally approved its continuation after August 1985.

Hitch became silent. "Those bastards," he said, "they're gonna try to put all the blame on me?"

Hitch was angry at the suggestion that he had been responsible for paying players from the start. Hitch was willing to take the blame for allowing the payments to continue—and he would keep Clements's name out of it—but he deeply resented being singled out as the cause of SMU's problems.

"I'm gonna have to think about this," Hitch told Kliever.

Kliever and Butch Worley met for an early lunch, then went over to Bob Thomas's office at One Main in downtown Dallas to meet Hitch. When they arrived, Thomas's secretary had already heard from Hitch that he would not be coming after all. From Thomas's office, Kliever called all over Dallas trying to reach Hitch—his office, his home, his car phone. Finally Hitch called back. He said he was talking to his lawyer and would decide within the next day whether he was willing to go through with this or not.

The next day, Hitch called Kliever again. He said that he had decided to talk after all. They were to meet him at the office of his friend (and lawyer) Steve Mahood on Wednesday, December 10, at ten o'clock.

* * *

MAHOOD'S OFFICE is on Preston Road in North Dallas. As soon as Kliever and Worley arrived, Hitch laid out his conditions: that there be absolute confidentiality at every stage, meaning no players' names, no boosters' names, no staff members' names, and especially not his name; and two, that there be no confirming interviews. They would have to take his word alone. If Kliever and Worley were agreeable, he was prepared to give them totals only: the total number of boosters supplying the funds, the total number of players being paid, the total amount received.

The NCAA is always willing to keep names a secret from the public. What Hitch was asking for was that his name and all others be kept secret also from the NCAA Committee on Infractions.

"It won't do anybody any good," Hitch said. "It won't serve any purpose."

"No way," Worley said, and got up to leave.

Then Steve Mahood broke in. He told Worley that Hitch did indeed want to share his information, but that he had to do it in his own way. He said that Hitch knew it sounded unreasonable, but they had to know why it was unreasonable. And so they reached a compromise. Hitch would tell Worley and Kliever what he was prepared to say, on the condition that it not be used unless Hitch authorized its use, which he would not do unless they agreed to his restrictions. When all parties agreed, Hitch began to talk.

He went way back. Soon after he arrived at SMU in 1981, Hitch said, he had discovered the existence of a statewide network of boosters who were supplying a slush fund that had assets in the six-figure range. He told them that as far as he knew, the network had been shut down sometime between November of 1984 and April of 1985, at the height of the last NCAA investigation. But in August 1985, when Bootsie Larsen was fired, Hitch said he was told by Larsen that there was still money in the pipeline. Not only that, but he had "a payroll to meet." Hitch told Worley and Kliever that at that time, he and Bobby Collins decided on their own they had no choice but to continue making the payments, for which they enlisted the help of Henry Lee Parker. It was a risky business but it was their only hope. Hitch expressed some remorse. He said he knew that what he had done was wrong, but that he had acted in what he believed were the best interests of SMU.

Worley was astounded. He thought he was finally getting the whole story about SMU, the one that the NCAA had been digging for since at least 1980. He questioned Hitch for two hours. Of course, Hitch made no mention of Bill Clements or Bobby Stewart or any other member of the board of governors. He was simply delivering the agreed-upon version of events.

Before he left, Hitch said he thought there was a chance that the booster who had been the whole source of funds might be willing to talk, but apart from that he insisted that his conditions still applied: no names and no confirming interviews. This would have to be the whole investigation, the beginning and the end.

Worley was impressed. He said he would have to go back to David Berst with all this and discuss the terms of their cooperation. But he was optimistic that Berst would find the conditions acceptable.

Bob Thomas was the only other person in the room that day who knew the essential fact that Hitch had failed to reveal—that Bill Clements was a party to the decision to continue the payments. Thomas kept quiet.

ON THURSDAY, Lonnie Kliever bumped into Bob Hitch at a Christmas party for athletic-department employees at Moody Coliseum. Talking in a general way, Hitch told Kliever that Kliever now knew about 95 percent of what had happened, and that the other 5 percent was unimportant. He also told him that the booster who supplied the cash to phase out the payments was Sherwood Blount.

WHEN BUTCH WORLEY brought the news of developments with Hitch back to Kansas City, the first person he talked to was Steve Morgan, David Berst's immediate supervisor. The terms of the agreement with the source were irregular, Morgan agreed, and yet here was the institution admitting to serious violations, actually handing the finished case over to the NCAA. It looked like this was the best chance they had to get the whole story, or enough of it, anyway. In the end Morgan was amenable to accepting Hitch's conditions, as long as some conditions of his own were met. Namely, that the institution be willing to accept Hitch's statement of the violations, and accept without dispute whatever penalty may be handed down by the Committee on Infractions. This forced Kliever's hand as well.

He would have to stand by the NCAA in asserting that this was a fair and accurate description of events.

WHILE MORGAN, apparently, was willing to go along with Hitch's conditions, Berst had to be convinced. He regarded Hitch's statement as a shocking development. First had come the news that SMU had deliberately broken the rules and lied about it by paying for David Stanley's drug treatment. Now he had learned that the latest round of violations went well beyond David Stanley to include many other players, and that the payments had been authorized and implemented by athletic-department staff members.

Berst wanted to make sure the board leadership fully understood what had happened before he would agree to make a deal. He was remembering the meeting with Cox and Hutchison and Corley in early December, when no mention had been made by anyone of institutional involvement in the payments. Through Butch Worley, he directed Lonnie Kliever to set up a meeting in Kansas City so that Ed Cox and the others could be informed. Berst asked Kliever, "Do you think the leadership knows that Hitch was involved?"

Kliever said, "I do."

ON THURSDAY, DECEMBER 18, Lonnie Kliever and Bob Thomas met with the board leadership at Ed Cox's office in the InterFirst building downtown, the same office tower visited so often in the past by Robin Buddecke, the booster who went there to collect recruiting funds from the chairman of the bank, Bobby Stewart. For reasons that Kliever did not yet fully understand, the board members were delighted with the prospect of the NCAA agreeing to accept Hitch's story. They had no reservations whatsoever about committing the institution to an endorsement of Hitch's findings.

As Kliever laid out Hitch's story—about Hitch and Collins taking it upon themselves to continue the payments—he was the only one in the room who did not know this to be false. Yet no one took the opportunity to set him straight. Kliever told the leadership that David Berst was so taken aback by the knowledge of Hitch's involvement that he wanted to meet again in Kansas City. Cox wanted to designate Kliever as his representative but Berst would not accept that. A return trip was scheduled for December 30.

On Christmas Eve, Kliever and the board members met at Cox's house to discuss their strategy for the meeting on December 30. Kliever had prepared a set of proposed sanctions, which he laid out for discussion. The sanctions he had in mind were severe. They included something from every category in the bag, including the loss of some athletic scholarships, recruiting visits, television appearances, and bowl-game privileges. It was not quite the death penalty. Still, the leadership was discouraged. By cooperating with the NCAA through Hitch, they had hoped to avoid stiff penalties. As far as they were concerned, the option of voluntarily terminating the program was no longer acceptable.

ON THE DAY BEFORE New Year's Eve, Ed Cox, Paul Corley, Lonnie Kliever, and Bob Thomas flew to Kansas City. Kliever had brought along a revised working paper that laid out a schedule of penalties somewhat less severe than those he had proposed on December 24. Everyone at SMU wanted very much for SMU to devise its own punishment, rather than be hammered again by the NCAA. The theory underlying Kliever's proposed sanctions was that SMU would be better served by sustaining severe limitations spread out over a period of five years rather than by simply giving up the program for two years and then having to face the prospect of a revival of boosterism after that.

When they arrived in Kansas City, it was clear from the start that David Berst was still highly distressed at the news about Bob Hitch. He told the SMU delegation that this was "the worst possible situation he could imagine," and recommended that SMU join the enforcement department in going ahead in recommending a one-year suspension of the program.

But after Kliever had explained his reasons for recommending a lesser penalty, Berst seemed to give ground. He said he would consider the possibility of the enforcement department joining SMU in arguing against the death penalty before the Committee on Infractions.

18 DEATH ROW

IT WOULD BE four weeks before the SMU delegation returned to Kansas City. The NCAA was vacillating. Director of enforcement David Berst was simply not yet able to accept SMU's unwillingness to release names.

Meanwhile, on campus there was a growing sentiment among faculty, students, and administrators that an investigation conducted solely by Lonnie Kliever and not by a broader committee more representative of the university as a whole was inadequate. Kliever, though widely respected, came under suspicion in some circles from those who felt he was too closely allied with the interests of the athletic department, Hitch in particular. At a time when factions at SMU were seriously promoting the idea that SMU withdraw from the Southwest Conference and abandon "quasi-professional athletics," Kliever's allegiance was suspect.

ON JANUARY 20 Kliever talked to the football team. In recent weeks there had been stories in the papers describing the team members as "zombies," so depressed were they over their future at SMU. Kliever had first met with the team in December, at the request of acting athletic director Dudley Parker, in an attempt to fend off the possibility of widespread defections at a time when it was by no means clear that the football program would be suspended. Kliever's message then was simple: "Stick it out until you know for sure. If after the penalties are announced, you would like to transfer, SMU will make every effort to assist you. If you decide to stay, SMU will honor your scholarship, football or no football."

Now Kliever came before the football team with a formal request that those who had been involved in rules violations come forward and make themselves known. Normally, such players would face the loss of their eligibility, but Kliever told them he was authorized by the NCAA to offer amnesty. By this point, SMU and the NCAA knew that there were at least three paid players who were still underclassmen. SMU thought it would strengthen their case if those players identified themselves. Kliever said he had no interest in talking to anyone about somebody else who was being paid—all he wanted was voluntary information directly from the affected players. He said he would be available in his office for the next two days, in case anyone wanted to talk.

After the meeting, Kliever and Butch Worley joked on the phone about the possibility that, say, twenty players would come forward, when they had been expecting only three. They need not have worried about that. Kliever sat two days in his office in vain.

ON JANUARY 27, a Tuesday, Lonnie Kliever and Bob Thomas returned to Kansas City alone to review the findings with the NCAA. David Berst had finally agreed to accept Bob Hitch's conditions. They would use only the information he provided, and there would be no names. As a result, Hitch had agreed to give the NCAA exact totals on the number of players paid since August 1985 and how much they had received. Now the challenge was to try to come to some sort of agreement on a draft of proposed sanctions. It was not a pleasant meeting. Kliever and Thomas were distressed at the severity of the sanctions proposed by the NCAA, so much so that Kliever said he could not endorse such penalties without first going back to Dallas and consulting with the board leadership.

In the end, Kliever and Thomas simply stood up and walked out of the meeting. "I don't know what the leadership is going to say," Kliever said on the way out, "but they may just decide to call the whole thing off."

KLIEVER AND THOMAS met for lunch at the S&D Oyster Company on McKinney Avenue on January 29 to talk over what went wrong in Kansas City. After they left, on the way to their cars, they paused for a moment to sit down on a low wall by the side of the restaurant and finish their conversation. Both agreed they had come too far in their joint investigation with the NCAA to back out now. Were the NCAA to conduct its own investigation, both men agreed, there was no telling what might turn up.

"The trail might lead to the governor's mansion," Kliever said, and Thomas nodded.

Later, Kliever would say that he was speaking loosely, based on rumors he had heard of the governor's participation in the early days of the slush fund under Ron Meyer and not on any precise knowledge of Clements's role in the affairs at hand. In any case, Thomas, who knew full well what an independent investigation by the NCAA might disclose, chose only to say, "You might be right."

SMU WAS LUCKY. Just when it looked like the joint investigation was in danger of breaking down, the NCAA—apparently afraid of what might happen if they were left to conduct their own investigation, deprived of the information they had received from Bob Hitch—gave ground. By February 6 Kliever was able to hand to board members a final version of the joint NCAA/SMU statement of violations and a proposed schedule of penalties, which did not include the death penalty. There could be no guarantee that the infractions committee would approve the enforcement department's recommendations, but Kliever and the rest of the SMU delegation had reason to be hopeful.

Bill Hutchison (who had now formally replaced Bill Clements as chairman of the board of governors), President Stallcup, Lonnie Kliever, and Bob Thomas all signed a final draft of the statement of violations, which contained information that only Kliever did not know to be false. Specifically, it was stated that the decision to continue the payments was made by "certain key Athletic Department staff members." No mention was made of Clements or any other member of the board of governors, the board of trustees, or the university administration.

ON THURSDAY, FEBRUARY 12, the four members of the SMU delegation—Hutchison, Stallcup, Kliever, and Thomas—made their way to San Diego, where they checked in at the historic Hotel del Coronado, a grand Victorian edifice on the beachfront. It was the day after national signing day, and for the second year in a row, SMU had signed no prospects. They were entitled to sign fifteen under the terms of their 1985 probation, but had decided to suspend assignment of all new football scholarships pending the outcome of the current investigation.

The winter weather in San Diego was brisk, too cold for swimming but good for walking on the beach. This was to be the final step in what had been a remarkably fast investigation. It was exactly three months since Channel 8's report had aired. Since then, four top-level administrators—the president, the athletic director, the head football coach, and the recruiting coordinator—had already lost their jobs. A far-reaching examination of the future of big-time athletics at SMU was under way, with its report due soon. It was possible that the committee would recommend SMU's withdrawal from the Southwest Conference and NCAA Division I. Now, as SMU prepared to take its case to the Committee on Infractions, even a best-case scenario had SMU facing severe limits on how it could conduct its football program in the future. Players, already angry, were threatening widespread defections. The image of the university had already suffered greatly, whatever the outcome would be. But SMU had one last wish and hope, and that was to avoid the death penalty.

SMU HAD A POWERFUL ally—the enforcement department. After much soul-searching and intense negotiations, the NCAA and SMU had agreed to together recommend a package of sanctions that, while severe, fell short of the death penalty. Now they had to convince the Committee on Infractions of the wisdom of their recommendation.

The Committee on Infractions, chaired then by University of Wisconsin law professor Frank Remington, is the judicial body of college athletics. It hears cases from the enforcement department and the member institutions and passes judgment. From the beginning, while the enforcement department had encouraged SMU to work with them, there was never any promise of a deal, no suggestion that even David Berst and Steve Morgan would be able to convince this independent committee of the membership to spare SMU and pass on the first opportunity afforded them to enforce the death penalty.

The package of proposed penalties agreed on by SMU and the

enforcement department called for four years' probation, two years with no bowls, two years with no TV, significant reductions in staff, scholarships, and paid visits by recruits, and the elimination of two nonconference games per year for two years.

The SMU delegation entered the ground-floor conference room at the Hotel del Coronado slightly after 1:45 P.M. on Friday, February 13. They would not emerge until 6:00. Inside, the west windows that gave out on the veranda and the Pacific Ocean were shuttered closed. As is typical, the three parties were arranged around a horse-shoe-shaped table, with the six-member Committee on Infractions at the head, SMU on one leg, and the enforcement department— including the director, David Berst, and the investigators who had had a hand in the case—on the other leg.

The Committee on Infractions had had a chance to review the briefs in advance. Berst opened the formal presentation by intro-ducing the case and describing how the university had first learned of the violations, up to the point where Kliever was asked to conduct the investigation. Berst emphasized that the enforcement depart-ment was standing with the university both in its statement of violations and in recommending appropriate penalties. After Kliever finished describing the progress of the investigation, the Committee on Infractions began to question both parties. Normally, the en-forcement department and the university would have used this opportunity to dispute their respective claims. In this case, they stood together.

The questioning from the infractions committee, four men and two women, none of whom were from a Southwest Conference school, was severe. If there was any doubt in the minds of any members of the SMU party whether the infractions committee was indeed independent of the enforcement department, those doubts were erased. The committee of lay people evidently took a far dim-mer view of events than the enforcement professionals.

Under harsh questioning from the committee concerning the terms of the deal between SMU and the enforcement department, David Berst stressed that had SMU not voluntarily provided all the evidence, the NCAA would probably not have been able to build a case on its own. The revelations by Channel 8 were dramatic but useless as evidence. And even though Butch Worley of the NCAA had talked personally to David Stanley, in the end Stanley had not allowed the NCAA to make use of his testimony; under the NCAA's own rules of evidence, they were obliged to ignore it.

The fact is, had SMU not turned itself in, it might well have been able to avoid the death penalty. "Hell," said a member of the board leadership later, "if we'd have known that, we wouldn't have co-operated." Those who heard him insist that he was joking.

THE SMU DELEGATION spent the night in San Diego and returned to Dallas the following day. Kliever's first contact with anyone from the NCAA was on Monday, February 16, when he learned that the infractions committee had stayed in session in San Diego longer than expected, extending their stay for at least an extra day. That seemed an indication that they had not simply rubber-stamped the enforcement department's recommendation and were evidently still trying to arrive at an appropriate penalty.

Later in the week Kliever talked to Butch Worley, who indicated informally that it looked like the penalties were going to be harsher than they both had expected. And on February 20 Berst told Kliever that it would in fact be a modified version of the death penalty. Berst said he thought SMU had been given a great deal of credit for its cooperation, as far as it went, but that in the end, the committee felt the violations were simply too severe.

On the afternoon of February 24, Lonnie Kliever, President Stallcup, attorney Leon Bennett, and presidential assistant Mark Sherouse met to go over plans for the press conference. At one point Stallcup raised the question of what would be an appropriate way to respond to the question of Clements's involvement, if it were raised. Bennett said he didn't think it would come up, and even if it did, they were under no obligation to respond. But Kliever said that Channel 8's John Sparks, for one, had already raised the question at an off-the-record press briefing on February 11.

Kliever thought that since the agreed-upon statement of infractions attributed responsibility for the payments to unnamed members of the athletic department, then they ought to be able to deny any involvement either by members of the SMU administration or the board.

Bennett and Stallcup knew better, but they both kept their mouths shut. Kliever was cautioned in a curious way, though, which he thought little of at the time but later agreed was significant. One of the lines in his proposed statement was, in effect, "we have solved all our problems." Better say, "solved all our problems that we knew about," Stallcup told Kliever.

THAT AFTERNOON, Kliever, Stallcup, Sherouse, Thomas, and Bennett met with David Berst in a conference room at the Doubletree Hotel on North Central Expressway in Dallas to receive the final report of the infractions committee. They were the first to learn officially that SMU would be given a modified form of the death penalty. Later, the board leadership arrived. The group made final plans for the press conference in the morning.

19 EXECUTION

AT 7:30 A.M. ON Wednesday, February 25, 1987, Larry White, the SMU sports information director, opened the door of the assembly room on the first floor of the Umphrey Lee Student Center and was met by a blast of refrigerated air. White was pleased, if that was the word. So far, so good.

The SMU football scandal had passed the stage by now where it could be called simply a sports story. For White, this meant that planning for the announcement was mostly out of his hands. That worried him. He wondered if the people in university relations appreciated the magnitude of this day and the interest it held for news organizations around the country. He knew from past experience that the Dallas papers—the *Morning News* and the *Times Herald*—would send eight or ten reporters and editors apiece. *The New York Times* was coming, the *Los Angeles Times*, *USA Today*, the *Chicago Tribune*, the *The Washington Post*, the list went on. Anticipating a large crowd, White had taken the precaution of asking a small contingent of campus security officers, some in plain clothes, to be on hand.

What really worried him, though, were the lights. So many television cameras with their bright lights would turn the cramped room into a hothouse in no time. And so White had arranged with maintenance the night before to override the building thermostat and kick on the air conditioning in the assembly room, bringing the temperature down to about sixty degrees. He figured the last thing SMU needed now was for the whole world to see them sweat.

* * *

NOT ALL OF the more than two hundred people packed inside the assembly room waiting for the press conference to begin were reporters. Standing in the back, behind the cameras, were a handful of SMU loyalists. They were boosters, not bagmen; lawyers, accountants, and real-estate brokers who put pony stickers on the windows of their Honda Accords and their Jeep Wagoneers; contributors to the scholarship fund, not the slush fund; men who wrote letters to prospects on the firm's stationery and stopped by Ownby Stadium on recruiting weekends for coffee and doughnuts with the players. They represented the soft core of SMU support, and today, they struggled to contain their resentment.

Who *were* all these reporters? So many were obviously from out of town. Wherever they looked, the SMU supporters saw "prissy" types who looked like they had never sweated in their lives. One of them wore suspenders and a yellow bow tie; he looked like someone who had canceled breakfast at the yacht club just so he could attend SMU's execution. Most of them weren't even sportswriters. No—and now they began to understand—these guys were the *national media*, the *Eastern press*, and from the look of them, they guessed that SMU was going to take a beating in the papers.

At 9:00 A.M. three somber men in sport coats and ties entered the assembly room, climbed two steps to the podium, and took their seats at a narrow table faced with blue cloth. On the table were clusters of microphones and portable tape recorders. A blue curtain, intentionally unadorned by the university logo, provided a plain backdrop for the cameras. A woman from university relations stood and briefly introduced acting university president Bill Stallcup, faculty athletics representative Lonnie Kliever, and David Berst, who would speak first.

Before he was an NCAA investigator, Berst was a baseball coach at a small college in Illinois. The way he sat in his chair—leaning slightly forward, feet flat on the floor, forearms propped on his thighs—he looked as if he were on a bench, watching a game. Speaking in a nasal, monotonous twang, he announced that the NCAA had counted thirteen players who were paid between $50 and $725 a month during the 1985–86 academic year and eight players who continued receiving payments until December 1986.

He estimated that the total amount paid out over sixteen months was $61,000. He pointed out that violations committed after September 1, 1986, were subject to new legislation, including (though he did not say it) the death penalty.

As Berst droned on, some of the people in the room were becoming more concerned with his appearance than with what he was saying. He looked terrible. His cheeks were pale and his eyelids pink. Pausing frequently to clear his throat or to sip from a Styrofoam cup filled with iced water, he seemed on the verge of losing his composure. Kliever, who was sitting to Berst's left (Stallcup was between them), was puzzled. Frankly ill at ease himself, Kliever thought it odd that Berst, of all people, would be the one to show his discomfiture. Didn't he do this sort of thing all the time?

Then Berst cleared his throat and made it official. "Regarding football games," he said, "the university will be prohibited from participating in any football game or scrimmage with outside competition in 1987. During the 1988 football season, the university shall be limited to no more than seven games ... none of which may be considered a home game."

So that was it. The death penalty. Later the nitpickers would point out that the death penalty as written—NCAA Enforcement 7-(f)-(1)—calls for a two-year suspension. Since SMU got only one year, well, it could have been worse. This distinction was lost on everyone who watched the news on TV that night and the millions around the country who read the newspapers the next day; it was missed by Larry White, whose summary, expressed to a reporter friend, was simply, "They gassed us"; and it was ignored by the SMU administration, which later went ahead and canceled the seven away games allowed SMU in 1988. The program was dead, it was that simple.

Hardly anyone had imagined it would come to this. Up until a half hour before the press conference, when White had handed out releases to all the reporters, the inside word was that SMU had been given a stay of execution. It was known that the NCAA enforcement staff had joined with SMU in recommending leniency before the Committee on Infractions.

The committee, though, stood fast. "Not only is Southern Methodist University a repeat major violator," the committee members wrote in their final report, "but its past record of violations is nothing short of abysmal." In the end the committee clearly felt bound to act in accordance with the consensus view of the mainstream of college athletics. Clearly, the mood of the country—not just the universities—favored tough measures to stop the cheating. In this, the committee's first opportunity to impose the maximum punishment, it did not back down.

One of the SMU supporters who was there struggled to contain his anger. "Oh, I tell you, I had some real serious anger," he said later. "I mean, I certainly was disapproving of David Stanley and our stupidity with all that. But to yank the program, I thought that was pretty strong medicine. The stigmatization of the entire alma mater, it was as severe as it could possibly be. The only thing that would have been worse would have been if we'd had some concentration camp underneath the science building that had only now been discovered and was being exposed. It was frightful. It was horrible."

What did it mean? Lost revenue, for one. Probably $2 million in ticket sales, another $300,000 in SWC distributions, more in gifts. There would be no lucrative television appearances, no bowl-game paydays. People would lost their jobs. Already the athletic director and the head coach had been forced to resign. The assistants were looking for work. So were secretaries, academic advisers, trainers. Within two months, the athletic department staff would be reduced by more than half from its pre-November 1986 level. And the players, the honest ones who weren't taking money, what about them? They had a choice—give up football or leave SMU.

Unavoidably, SMU's reputation would be damaged. How much, who knew? Would SMU be judged by the excesses of its football team? How could it not be? This wasn't something that could be foisted on overzealous alumni, not this time. Athletic administrators were known to be responsible. The president had resigned—ill with diabetes, yes, but clearly weakened by events. Already there was talk that the truth was more disturbing still, that ultimate responsibility would be attributed in the end to certain individuals at the highest levels of trust in the university. And all of this had happened in the year marking SMU's seventy-fifth anniversary, the year, many hoped, when SMU's standing in the academic community would finally catch up with its self-image. "Embarrassment is a mild way of putting it," Leroy Howe, a professor of religious studies would say later. "It's just downright humiliating—and shameful."

Now Berst was wrapping up his remarks. "I believe that the Committee on Infractions has imposed a penalty that was intended to eliminate the elements of a program that they did not believe should be continued," Berst said, somewhat obtusely, "but also provided the hope that a program can be reconstructed at the institution . . . and can be built on a foundation of integrity."

Berst said, "Thank you," and sat back in his chair. Beads of sweat glistened on his forehead.

KLIEVER, READING FROM a prepared statement, began with an apology. "We are all deeply embarrassed and regretful over the recently discovered violations and newly imposed sanctions within our football program," he began. "We were and are troubled by the fact that those who have brought this bad day on our university must remain unnamed," he said. "But we believed that the time had come to discover the problems in our football program, even at the price of limited public disclosure of the individuals involved."

But for those who sat listening to Kliever's summary statement, many questions remained. Who were the players who had accepted money? Which boosters contributed to the fund? Kliever gave an unsatisfying, if familiar explanation: Because neither the NCAA nor SMU has the power to compel testimony or subpoena documents, they had to rely on voluntary cooperation from confidential sources.

Kliever took less than eight minutes to complete his remarks. The final speaker would be Bill Stallcup. Before Stallcup could begin, Berst pushed back his chair and made an effort to stand. He said something to Stallcup and Kliever that the microphone failed to pick up, but which Kliever later remembered as "I need to get out of here." Then, with Stallcup's assistance, Berst stood. Sweat ran now in rivers from his brow. Stallcup walked him to the edge of the podium. Berst took one step on his own and collapsed.

HANDS COVERED mouths in horror. Reporters craned their necks and then left their seats for a closer look. John Sparks, the producer for WFAA-TV who probably more than any other person in the room was personally responsible for the day's events, felt a stab of remorse. Berst had suffered a heart attack, he felt sure, and it was his fault.

When Berst fell, he fell into the arms of White, who had been watching Berst wipe his brow and wondering if the assembly room was cold enough after all. White, with the help of his security officers, carried Berst across the hallway to another room and laid him out on the floor. Someone called an ambulance. Ann McCartin, a university nurse whose son was on the football team, loosened Berst's tie and unbuttoned his sweat-soaked shirt. His skin was the color of chalk.

In time Berst opened his eyes and looked directly at Nurse McCartin, who sat leaning over him, fanning his face.

"Who are you?" Berst asked.

"I'm Ann McCartin, mother of a walk-on football player at SMU," she replied."

White was afraid for an instant that Berst would pass out again.

BACK IN THE assembly room, Stallcup and Kliever consulted with each other over how to proceed.

"Shall we just continue?" Kliever asked. The sound of an approaching siren could be heard.

Stallcup nodded. "We'll ask people to wait here."

Then Stallcup spoke into the microphone. "If we may continue—David Berst has not been in the best of health, and I am concerned that suddenly he has been taken ill. But our people, I'm sure, will see that he's well taken care of."

Stallcup, a white-haired, balding man of sixty-six, with thin lips and a turned-up nose, grimly read his statement. He spoke of "the distress we all feel at this university," and of the "many fine young men who are guilty of no wrongdoing, and who now face uncertain futures." He reassured the players, many of whom were gathered at Ownby Stadium, watching on closed-circuit TV, that SMU would honor their scholarships should they wish to stay and complete their educations. "The thousands of fine people who are associated with this university," Stallcup concluded, "—faculty, staff, students, members of the board, alumni, friends—will ensure that SMU will restore to its athletic programs the integrity and quality for which the rest of the university is known and respected."

Five minutes into the question-and-answer period that followed

Stallcup's statement, Berst reappeared at the door of the assembly room. He walked slowly and with evident determination to his place at the table and sat down. The room fell silent.

"Apparently I am fine," he said, provoking a loud burst of tension-releasing laughter. "There must be some line that you ought to have on occasions like this, but I don't. . . . It's more embarrassing to me, I think, than anyone else. You may have even enjoyed that" (more laughter).

Berst had not had a heart attack. His fainting spell was later attributed to hyperventilation, low blood sugar, and anxiety. He evidently had been suffering from the flu.

WITH BERST BACK in his chair, the question-and-answer period resumed. Sparks, sitting in the front row next to Dale Hansen, his on-camera colleague, stood and addressed himself to President Stallcup. "John Sparks, Channel 8," he said, with a soft, homey accent. "I refer to page two of the NCAA handout here. Specifically it mentions, 'in August 1985 certain key athletic-department staff members agreed that promises made to student-athletes prior to the 1984–85 academic year would and should continue to be fulfilled.' Did the university's investigation determine that Texas governor Bill Clements in August 1985 was aware of that, or did he participate in the meeting in which that decision was made to continue those payments?"

Stallcup was silent for two beats. On December 1 he had been at Ed Cox's house with board members Bill Hutchison and Paul Corley and university counsel Leon Bennett. Together they had listened to athletic director Bob Hitch tell his story of the famous parking-lot conversation in August 1985, when Bill Clements instructed Hitch to continue the payments. Yet on February 6 he had signed the final version of SMU's statement of facts to the NCAA committee on infractions, which specifically omitted any reference to Governor Clements and which Stallcup knew to be false.

"Although I have not been involved directly in the investigation," Stallcup now told Sparks, "I have been kept informed of the various steps that have been taken, the information that has been brought to light. I did attend the meeting with the infractions committee in Coronado ten days or so ago. There is no evidence that Governor Clements was involved. As a matter of fact, the name has not appeared in any of the investigations, nor did it appear at that conference."

Kliever, listening to Stallcup, was himself anxious to respond. Rumors about the governor's involvement had been floating around Dallas—and Austin, for that matter—for months. Kliever had already been asked the same question by Sparks in private. Then, he had told Sparks that yes, he'd heard the rumors, but he had no reason to think that they were true. Earlier this morning, Kliever had addressed a special meeting of the SMU board of trustees, and again the same question had come up. Kliever had told the trustees exactly what he told Sparks now.

"What I can affirm," Kliever said, "and what I am interested in getting on the record is that there were no allegations and no evidence of the governor's [involvement]—or any other member of the board of trustees or the board of governors of this university—in any of the problems that we identified."

When Kliever said the governor was clean, he was misinformed. When Stallcup said the governor was clean, he was lying.

UCLA RECRUITING COORDINATOR Bill Rees was in Detroit on Wednesday afternoon when he heard the rumors about SMU. He called his boss, Terry Donahue, who urged him to fly to Dallas as soon as possible. The SMU football program had been shut down, meaning it was open season on approximately one hundred Division I football players. Not prospects, but proven performers.

By the time Rees got through to Pac Ten conference headquarters to see if there were any special rules he ought to know about, three other schools had already called with the same question. Reese was on a plane to Dallas that night. He checked into a two-room suite at the Hilton on Mockingbird Lane, within sight of Ownby Stadium. In the lobby, signing for his room, he ran into two coaches he knew, one from the University of Oklahoma and another from the University of Arizona.

It was raining again on Thursday morning, the day after SMU received the death penalty. Bill Rees was the first coach to arrive at Ownby Stadium. He had spoken to a woman who used to go to SMU—a friend of a mutual acquaintance—and from her he had learned the name of Coach Collins's secretary. The secretary informed Rees that he was in luck; this happened to be the day when the monthly room-and-board checks were passed out to scholar-ship athletes. All he had to do was wait. Sooner or later, they would all be here.

By midmorning, scores of coaches from all over the country had descended on Ownby Stadium. They stood in clusters in the parking lot, on the terrace outside the football office, in the football office. They wore suits and ties and crew-neck sweaters and polo shirts of every shade in the college-football rainbow. No man under twenty-five and over two hundred pounds was safe. They were pulled aside and interviewed in the hallways, the locker room, the weight room, as they were coming out of the shower. There were reports of tugs-of-war. One school, Alabama, had sent *six* coaches to Dallas. They worked as a team, with stallers trapping the com-petition in idle conversation while salesmen delivered their pitch to the players in private. At least two former SMU coaches were back representing new schools—Whitey Jordan with Wake Forest and Ken Pope with Oklahoma State. The most often heard question was, "What does so-and-so look like?"

If Rees had an advantage, it was that he knew which players he was after and what they looked like. He set up appointments with all six at the Hilton, beginning the following morning at 9:00 A.M. That afternoon, he called Coach Donahue in Los Angeles and told him to come to Dallas. Ultimately, Rees would sign two players, David Richards and Ben Hummel. Both would finish out their col-lege careers as UCLA Bruins.

FOR THE SMU alumni who stood in the cold rain outside Ownby Stadium that morning, the sight of all those unfamiliar coaches from God know's where picking over the remains of the team was the saddest episode in the whole sorry ordeal. Somewhere between yesterday's surprise announcement and today's unexpected sequel, shock had given way to pain. And now this.

"Yeah," says a loyal son of SMU, "all the vultures swooped in from everywhere. I left work early, I went over there. Those were *our* guys, you know? Guys that you've been through recruiting bat-tles with. You get them, they're yours. And then to see them being picked over ..."

It was terrible. And what was worse, some of the players actually seemed to be *enjoying* themselves. Sure, the rug had been pulled out from under them. But it wasn't the end of the world. They could see that now. So they were no longer SMU Mustangs? All they had to do was give the word and they could be Georgia Bulldogs, or Arizona State Wildcats, or Missouri Tigers. There would be another day.

But not for the alumni. For them it was over. And on this day they felt a kinship with spurned fans everywhere: the ones in Baltimore, abandoned by the Colts, who left town in a moving van in the middle of the night; and in Brooklyn, where you can still find faded team photographs of the '55 World Series champion Dodgers in store windows on Atlantic Avenue. If anything was obvious to the loyal SMU fans, it was that everything that meant so much to them—the red-and-blue school colors, the Mustang mascot, the brick-and-slate campus—didn't mean very much to anybody else, and probably never had. Not to the coaches, anyway, who were just passing through. And not to the players who had been bought.

EPILOGUE

ON SUNDAY, MARCH 1, just four days after the death-penalty press conference, Bob Hitch's cover was blown. The headline on page one of *The Dallas Morning News* was "Hitch reported aware of payoffs; Boosters, co-workers say ex-SMU official knew all." Reached for comment, Hitch told reporters for the *Morning News*, "It's a long, difficult, drawn-out situation. This whole affair is unbelievable the way it has come out. I have to sit and take the shots. Somebody has got to take the blame."

Bill Clements was next. Confronted with rumors that would not go away, Governor Clements sat for a secret interview in Austin on Monday, March 2, with Burl Osborne, president and editor of *The Dallas Morning News*, and Scott Bennett, a *Morning News* editorial writer. Clements gave them a primer on the history of the slush fund. He mentioned several boosters by name: Jack Ryan, George Owen, and Sherwood Blount.

"There are 12 or 15 of these principal players that we're talking about here," Clements said. "[S]omehow or other, coming from totally different directions, they are motivated to do these crazy things and get us in trouble.

"As far as I know, Ron Meyer recruited every one of them. . . . And he put this whole system into place."

As for the decision to continue the payments after August 1985, Clements said that any promise made by an SMU official or booster to an athlete during his recruitment was a "contract," which "we" felt obliged to uphold.

"[A]nd I want to emphasize we," said the governor. "Under no circumstances should anyone ever consider that this was an unilateral decision by Bill Clements as chairman of the board of governors at SMU. That's not the way we worked, I have never worked that way, and this wasn't the way that decision was determined."

Later, Clements acknowledged that the "kind of detailed discussion on the specifics, ... the board in formal session has never gotten into all of this." But he said that "at least half" of the seventeen members of the board understood the details. "[T]he other half accepts in good faith that we in a judgmental sense made the right decision in the interest of the institution. And I think we did."

ON TUESDAY, MARCH 4, Governor Clements held a news conference in Austin, at which time he announced publicly what he had shared privately the night before with the *Morning News*. The news that the governor of Texas had personally approved payoffs for SMU football players was front-page news in newspapers all over the country. On campus SMU deans and vice presidents issued a statement expressing "shock" at the governor's revelation and calling for the resignations of all those who had been a party to the decision. Board members who had been unaware of the payments called on Clements to clear their names.

On March 12 a special committee consisting of five bishops of the South Central Jurisdiction of the United Methodist Church met for the first time, beginning a three-month investigation aimed at determining which current and former members of the SMU board of governors and SMU administrators "participated in and/or were aware of decisions to make and/or continue payments to student athletes in violation of NCAA rules."

The bishops' forty-eight-page report, released on June 19, identified board members Bobby Stewart, Ed Cox, Paul Corley, and Bobby Folsom, and president Donald Shields, as those who had knowledge of payments to SMU athletes prior to August 1985. Cox, Corley, Bill Hutchinson, and Bill Clements were singled out as conspirators in a plan to deliberately conceal Clements's admitted role in the decision to continue making payments. Acting president Bill Stallcup, attorney Bob Thomas, and "to a lesser extent," SMU vice president for legal affairs Leon Bennett were singled out as participants in the cover-up.

On March 21 the SMU board of governors was abolished by a

vote of the trustees. Later, thirty-one of the most senior members of the board of trustees resigned, making way for a new generation of leaders at SMU. The new board of trustees, elected almost one year later, was a younger, far more diverse group than the old guard of Dallas businessmen that had dominated affairs at SMU since its founding. Eighteen new members of the current forty-one-member board are from outside of Dallas. Nine are from states other than Texas.

ON MAY 14 1987, the University Committee on Intercollegiate Athletics completed its study of the future of SMU athletics, which was undertaken at the height of the scandal. The committee considered a proposal that SMU athletics be reorganized under NCAA Division III; that is, with no athletic scholarships and an emphasis on participatory rather than spectator sports. In rejecting the proposal, the committee cited "SMU's institutional identity, and the implications of a major alteration in that identity."

According to the majority opinion of the committee, "there is concern that a large segment of current and prospective SMU students are attracted not only by the institution's academic standing, but also by the balanced array of student life opportunities it offers, including, prominently, football and other major college sports. A shift to Division III ... might well affect this segment and alter the university's enrollment and overall institutional health."

The committee further cited its obligation to the alumni "who chose to attend SMU and who continue to relate to the identity of the university as they know and understand it." To alter that identity, the committee warned, "by way of giving or in other dimensions, may adversely affect the health of the university and all its undertakings."

RON MEYER WAS fired by the New England Patriots in 1984 and returned to Dallas, where he and former assistant Steve Endicott founded Athletic Associates, a venture underwritten by Sherwood Blount. In 1986, soon after the report on David Stanley aired, Ron Meyer left Athletic Associates to become head coach of the Indianapolis Colts.

After he resigned from SMU, Bobby Collins returned to Hattiesburg, Mississippi, where he currently helps raise funds for the University of Southern Mississippi athletic department. Henry Lee Parker is a truck salesman in Knoxville, Tennessee. Bob Hitch still lives in Dallas and is selling "oil and gas investment opportunities," a job he describes as "no harder than selling tickets for SMU sporting events." In December 1987 an investigation by the Texas attorney general's office into whether SMU had acted properly in settling the contracts of Collins, Parker, and Hitch turned up unexpected evidence that an unnamed employee of the SMU athletic department may have been involved in a "misapplication of theft" of at least $10,000 in university funds. The investigation was later abandoned.

ON MAY 29, 1987, A. Kenneth Pye, a former law professor and chancellor of Duke University, was selected as the ninth president of SMU. He brought to the university a commitment to high academic standards in harmony with big-time athletics. In October, Pye hired Doug Single, a thirty-seven-year old Stanford graduate who was formerly athletic director at Northwestern. Together they are committed to a policy of restoring integrity to SMU athletics; in Single's words, "emphasizing the student in student athlete." Strict new standards—in comparison, at least, to other Division I football powers—require a minimum grade-point average of 2.0 and a combined SAT test score of 900 for all SMU athletes.

Whether SMU can compete with the new self-imposed limits remains to be seen, although expectations are high. In January 1988 Single hired former Green Bay Packers head coach Forrest Gregg, SMU '56, to rebuild the SMU football program. When Gregg was introduced to the SMU community in a press conference on campus, he was asked by an SMU alumnus, "How many years before the Mustangs return to the Cotton Bowl? Five? Ten?"

"A lot less than ten," Gregg answered. The room erupted in cheers.

INDEX